The Doctors' DOCTORS

Baylor College of Medicine
DEPARTMENT OF PATHOLOGY, 1943-2003

The Doctors' DOCTORS

Baylor College of Medicine

DEPARTMENT OF PATHOLOGY

1 9 4 3 - 2 0 0 3

Amy Storrow

Texas Review Press ■ Huntsville, Texas

Requests for permission to reproduce material
from this work should be sent to:
Permissions
Texas Review Press
Sam Houston State University
Huntsville, TX 77341-2146

Cover photograph by Jennifer W. Shuler/Photo Researchers, Inc.
Jacket and text design by Kellye Sanford

Library of Congress Cataloging-in-Publication Data

Storrow, Amy, 1963-
  Doctors' doctors : Baylor College of Medicine Department of Pathology,
1943-2003 / Amy Storrow.
    p. cm.
  Includes bibliographical references and index.
  ISBN 1-881515-57-5 (alk. paper)
  1. Baylor College of Medicine. Dept. of Pathology--History. 2.
Pathology--Study and teaching--Texas--History. 3. Oral history. I.
Title.
  RB37.5.S86 2004
  616.07'071'1764284--dc21

                                                    2003001140

CONTENTS

Preface   VII

Acknowledgments   X

1. The Accidental Pathologist   3

2. Leadership   29

3. Teachers and Students   79

4. The Doctors' Doctors   105

5. Larger Than Life   115

6. In the Lab   143

7. The Business of Pathology   175

8. Derring-Do   191

9. Water   203

10. The Future   227

Afterword by Michael W. Lieberman, M.D., Ph.D.   235

Chronology   239

Roster of Faculty and Staff   259

Roster of Residents and Fellows   267

Illustration Sources   269

Index   271

PREFACE

Dr. Jack Titus, the third chair of the Baylor Pathology Department, ushered me into a room containing 15,000 preserved human hearts, all in plastic bags, hanging on rods. I'd flown from Houston to St. Paul, Minnesota, to interview him, where he now heads up the Jesse E. Edwards Registry of Cardiovascular Disease at the St. Paul Heart and Lung Center. I hadn't thought through what a "cardiovascular registry" might be. "You see how little formalin is in the bags?" he said.

I nodded.

To him, this detail was obviously important. But I was still back in the fact of a room containing 15,000 human hearts. It reminded me of the catacombs in Paris, where millions of bones sit in perfect geometric crosses, triangles, and starbursts, with each bone chosen carefully for size. At the entrance to the catacombs, a sign announces, "Stop. This is the empire of death." I'd wondered what they'd done with the bones that didn't fit into the designs. And I felt that—if such a thing is possible—I understood the French better for seeing how their artistry could appear in the most unlikely places.

Dr. Titus and I stepped into a laboratory. Water gushed in the sink. Inside bobbed three unmistakable objects.

"I thought hearts would be smaller," I said. I held up my fist. "I mean, I know how big they are, but I guess I'd always imagined them being the size of the curled fingers, rather than the whole hand."

"Well, that one's enlarged," he said. He pointed to a heart drifting in the water, over to the left.

The one down near the bottom was all black and pocked and weird-looking. It was roughly the same size as the others, but it must have caused a horrendous death. "That one's in terrible shape," I said.

To his credit, Dr. Titus didn't laugh. "That's a lung," he said. He snapped on a glove and picked up one of the hearts. He held it an inch from my nose. "Smell that."

I did. It smelled a little like chicken. "It doesn't smell like much," I said.

"That's because the water gets out the formalin smell."

Formalin again. I was back with the chicken smell. I was back with having had a human heart an inch from my nose.

The whole time I've been compiling the history of the Baylor College of Medicine Pathology Department, I've also been writing a novel called *When Strange Was Normal*. When my narrator is 15, visiting Houston for the first time, her hostess asks if she'd like to go ice skating in a mall, see a house covered in beer cans, or go to a museum about the orange. My narrator thinks that Houston is a place where strange is normal.

That morning in St. Paul, Dr. Titus saw "normal" and I saw "strange." Indeed, every culture is, in some sense, normal to its insiders and strange to its outsiders, and pathology as a discipline demonstrates this dual nature more readily than most. During the course of this project, I felt privileged to peek inside its normal, everyday culture.

When I agreed to take on this project, most of my ideas about pathologists had been formed by that 1970s TV show *Quincy, M.E.* I knew, of course, that most pathologists were not medical examiners. I knew that they did not inevitably work themselves into lathers of righteous indignation to give their stories good endings, as Quincy did a few minutes before the end of each episode. But what did I know? Not much.

To be honest, I took on this project because I thought it might be interesting—

a pathologist friend had even rather firmly informed me that it would be fun—and I liked the autonomy it offered. I did not expect to fall in love with it. But as I heard story after remarkable story and saw how they pieced themselves together, I often found myself in awe.

I began to understand that the story of the Baylor Department of Pathology is itself an exemplum of the revolutions in medicine since the 1940s. Here we witness the rise of medical technology—and the rise of Medicare and managed care. Because pathologists are the "doctors' doctors," their story is the story of American medicine, and this book is (in literary terms) a kind of synecdoche, in which the part stands for the whole.

What follows are the stories that members of the Baylor Pathology Department have told about themselves, each other, and their work. It is mostly in their own words, except for a brief introduction to each chapter to guide readers outside the Department. My goal has been to create a composite portrait. To give it a manageable size and shape, some stories could not be included in the book, but the missing bones, so to speak, are in the Baylor College of Medicine Archives. What remains looks forward, as well as back, and reveals the considerable artistry of the Pathology Department's faculty and staff.

—Amy Storrow

ACKNOWLEDGMENTS

Every book is a collaborative enterprise, and this book would not have been possible without the talents and time of many people. First and foremost, I would like to thank Michael Lieberman for the idea for the book and for helping me at every step along the way. Susan Rossmann read each page in draft, offering insightful criticisms and saving me from myself more times than I can count. Gail Donohue Storey also lent her expert eye to each page, as did Brian Howard. Kellye Sanford's vision for the book's design far exceeded my expectations and transformed every page. Paul Ruffin published it through Texas Review Press. James (Jamie) Davis, Milton Finegold, and Thomas Wheeler were especially generous with their time. Hinda Simon and Marilyn Jones were my anchors.

I would also like to thank Will Kyle, Becky Patrick, and Shirley Baker for smoothing the way. Elizabeth White and Sara Holland of the McGovern Historical Collections at the Houston Academy of Medicine-Texas Medical Center Library (HAM-TMC) and Diane Ware, JoAnn Pospisil, and Timothy Kirwin of the Baylor College of Medicine Archives provided invaluable expertise and information.

The following people graciously agreed to be interviewed, sometimes more than once:

Bobby Alford, Dawna Armstrong, Gustavo Ayala, Eugenio Bañez, Roberto

Barrios, William Butler, Philip Cagle, Deborah Citron, Jill Clarridge, Gretchen Darlington, Jamie Davis, Joyce Davis, Michael DeBakey, Robert Edwards, Robert Fechner, Ralph Feigin, Chris Finch, Milton Finegold, Robert Genta, Linda Green, Geetha Habib, Grace Hamilton, Edith Hawkins, Judy Henry, Michael Ittmann, Faye Jones, Ginger Jozwiak, Han-Seob Kim, Bhuvaneswari Krishnan, Will Kyle, Rodolfo Laucirica, Juan Lechago, Michael Lieberman, Mark Majesky, Graeme Mardon, Martin Matzuk, Philip Migliore, Dilzi Mody, Dina Mody, John Moran, Sandy Oaks, Robert O'Neal, Ibrahim Ramzy, William Roberts, Mary Schwartz, Richard Sifers, Harlan Spjut, David Titus, Jack Titus, Jochewed Werch, Dayton Wheeler, Thomas Wheeler, Yolanda White, David Yawn, and Edward Young. Thank you for your time and your stories.

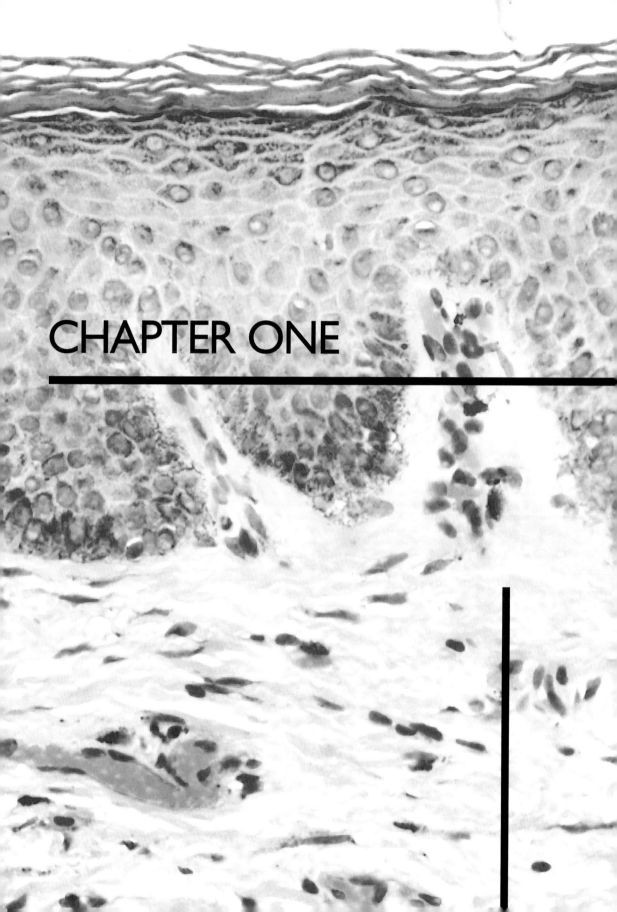

CHAPTER ONE

THE ACCIDENTAL PATHOLOGIST

It is safe to say that most students do not enter medical school intent on becoming pathologists. Of all the pathologists I interviewed, only one, Phil Cagle, had that goal from the get-go. Yet virtually all of them are very happy in their career choice. How, then, did they end up as pathologists? And what draws people to Baylor?

The Accidental Pathologist

I immigrated here from India in 1981, and by the time I got here, it was mid-May, so that was too late for the Match. Even the people who hadn't matched in the Match had matched. So, basically, by the time I got my paperwork together it was early June, and I said, "OK, well, there is no hope of anything this year." So I started working on my application for next year. Since I was doing internal medicine back in India, well, naturally, I was going to go into internal medicine here. I had no intentions of pathology. Pathology in India was restricted to just doing autopsies. There was not much clinical pathology, and the blood bank was still pretty primitive. I was really clinically oriented.

I went to Baylor, and I picked up my application. In those days, in certain departments, you had to go to the department to pick it up, but the main application I picked up at Baylor. The lady who gave me the package said, "Oh, you're really early."

I said, "No, that's fine, I'm getting my paperwork together." It was a huge, long office. There were two ladies in the next room talking about some resident in Pathology who had been going to start July 1, but wasn't going to show up. Somebody was not too happy about it. I said, "Hey, y'all have an opening?"

They said, "No, no, it's Pathology."

I said, "Well, I could look into that. You know I'm going to be sitting at home for a year."

They said, "Well, you know, we don't do any of the pathology stuff here. You need to talk to the Pathology people. You've got to go to Methodist." They basically directed me right here on the second floor and said I had to go see a Dr. McGavran. And, of course, I said OK. It was around 4 p.m. I still didn't have my driver's license. I had been in this country for 15 days. My husband wasn't picking me up until 6, so I said, "OK, well, I will go over."

So I came to Methodist, and there was the secretary. She said, "Oh, you know, Dr. McGavran's not there, but why don't you come tomorrow at 1?" The next day at 1 o'clock I was here, and I walked down this hallway. It was the last office in the hallway. Now it's occupied by Dr. Cagle. I knocked and knocked on the door, and there was no answer. And finally, I opened the door and put my head in.

Then somebody tapped me on the back and said, "Hi, I'm Dr. Malcolm McGavran."

I was really embarrassed.

He took me to the office and asked me to sit down. He said, "So you're from India?" And he started speaking to me in Hindi. I mean, pure Hindi. Now, Hindi was my third language. My main language, primary language, was English, and then the second language was Gujarati, and then the third language was Hindi, and the fourth language was French. So my Hindi was pretty bad. I knew just enough to get by. So basically, that interview was reduced to monosyllables.

But anyway, he thought that I was OK. He asked me, "Why do you want to go into pathology?" I was very honest, and now when I think about it, I was so

1. Mary Schwartz, M.D. (left), Abe Ramzy, M.D., and Dina Mody, M.D., became friends and colleagues in Methodist Hospital's Department of Pathology.

stupid. I said, "Well actually, you know, medicine is what I was doing, but this is one year that I'm going to be sitting at home, so why not?"

He said, "OK." Then he set me up for some other interviews. I came back and I interviewed with a bunch of people, and every one of them asked me, "Why do you want to go into pathology?" Now, in retrospect I'm thinking, "God, how dumb could I have been?" But I was just honest, and I told them my story. I don't know what they thought, but it was rather late, so I was in the program two or three days before the whole thing started. We had orientation on June 25th or something, and June 21st or 23rd I found out that I was going to be in pathology.

Once I started pathology, I really started liking it, though I actually did fill out my internal medicine application. I went through the process, but as time passed, I really enjoyed what I was doing. The way things worked out, I think it was good that I'm in pathology and not in internal medicine.

I'm truly the accidental pathologist. It turned out that there are some pretty famous people, like Dr. Ackerman, Dr. Spjut's mentor, who were accidental pathologists, too. He was something similar, surgery or something. And Dr. Spjut was doing something else and then sort of stumbled his way into pathology, too.

I feel an immense commitment to Baylor. I was an immigrant, and Baylor gave me my first job. Here I was in a situation where I had to be in Houston. My husband was in the oil industry, and Baylor gave me that break, and there is that immense gratitude and commitment that comes with it.

—*Dina Mody, M.D.*

Original Intent

I decided to be a doctor when I was in high school, probably during a physiology class that I took. When I was in the ninth grade, originally, I'd decided I was going to be a lawyer. A good friend of mine and I, we both decided we wanted to be lawyers. So he became a lawyer, and I branched off. I went to the university and went into pre-med. There were no flashing lights from heaven or anything. There were no physicians in my family, so it was just out of the blue.

I was in the medical corps in the Army in '47, '48, and '49. I was in the Philippines. I was a general medical officer, just general practice. My original intent after I finished my internship was to be a pediatrician. Then there were some experiences I had with newborn babies, trying to give them transfusions. I decided, "This is not for me." At that time we were giving transfusions through scalp veins, and it's hard to see a scalp vein. So I gave up on pediatrics.

When I got out of the Army, I wanted to go into internal medicine, but I got out of the Army at an odd time, so there were no available positions. That was in Salt Lake. I went and visited a friend of mine who was in the Veterans Hospital in Salt Lake. He was in the same situation I was. He was working in pathology at the Vets' Hospital. He said, "Why don't you come up here and spend the next six months up here?" So I started that way and went into pathology up there, and I just stayed there.

—*Harlan Spjut, M.D.*

It Turns Out

My interest in chemistry goes back a long way, back to my high school education. It has always been a favorite subject of mine, and I had always done well in

2. Harlan Spjut, M.D., decided to be a doctor in high school. "There were no flashing lights from heaven or anything. There were no physicians in my family, so it was just out of the blue."

it. I think if I hadn't gotten into medical school, I would have proceeded to go into graduate work in the chemistry area. That was a given.

I don't know of any other subject that I enjoyed as much in medical school as pathology. I don't know if I had an immediate indication on my part that I was going to become a specialist in pathology, if you will. But it was a subject that I always enjoyed.

One of the reasons was that of the courses taught at the University of Pittsburgh at that time, it was taught in a different way. It was because of that and the reputation of the department and the people involved, some of whom have become very well known internationally. I guess I leaned towards all that at the time.

There was still a doctor draft then. This was in the '50s. I graduated from school in 1956 and finished my internship in '57. While most people didn't worry about it, there was always a possibility that you could get drafted, and on that basis you took what you were given.

3. "For me, fate plays a large role in what happens in your life," says Phil Migliore, M.D. "I ended up at M.D. Anderson Hospital in a training program there, and from there I came to Baylor."

I was exempt from the draft until I finished college, which was the rule in those days. Then I was fortunate enough to get into medical school the first time I applied. In those days, many people applied five or six times and maybe never got in, or got in only after many attempts.

I felt an obligation to all those people and to my country to do some service. So I signed up for what was called the Berry Program, named after the gentleman who wrote the bill. It allowed people to sign up for military-services duty and select the service that they would prefer and to do a lot of other things. If you joined this, then you could make a choice about when you would like to enter the service, which I did right away.

I asked for an assignment as soon as placements were available. Within three months of my first internship, I was given my orders. I chose the United States Air Force. Then I got to choose the base where I wanted to serve, and I ended up in San Antonio. I'd grown up in the Northeast, so I wanted to get to some other part of the country. It was very fortunate for me, because I ended up at Kelly. Randolph Air Force Base was very well known at that time; it was a private training base. It turned out that Kelly was right down the road, so to speak, from

Randolph, and I ended up there for two years. Kelly Air Force Base had a relatively small contingent of military people at that time, 5,000 perhaps. But they had 30,000 civilian workers working on military jets. So we had a relatively small group of medical personnel. There were actually three of us in the flight-services office.

One of them was due to leave shortly, so that left two. As it turned out, I arrived at the base one day ahead of the second fellow to arrive, who was in my class at the School of Aviation and Medicine, so I was his senior. When the decision was made to move one of the flight surgeons to another base, he was low man on the totem pole. So I remained at Kelly.

When this other gentleman left, I became the base flight surgeon, which gave me a lot of privileges. I was given top-secret clearance. I had to have it to fly with the group that flew out of Kelly. They were flying all over the world, and many of the bases were secret bases. So I was the base flight surgeon, I ran my own office, I had a bunch of corps men under me, including an optometrist, and I had four secretaries.

So that's how I ended up in Texas and San Antonio. I guess having lived here for two years, I got to know something about the scene. After I left the Air Force, I decided to return to Pittsburgh, rather than try to start in a new location. It was in pathology. I stayed there two years. And during that two-year program, I began to look at alternate programs in some other parts of the country. Well, it turns out that of all the places I had applied to, I had the most favorable response from M.D. Anderson Hospital. For me, fate plays a large role in what happens in your life. I ended up at M.D. Anderson Hospital in a training program there, and from there I came to Baylor.

—*Phil Migliore, M.D.*

I Learned That I Loved It

Mentoring is really crucial for people in deciding what they are going to be. Where I went to medical school in Rochester, the school was founded by a pathologist, a Nobel Prize winner named George Whipple. He had trained at Johns Hopkins University with William Welch, who was the founder of serious pathology in the United States. Whipple had previously been at San Francisco. The basic science was taught at Berkeley, which is across the bay from the hospitals in San Francisco. And having come from Hopkins, where the medical school and the hospital were physically connected, Whipple found this intolerable. He started something called the Student Fellowship in Pathology to bring the students in their clinical years back into basic science. It turned out to be very suc-

4. Although he had not doctors in the family, Milton Finegold, M.D., set out to be a physician. Then he learned that he loved pathology.

cessful, because in the 1920s, pathology was still the one place where you were doing fantastic research. Not as fantastic as it has become because of the technology. It was the place for scientists. So when I went there, I was motivated by that concept.

The first class at Rochester was in '29, and Whipple was the dean until '53. The program kept on going. When I got there in '55, they had the tradition. So when I studied pathology, many of our teachers were the students who were one year ahead of us, who were taking a year off. That was very stimulating for a student to see that one year later, you could know so much. They were not our only teachers, of course; there was a professor and chairman. They were all very inviting. It was a small school with 72 students in a class.

I had no physicians in my family, so I had no experience of what it was like to be a doctor. When I went to the clinics in the third year, I was uncertain about what I wanted. I ruled out psychiatry because I found I was impatient. I needed something more active. I went through all the fields and didn't really find one that appealed to me. So I applied to do a fellowship in pathology. I'd use the year to learn more pathology and decide on a field. That was a wonderful time, where I did research for the first time and made some very interesting discoveries. And I learned that I loved pathology. But when I went to medical school, I had gone to become a practicing physician.

I thought of surgery. There was a really superb hand surgeon, and there was plastic surgery that worked with reconstructive surgery. I really fell in love with it. I thought, "That's what I want to be." That's why I applied in surgery.

After several months I looked around and realized that what I wanted to do was not the work but seeing the nerves, tendons, ligaments, and tiny blood vessels in the fingers. And I looked at my appendectomy patients when they came back and what their sutures looked like. They looked messy. And I looked at my 15 or 16 colleagues and the neat quality of their work—and the way they worked. I decided this was not for me.

Surgery was wonderful, and I still think it is wonderful. It takes a talent to do it, like Dr. DeBakey has. It is a gift to be able to do this.

There were other types of surgery to do. You could sew bowels together, anyone can do that. You could take out brain tumors, that's not hard to do. But doing ocular muscles and the hand—a lot is at stake. If I couldn't do that, I already knew that I loved pathology. The problem-solving and the teaching were appealing, and the research was also appealing. So that's how I made my choice.

I am always interested in how people come to where they are.

—*Milton Finegold, M.D.*

A Calling

I was the oldest of four girls and was always told by my mother that I could do anything I wanted to, if I wanted to do it badly enough. At age 13 at a church camp, I felt that I was being called by God to become a physician, and even perhaps a missionary physician. I think I may have commented about that on my application to medical school, but I wasn't getting in.

Anyway, I was valedictorian of my high school class, which was not a very big class. I probably would not have made it in this day and age. So I had a scholarship for the first year at Baylor University in Waco. And since I had decided that medicine was the thing I needed to do at that time, I started in the summer after I graduated from high school. I went straight through for three years.

Then I went to Baylor in Houston. I probably chose pathology due to Dr. Paul Wheeler, who was in the Department back when I was a student. He was interested in everybody in his classes, but particularly in the women. He treated us as equals and perhaps even as a little special. He advised us in terms of where to take internships. I don't know that we had a formal internship advisory kind of situation, but he is responsible for a lot of our class usually ending up in St. Louis, which is where he had taken his training. I ended up, on his advice, taking a year in pathology as the basis for whatever I wanted to do. I liked it, and then I ended up back in Houston.

—Joyce Davis, M.D.

Time to Go Back to Work

I am from Georgia and went to medical school at Emory. I'd had an internship in Atlanta, and then I stopped and had children for 10 years. But my husband came here as an ophthalmologist, and so I came with him. At the time I was just staying home taking care of the children. Joyce Davis was my Sunday school teacher, and she decided that it was time for me to go back to work. She had me call in there one day a week, and I followed her around as she set up the lab each Wednesday. And then the next year I became a part-time resident.

At the time I came, they were between chairmen. I started in 1971. I think that was the only reason they let me do it part time. Because they didn't have a chairman, they weren't attracting many residents. I thought it would take me eight years, but at the end of about three years, Dr. Titus came in as chair, and he was a little bit taken aback to find a part-time resident. At the end of five and a half years, Dr. Titus and Dr. McGavran decided to communicate to the American Board of Pathology. They filled out everything, so I was qualified, and I went ahead and took the board exams at the end of six years.

At the time I first met Joyce Davis, she was involved in the teaching program. But then she left and went to A&M and was head of the department there later. She is really a nice and smart woman. One of the better people I have ever known, I think. She has a very strong faith, but you learn her faith more by the way she acts. She doesn't preach to people. She just lives a good life, and as you probably realize, that is the way to go.

—Edith Hawkins, M.D.

5. While he was in training, Tom Wheeler, M.D., realized that he wanted to be the guy who speaks last, the guy who says, "This is the answer."

Never Work a Day

Dr. Joyce Davis was a faculty person here at Baylor, and I grew up two doors down from her, so I grew up with her children. She had four children, three boys and one girl, and we had five boys in my family. My dad was a doctor. She was a pathologist, and her husband was an internal medicine doctor. We were very close, and she probably influenced somewhat my decision to go into pathology once I became a doctor.

Edith Hawkins was my teacher in medical school for the laboratory. She was one of the instructors in the lab session, with a small group of students. She had gone to medical school and then dropped out of medicine to raise her family. Edith Hawkins came back as a resident right about the time I was a student in 1974-75. She had just started back in medicine. Joyce Davis was a big influence with her. Now she's a professor of pathology at Texas Children's Hospital.

When I went to medical school, I thought I was going to be an internist. For my rotation in internal medicine, I was at the VA for most of the meaningful part of the rotation, and I found it was a lot of work. I don't mean work in the sense of hard work. I worked hard in pathology. But it seemed like work; it wasn't spontaneously fun. I was always looking for another consultant to give a patient to, you know, triaging.

I remember reading the Clinical Pathologic Correlation from *The New England Journal of Medicine.* They have a clinician stand up and discuss a case that he's given maybe a month before, with the history, and then you try to figure out what is wrong. Then at the end of the hour the pathologist gets up and tells you what the patient has—these are the biopsy findings or the autopsy findings. The pathologist spoke last, with the final word, and everything was settled. I thought, "That's neat. I think I'd like to do that. I want to be the guy that says, 'This is the answer.'"

That's how I ended up in pathology, and it's been a real fun and exciting career. Confucius made a statement: Choose a profession you love, and you will never work a day in your life.

—*Tom Wheeler, M.D.*

Expansion

When I was in college, I was interested in history and in possibly being a writer, but I also had an interest in a lot of different areas in biology. I discovered that I could include all of those areas of biology that I enjoyed, things like anatomy, histology, and microbiology, under one career if I did something called pathology. And so I discovered the field of pathology as a sort of abstract idea, and that's when I decided to go to medical school. I went to medical school with the intention of going into pathology and with the intention of having an academic career. I did not even know a pathologist when I first made this decision. I enjoyed and concentrated on my clinical rotations when I did them, but I still knew that I intended to have a career in pathology.

As I was finishing medical school at the University of Tennessee, I went around interviewing at a number of pathology residency programs. I had to pick in the general Southern region just because I had to drive to interviews, but I interviewed

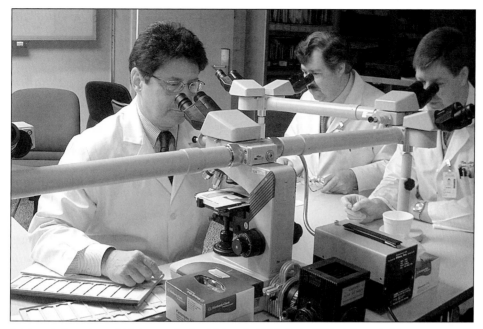

6. Interests in anatomy, histology, and microbiology led Phil Cagle, M.D. , *left*, to decide on a career in pathology before he had ever met a pathologist.

in quite a variety of programs. The one at Baylor really struck me as the place I wanted to go, both because of the quantity and quality of the training, the numbers of different types of hospitals included in the program, and then the people themselves.

When I interviewed, several people particularly impressed me: Dr. Malcolm McGavran, who was head of the residency program at that time; Dr. Finegold; and Tom Wheeler, who was the chief resident. He showed me around. When he asked me where I was in medical school, I said, "UT in Memphis."

He said, "Well, I didn't realize that the University of Texas had expanded that far." That did it. So, really, after I visited Baylor, I knew that was the one.

—*Phil Cagle, M.D.*

Hiding in Pathology

I always wanted to do something related to languages. I lived in many places. When I was 18, I already spoke five languages fluently. I wanted to do a job related to that, but it wasn't practical because linguists didn't make money. So I decided that I would do medicine, then try to go somewhere. My idea was an international organization where I could travel. Oh, the dreams of the young.

During medical school I continued to do my language things, and I studied Chinese. I did my thesis in Taiwan to practice my Chinese, which was not very successful, but anyway, and then I went back to Italy, where I'd started. I spent a year in an institute for the deaf in Copenhagen with a fellowship from the Danish government to study the perception of phonics by deaf and well-hearing people. Then I went back to Italy.

7. When Bob Genta, M.D., decided to pursue further medical studies in the U.S., he "hid" in pathology partly because he did not know English well—although he spoke more than five other languages.

I'd decided not to do anything related to medicine, but just then I met somebody who had this fantastic volunteer job in Yemen. And so I went to Yemen, with the idea of staying two years in this voluntary hospital. It was sort of a medical disaster, because it had been built by a Catholic group without really thinking of how they would staff it or what work they were going to do. The governor in that province wanted to be seen by nuns. He had been to Italy many times because he had diabetes. So when he knew that Catholic Relief Services offered a relief situation in Yemen, he contacted them and said he wanted a hospital with nuns. So they built a giant hospital, and then they staffed it as they could—by finding people here and there, with no organization, and no experience.

The doctors were myself and a guy who had just finished being a Jesuit and then became a doctor. There were a number of Irish nurses. None of us knew any medicine, and we were running a hospital. There was an American nun who was a pharmacist and seemed to be the only one who knew something. She always told me that what I should do was go to the United States, get trained, and then come back if I wanted to—if not here, then somewhere else. So I went after a year. I prepared for the test foreign graduates have to take. I thought that from what I knew of, say, internal medicine, they would probably kick me out the next day. I'm sure I was right.

So I decided to hide in pathology for at least one year until I learned more medicine, and I learned more English, and then I would make the next step. I did that and got a residency in pathology, and then I studied. Then I started liking it. I started doing research in tropical diseases, parasites, always with the aim of going to the tropics at some point. I did participate in projects overseas, but I never really did what I had planned to, which was to live in some exotic place and do good. So, that's how I got into pathology.

I spent three years at the National Institutes of Health. I was working on a worm called *Strongyloides stercoralis*. This is a parasite that is found in the tropics and also in some regions of the Appalachians. I was working with a doctor at the VA in Cincinnati. He was in infectious disease. He asked me if I was interested in a job there because my time at NIH was finishing, and so I went to see him. I ended up spending eight years there, working on the worm. Then I became bored with the topic and decided to do a fellowship—like a sabbatical—at the University of Washington, in gastrointestinal pathology. While I was in Seattle, a gastroenterologist at Baylor, David Graham, who is one of the first believers in *Helicobacter pylori*, was looking for a pathologist to work on this new bug. My wife and I came to Houston to visit, and we sort of liked it. Actually, we didn't like it the first time, but then we liked it the second time. That's how I got to Baylor.

—*Robert (Bob) Genta, M.D.*

No, No, No

I was in the Department of Cell Biology at Baylor as a post-doc. Dr. Savio Woo, my adviser, was one of the first Howard Hughes investigators, and I was in with him. I found out about this department through interaction and collaboration I had with Milton Finegold. He organized most of the morphological work done in that lab. I was applying all over the country for an assistant professorship, and I had gone to a couple of interviews. The common thread was that they all wound up coming back to Baylor College of Medicine. I thought to myself, "Why am I leaving Baylor College of Medicine if people want to come to this place?"

So one day, Milton Finegold called me and said, "Why don't you stay here?"

And I said, "What? Where?"

He said, "Pathology."

I said, "Well, it's kind of personal. Pathology is a group of old men wearing white coats looking at dead people." That is how I viewed Pathology.

He said, "Oh, no, no, no. We are bringing in a new chairman, Mike Lieberman, and he wants to start a research program."

And I said that I'd look into it. So I interviewed with Mike. We had a nice discussion. I looked over the facilities and talked to my family about it, and we decided to stay. He made me a very nice offer. I had some really good offers from other places, too, and I told him, so he matched it. So I learned something there, too.

—Rick Sifers, Ph.D.

Galen and I

I had no idea I was going to be a pathologist. I knew I wanted to be a doctor from the age of 9. I think it was because I was very fond of our pediatrician, and

8. Before he began his work in the Department, Rick Sifers, Ph.D., thought of pathologists as "old men wearing white coats looking at dead people."

9. Michael Lieberman, M.D., Ph.D., started medical school with the idea of becoming a practicing pediatrician, but he discovered pathology suited his interest in the mechanisms of disease.

he enticed me into medicine. Then I went to college with the notion that I was either going to be a chemist or a poet. It was incomprehensible and odd, as those two choices seemed juxtaposed, but I ended up majoring in the social sciences and going into medicine.

I went to medical school thinking I was going to be a practicing pediatrician. Do well-baby pediatrics. How far I've come. Between my second and third years in medical school, I spent that summer doing pathology. Those were the days when you had your summers off. I realized I had done very well in the pathology course the spring before, and I realized that I loved pathology. I came back that fall to my first rotation, which was pediatrics, and it only took—because I'm a slow learner—48 hours for me to realize that I wasn't going to be a pediatrician, and I was going to be a pathologist. When I retrofit my explanation for this onto the actual preferences, what I say to myself is that I realized that I was more interested in mechanisms of disease than in sick patients. Once I realized that, my career choices became clear.

I purposely stayed at the University of Pittsburgh for my residency because they had a strong program in both hospital pathology and in research. I knew I was interested in research, but one day the head of Anatomic Pathology came in and saw me dissecting the arteries off a heart from somebody who had had a heart attack. I was slicing the arteries bread-loaf style, looking for the clot. Normally what happens is that people open the artery lengthwise, as if one were cutting a straw lengthwise, but the problem is that the scissors go forward. They push the clot or disturb it, and so you don't get the geometry of the effect, and you also can't tell how much of the surface is occluded. So, bread-loaf style is just a much better way to do it. But when I was in training 2,000 years ago—Galen and I went to medical school together—people didn't routinely do that.

The chief took one look at me, and he said, "I think you are a researcher. You need to go talk to the chairman of the department, Dr. Farber. You need a research project."

Before I knew it, I had had a one-hour conversation with Farber, and he told me that there was no way one could do research unless one had a Ph.D. in biochemistry as well, and so I ended up in a joint residency-Ph.D. program at the University of Pittsburgh. My career has just unfolded from that very propitious bit of advice, although I probably would have gotten there anyway.

—*Michael Lieberman, M.D., Ph.D.*

Ridding Oneself

10. Mark Majesky, Ph.D., switched from a career in toxicology to vascular biology.

As an undergraduate student, somebody advised me that the way to ensure yourself a career in science was to study toxicology, that the government was going to fund a lot of toxicology positions in the future, and you would have a good chance of getting a secure living. And so I enrolled in a pharmacology program at the University of Washington, which is where the toxicology program was based. It took me about six months to realize that I really wasn't interested in learning how things die. What I really wanted to know was how living things work. Fortunately, at the University of Washington, there was a very strong vascular biology group nearby that was actually part of the training program. It really grabbed my attention very early on. Even as a graduate student pursuing a Ph.D. degree, I knew the general direction I wanted to go. Once I rid myself of these ideas that I should be a toxicologist, it was really pretty much of a focused pursuit after that.

—*Mark Majesky, Ph.D.*

They Called Me Mitochondria

I always knew I wanted to be in something related to science, that was for sure. Hey, I had my first microscope—my first chemistry set—when I was 6. I was a total nerd until I was about 19. In high school and after I'd graduated, I wanted to do nuclear physics.

I'm from Paraguay. I went to the American School there, and I had a scholarship to come to Boston College, but I was in love, and I didn't come. I remember my school principal talked to me and said, "You know you've got to choose a career in which you're going to be your own boss. In nuclear physics, you're just not going to be able to survive here. There's nothing for you. Why don't you choose something that will let you survive and still do science?" So I went into medicine.

I always looked a little bit further into mechanisms than most medical students. They used to call me "Mitochondria." During the first year of med school, I loved histology. I was a tutor for the next three years in histology. But when I went into pathology, I didn't like it at all. Probably I had a bad experience. It wasn't well-taught, and it was torture. I was going to be an internist.

One of the guys who really influenced me was Dr. Cubilla, who was a pathologist at Sloan-Kettering. He went back to Paraguay, and he suddenly ended up being my mentor. So during that year, during the year I did pathology, I would go to his lab and look at slides with him and work with them. He influenced me a lot, because I saw in his life what I wanted to do. I mean, he was being a doctor, but at the same time he could do science. It's a six-year medical school there, and the last year I decided to go into pathology, but it was nowhere near my original plans.

I graduated from med school in Paraguay, did part of my residency over there, then came over here, restarted and completed the residency at Georgetown, did a fellowship at Yale, and then I went to Allegheny University of the Health Sciences in Philadelphia. I started looking for a new job, and I accepted a position verbally at the University of Medicine and Dentistry of New Jersey, which is part of Rutgers, but they never sent me the paperwork. Meanwhile I was also looking at Baylor. So I called Dr. Lechago, and he said, "Do whatever you need to do, but still come." And so I came. I finally got the contract from UMDNJ the day before I flew to Houston. So I came here with contract in hand. That was so relaxed. Everything went so well here. There was no tension. It was just natural.

—*Gustavo Ayala, M.D.*

Teaching and Medicine

I had a brother and sister who were doctors, so I think I was influenced by them. Doctors were very important people to me, and I think that was probably why I chose medicine. I like science. I also liked the idea of teaching. It was always in the back of my mind, whether I should be a teacher or in medicine. I thought that it was more important to teach people—it was more difficult to teach people than to look after their bodies. I thought that I probably could look after their bodies better than I could influence their minds, so I thought that would be a better choice for me. I didn't think I would be able to teach. I spend a lot of time now teaching, which is funny, but that was my reasoning. I still think it's by far the most important thing, teaching.

I'm a visual person, and I'm really intrigued by the way the body is put together, visually, and so pathology really appealed to me. I also had some very fine pathology teachers, and I admired everything about them. I never really thought I would do pathology when I was studying it, and after I did my rotating internships, I really enjoyed all the subjects. I really like patient contact, but I married at the beginning of my internship, and I decided that I could do pathology during the day and then leave it at the hospital, perhaps. I really couldn't do that, though. I thought pathology would suit my temperament better. I think that's true.

—*Dawna Armstrong, M.D.*

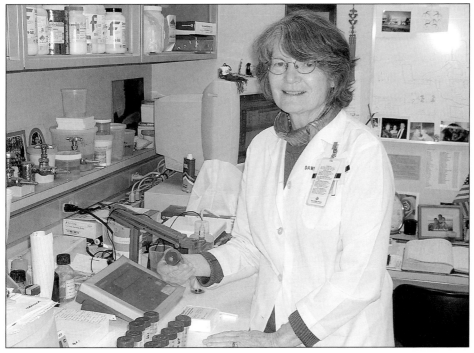

11. Dawna Armstrong, M.D., chose a career in medicine over teaching because she thought she could "look after bodies better than I could influence minds." As a pathologist who has had a long teaching career, she ended up with the best of both worlds.

Just to See

I was always interested in science. I got a degree in biology and psychology. Back then—I graduated from college in '75—I toyed with the idea of medical school or vet school, actually more seriously vet school. It was very difficult to get into either, even more difficult to get into vet school at the time. This was in Missouri. I just didn't pursue it. I wasn't exactly sure what I wanted to do. I ended up meeting my husband in organic chemistry lab at this small state school, and he got a degree in chemistry, and we ended up moving to Houston in '76 because of his job. He was hired by an oil company.

I decided as we were talking about moving to go to nursing school. I had friends in Missouri who did that and liked it reasonably OK. So, as soon as we moved here, I started nursing school at St. Thomas. I was in nursing for 10 years. Most of that time was in a private family practice with the same physician. I was still subconsciously, I think, thinking about medical school, but my husband had a career change from working in a chemistry lab at an oil company to dental school. He started dental school here in Houston and graduated in '87. I finally got to the point where my boss badgered me into applying to medical school. I really didn't think they would seriously consider me, because I had been out of school so long. My grades were good, but I just wasn't sure I was medical school material, and I wasn't sure how badly I wanted to do it, either. Because of my husband's work, I wanted to stay in the Houston area. But when I got in, I decided to go to UT-Houston without much hesitation.

12. After a difficult first year as an older medical student, Chris Finch, M.D., found pathology class was the first "where I had any glimmer of hope or enjoyment."

I was 36 when I started medical school, so everybody else was about 10 years younger. It wasn't a huge difference at that time. I really didn't feel that much older until I started residency. Then I felt very old. I really intended to go into family practice and go back and work with the physician I had worked with for about 10 years. We had talked about my buying his practice, since he's about 20 years older than I am.

The first year of medical school I absolutely detested, because I just hadn't been in an intensive academic setting in a very, very long time, in fact, for about 15 years. I thought I would really like anatomy, and I just hated it. I had never had biochemistry before, and the majority of my class had. It was nearly the end of me. Every day I would try to decide whether I was going to drop out then or wait another day. I went through the first year that way. I formed some close friendships, however, with a couple of people, and I think that was helpful. One person—she had been an engineer at NASA—was a little bit older. I became friends with another ex-nurse.

I started the second year, and that was when I had pathology. That was the first course where I had any glimmer of hope or enjoyment. I did very well compared to how much I had struggled the first year. One of my classmates had a husband who was a pathology resident, and she really liked pathology. Then I ended up talking to him some, and I decided that I would try an elective in pathology just to see what it was like. So the second year was much better in general. The pathology course lasted all year long, and some of the other courses I liked, too.

Then the third year started, where we start rotation in clinics and had on-call. I had already worked pretty intensely with patients for 10 years. When I was reintroduced to it, I just decided that I'd enjoyed it while I did it, and that was enough. I detested calls all night, which of course most people do, but I really have to think that it is more burdensome as you get older. You just don't adapt quite as well to a miserable schedule like that. So that convinced me even more that I should take a serious look at pathology.

And now here I am at Baylor.

—Chris Finch, M.D.

Very Important

People ask me all the time why I became a doctor. I suppose it's an easy question to ask. It is a natural question to ask. I have never been able to come up with a really good, witty-sounding answer. I couldn't even say, "Oh, because I wanted to help humanity." I have never said that. I have never said about being a doctor, "Oh, I wanted to experience the feeling of being able to save a life" or whatnot. I have never said that, and I have never felt that way.

I was thinking about that this morning: Wouldn't it be nice if I could say that and be honest about it? No, the truth is, it looks like I never had a choice. Ever since I could remember as a child, I have always said, "I will become a doctor." As I was driving in this morning, I was thinking, maybe my mother may have planted it in there without me knowing, or it could even be my uncle, who was a doctor also. Could there have been an influence there?

About pathology, the story is a little bit more positive than about becoming a doctor. Pathology I thought was the area that was most intellectually challenging. It is a very important undertaking, what pathologists do. I firmly believe that. And what pathologists do is always interesting. There is nothing routine or run-of-the-mill about what we do at all, even if we do it on a daily basis, because I think that, by definition, if it comes to pathology, it must be very important. It was important enough for the physician to bring it to us, to consult us.

—Eugenio (Gene) Bañez, M.D.

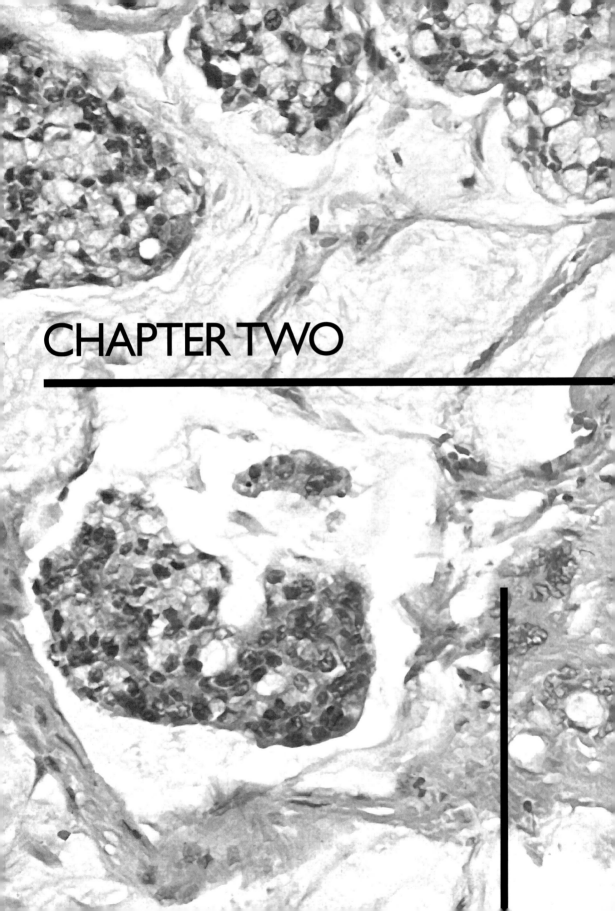

CHAPTER TWO

LEADERSHIP

The story of the Department's chairs is the story of the expansion of medicine from the 1940s until the present. Stuart Wallace, the first chair of the Department here in Houston, left behind a legacy as a superb teacher of medical students. That first year, there were only two full-time employees. Bob O'Neal, his successor, spent much of his time recruiting new faculty members and laying the groundwork for a research program just as research, thanks to the electron microscope, was itself being revolutionized. Jack Titus, his eventual successor after a stint by Harlan Spjut as interim chair, consolidated the Department's affiliations with area hospitals and built a first-class faculty devoted to patient care. Michael Lieberman, his successor and the current chair, has vastly expanded the research scope of the Department as well as the Community Pathology Associates program for outlying hospitals.

The astonishing thing is that each chair was exactly the right person to modernize the Department, according to the definition of "modern" at the time.

13. In the early 1950s, students called Stuart A. Wallace, M.D. "The Shadow," referring to a popular radio mystery program in which The Shadow always knew how to solve the problem.

Stuart A. Wallace, M.D.

Fulbright Professor and Chairman, Department of Pathology,
Baylor University College of Medicine, 1943-1961

Always a Gentleman

Pathology was a major course in the second year at Baylor. It met each morning for four hours throughout the year. We had general pathology for the first two-thirds of the school year. Our studies included a lot about syphilis and tuberculosis. In those days, there was no good treatment for either of those diseases. We encountered the various organ systems and their maladies in systemic pathology during the last one-third of the course.

In the mid-'40s, there were four full-time faculty members in the Department. The chair was Dr. Stuart A. Wallace, from Canada, who had been on the faculty before the medical school moved to Houston from Dallas. He was from New London, Ontario, and was a bachelor. A quiet man he was, well-respected by his colleagues, an elder in the Presbyterian Church, and a generous soul. He gave most of the lectures in general pathology. His sister would come from Canada to visit him from time to time, as did a niece. I do not know much more about his family except that his forebears had come to Canada from Scotland.

In later years, I would see many of the pathologists from other Houston hospitals bring a case to Dr. Wallace for his opinion. After careful review, he would give them his diagnosis. When Dr. Ellard Yow had a lymph node removed, the diagnosis of Hodgkin's disease was disputed, as it was a lymphocyte-predominant pattern. Dr. Wallace made the correct diagnosis, as the subsequent course of the disease proved.

His assistance to the residents in Pathology was legendary. He loaned my husband and me one of his cars for an extended time while he continued to pay the insurance. And he had us all to dinner at the San Jacinto Inn for all the seafood we could hold at least every year, or occasionally to some other fancy restaurant.

After taking a year of pathology as a resident in St. Louis, I discovered I liked it. When I ended up back in Houston, I asked Dr. Wallace if I could work part time, just to keep my hand in. I worked at Baylor for a while in the Department of Pathology. It was interesting. Dr. Wallace always wanted to make sure that the others—the men—made more money than I did. That's all right. It didn't bother me. I began to go over to Jefferson Davis to participate as a regular resident in pathology. This allowed him to write a support letter for me when I went to take the boards in pathology. It turned out to be a wonderful field because of its wide range of interests and the intellectual challenge that it had. And I enjoyed teaching the medical students, something I never thought I'd do. So it worked out pretty well.

He signed papers that allowed a Korean physician, who was my husband's interpreter when he was a medical officer in Korea, to come to the United States to study pathology at my husband's and my request. That man completed his pathology residency, served as a neuropathology resident under Dr. Buster Alvord, and ultimately finished his career at the Veterans Hospital in Cleveland, Ohio.

I never saw Dr. Wallace do an autopsy, but we residents learned the importance of careful study of a case and not to make snap diagnoses in difficult cases. After Dr. O'Neal became Department head, Dr. Wallace continued to serve as a faculty member until his death. He seemed never to discard any of his mail, and when I became a junior faculty member, it became my self-appointed duty to try to clear some of the junk mail and old journals from the top of his desk.

He was always a gentleman.

—*Joyce Davis, M.D.*

The Shadow

When I was a student, Dr. Wallace was the Pathology chair. He was a very devoted teacher and extremely well-respected in the community for his professional expertise as a pathologist. He was also well-liked by the students.

In those days—the early '50s—in the pathology laboratory, the students had four cubicles on the second floor. There would be about 21 or 22 students per cubicle. It was arranged in two rows of desk-like cabinetry where a microscope could be put on top of the desk with drawers for the slides underneath the top. Students sat across from each other in these two rows of cabinets in each of the cubicles. Dr. Wallace would come by and regularly take roll.

Dr. Wallace was often referred to by the students as "The Shadow" because there was a radio program, a mystery program, that always started or maybe ended, I don't remember which, with "The Shadow knows." He was the one who would solve the mystery of the pathology problem.

There was a student in my class who came to medical school from a small East Texas town. Actually, he was a fellow student with me at UT, and I was a little surprised that he was in my class at medical school because I had never thought of him as being a really good student. Well, when he came to medical school, from Day 1 he said he wanted to be a psychiatrist, and in order to be a psychiatrist he had to go to medical school. He only did enough to get by. He didn't show up for pathology lab very often. Dr. Wallace would come by and check the name off of the person as he passed behind his stool in the lab. He came to this fellow's seat, and he paused. We all knew that there was going to be an interesting pause, because this person rarely came to class. Dr. Wallace looked at his book, and he

14. Walter Moursund, M.D., left, Irene Fulbright, and Stuart Wallace, M.D., admire portraits of the Fulbrights upon the endowment of the Fulbright Professorship of Pathology, Baylor's first endowed chair, held by Dr. Wallace.

looked at the student. Then he reached slowly into his pocket. We were all watching to see what was going to happen. As he reached in his pocket, he said, "Mr. So-and-So, if I give you a quarter, will you come back tomorrow?" Of course, everybody started to cheer. Dr. Wallace had quite a wit about him.

You wouldn't say he was laid-back, that's not right. I started to say he was slow, but then people might think I was talking about his intellect. He sort of crept along. I don't know when his heart disease appeared, but you never saw Dr. Wallace in a hurry. He talked slowly, also. His mannerisms were those of a very reserved person. He was a bachelor.

His examinations were all essay-type exams. You could be exempt from the final exam. Pathology in those days, in the early days when Baylor was here, was split between the first and the second year, and the final grade was an average of the two parts. When Dean Olson came in as dean, he changed the pass point. The pass point had been 70, and he made it a 75. Now, if you made a 71 on the first part of pathology, which was passing, and you made a 76 on the second part of pathology, which was passing, but the final grade was an average of the two, you failed. Many people failed because of that in their second year.

You could be exempt from the pathology final if you had done sufficiently well on other examinations and you made top grades on the slide exam. At the end of the pathology course, there was a final slide exam which was over all the specimens. Dr. Wallace's essay exams were very arduous. I wanted to do everything that I could to avoid that exam. As an incentive to students, Dr. Wallace said that if you did exceptionally well on the slide examination, then you could be exempt from the final exam, if the other exam scores up until that time were of a certain level. I don't remember the details, but I was in the category with good enough exams to exempt it if I could pass the final slide exam. It was only on 10 slides, and each slide had two scores. One score was for the tissue, and one score was for the diagnosis.

15. Chairman Stuart Wallace, M.D., moved a superb collection of anatomical specimens in jars from Dallas to Houston in 1943.

I thought going in, "Well, I'll just have to take the essay exam." The first slide I knew. I thought, "Wow, this is terrific." The second slide I knew. And I went on through. I quickly went through the 10 slides before I started writing down the tissue and the diagnosis. When I got to the 10th slide, I realized I knew all 10 slides. I thought, "All right." Then I thought, "Oh gee, I must be making a mistake." I went through it one more time and checked all those answers, and they were all correct. And then I thought, "Well, it's probably not smart to make a hundred." I'm serious. I was having this debate with myself.

Everybody was terrified about this slide exam, because it was always known to be *the* toughest exam. I finally decided I would miss half of one slide, so that I couldn't make a perfect score. I thought, "Maybe there would be a lot of people, but I'm not going to stand out."

It turned out that only one other student—Morton Adels—and I made that score. Dr. Wallace was so proud of us. He just thought we were geniuses.

He got up in front of the class and said we were exempt, the two of us were exempted from taking the written exam. It was embarrassing. When we left the room, the class was saying, "Grrrrr."

—Bobby Alford, M.D.

A Fine Gentleman

I recall him really quite well. He was a very fine gentleman who was rather quiet, but he was liked, certainly, by faculty members, and from my understanding about students, he was a good teacher.

He also had brought down a lot of specimens from Dallas, anatomical specimens in jars and so on. He had a little bit of a museum in the Department. What happened to that, I have no idea.

—Michael DeBakey, M.D.

Last Moments

I was sitting next to Dr. Wallace when he died in '65. It was in the conference room on the second floor at Baylor. Harvey Rosenberg was giving a lecture about primary pulmonary hypertension. Suddenly Dr. Wallace went *uuuhh, uuuhh, uuuhh,* and then he was dead. Zack Blailock gave him CPR, and meanwhile Joyce Davis ran down the hall to get Ray Pruitt. Dr. Pruitt came in with a syringe of epinephrine and stuck it in his heart.

That was when the conference room was where the main office is now. Stuart Wallace died in the Jack Titus Conference Room.

—Harlan Spjut, M.D.

16. Robert O'Neal, M.D., *front center*, enlarged the Department's residency program. Department members of 1963 include Joyce Davis, M.D., *front row, third from left*, and Stuart Wallace, M.D., *front row, fifth*.

Robert M. O'Neal, M.D.

Chairman, Department of Pathology,
Baylor College of Medicine, 1961-1969

TB and Pathology

I was in Memphis in the mid-'40s. I had TB, and it had interrupted my internship. I'd interned down in Panama. We had a lot of terrible tuberculosis down there, and I was assigned to the TB ward for a while. It was down there when I really first got sick and had fever. So it's possible that I got it from patients in Panama. The TB ward was just people that were draining sinuses. There wasn't much treatment, just bed rest. TB guys were dying every day.

My dad had been sent down to Venezuela during World War II as an agricultural consultant. He was a veterinarian and kind of a politician, too. Some man down there had a 25,000-acre ranch, and my dad came back saying he had a half interest. So I decided I would go down there. I decided I needed to know something about tropical medicine, so I would intern in Panama. My Spanish wasn't good, but I could say, "¿Cuántos tiempos usted va urinar por la noche?"—"How many times do you get up to urinate at night?"

When I finished, I found I was a little more ambitious in medicine than I had been before. It just changes you when you have something like tuberculosis. I decided I would just start out trying to learn everything about medicine that I had failed to learn before. I started out with a residency in pathology, and I ended up at Washington University. And I liked it. Even after I broke down with TB again, and I'd spent a few years straining with chest disease, I still wanted to go back to pathology.

—*Bob O'Neal, M.D.*

We met in Memphis. I graduated from Baptist Hospital School of Nursing, and he interned there. He ran me all over the place. He broke down again after we got married. We got married in June 1947, and then by the first of the year, the next year, he was at the sanatorium. I had to resign my job at the hospital and go out and buy a trunk. We did not have much. We put our possessions in it, and that night we got on a train to the sanatorium in Mississippi. They put us off the train out in the middle of nowhere. There I was with a trunk and a sick husband.

Two years he was in bed. I could only visit for two hours a day, but I nursed there at the sanatorium for a while. I did not know it, but I was pregnant when we went there. So I had to quit when I was about seven months pregnant.

—*Mildred O'Neal*

A lot of doctors who got TB went there. It was a cottage-type sanatorium where they got the patients to chop wood and live a good, clean life.

—*Bob O'Neal, M.D.*

From St. Louis to Houston

We both came down from St. Louis. We were both at Washington University. I was in surgical path, and he was in general pathology, which were separate entities. I arrived in St. Louis in 1953. I don't know when I met Bob O'Neal, between '53 and '62 or '61. We were friends. When he came down here, he came as chairman. Dr. Wallace was chronically ill, so he had retired, and Bob O'Neal was recruited. He had a strong interest in cardiovascular pathology and pulmonary pathology, which fit well with DeBakey's interests. After about a year, he got hold of me and asked me if I wanted to come down to Houston. I had never even thought about going to Houston. I said I'd come down and look. So he recruited me. He is just a real nice person. He's a tall, sort of gangly guy, about 6'2" or 6'3", slender, born in Mississippi. He has a Southern accent, and he's easygoing. He was pretty active in getting this Department on its feet.

—*Harlan Spjut, M.D.*

Near-Distance Learning

I think Dr. Wallace did an exceptional job of putting together a group of very serious-minded and religious people. They were very dedicated. And I think that, probably, I was too hard on him. I should have been more appreciative of other people there. We changed the Department to be a little more aggressive and more research-oriented, a little more organized. Instead of having just one person running everything, we distributed the responsibility. I think the best thing I did was the organization of the Department.

I didn't have a whole lot to work with. When I came there, there was a Scottish pathologist in charge of the lab at Jefferson Davis Hospital, the teaching hospital. Everything I suggested to him, he'd say, "We already tried that, and it didn't work."

We had a young fellow who came down with me, Gordon Adams. I think he was from Utah. He had worked, from when he was quite young, in a radio station, and he was self-taught in electronics. He put together a television station for the students, and he arranged a couple of monitors for the broadcasting of lectures. I had hoped to record the lectures, but it turned out to be a dull way to get information. We never did do it. I tried to watch some of the lectures myself, and I found it very dull.

—*Bob O'Neal, M.D.*

17. Bob O'Neal M.D., in suit and tie at center, examines a specimen during a regular Friday afternoon slide conference. Harlan Spjut, M.D., watches over proceedings from the back of the room.

Expansion

We had a remote TV system, probably the first one at Baylor. Gordon Adams had a TV in the core lab, and it eventually got to the point where we had four labs, each with TV monitors.

Gordon had set up the system so that somebody looking through a microscope, looking at a slide, would see something. They would discuss it as it was projected onto each of these monitors. There was also a system whereby a gross specimen would be put on a plate, and again a TV camera would see it, and then the eight monitors could also see it. That was innovative and new.

There was a residency program here at Baylor before then, but O'Neal modernized it and stimulated it. Instead of having one or two residents, we were now having four, five, or six. At the same time when he came, he recruited some young pathologists, Erwin Rabin and John Ghidoni in particular. John Ghidoni is still

18. Working under Bob O'Neal, M.D., front row, second from left, in 1968 were Joyce Davis, M.D., and Don Greenberg, M.D., front row, third and fourth from left.

at UT-San Antonio. They were interested in cardiovascular diseases. Then he brought Minoru Suzuki down from St. Louis. His office used to be a couple of doors up.

O'Neal expanded things gradually. There were no Nobel Prize winners or anything, but he expanded it. He got, I think, three electron microscopes while he was here. At that time in pathology, electron microscopy was the pinnacle of what one should do. There were three. He was trying to build a base of research.

He expanded the faculty slightly and strengthened the residency program with Joyce Davis. Joyce had gone through the residency program at Baylor before O'Neal. At that time she was in charge of the teaching program. She, with Bob O'Neal, modified the program.

—Harlan Spjut, M.D.

Salaries

When I went there, Joyce Davis was part time because of her family, but she was doing as much as anyone else. So one of the first things I did was make her full time. I said that I didn't care how much she came in. She had been on half salary. And she accepted it and was glad of it. When I went there in '61, Dr. Wallace, who was a wonderful man and the first head of Pathology, was making $12,000 a year. His salary hadn't been raised since 1943. I asked Dr. Olson, the dean, about giving him a raise, and Dr. Olson said he had never asked.

—*Bob O'Neal, M.D.*

Fudge Factor

Bob O'Neal and I had frequently commuted from Baylor over to the old— well, not the *old*, old Jefferson Davis, but the one that was torn down recently. On the way, the speed limit was 35 mph, and Bob would drive about 37 mph. He called that the O'Neal Fudge Factor. So we still call it the O'Neal Fudge Factor.

Bob encouraged me to try to involve myself in more research, because I really had been mainly involved in the teaching service.

—*Joyce Davis, M.D.*

Politics

We changed deans while I was there. Dr. Olson was there for my first four years. I felt he was a good dean, but the whole school had felt that he had been there too long. He was the one who really firmed up the relationship between Methodist Hospital and Baylor. He was the main one, although DeBakey's influence was maybe more important. Olson did administrative work. We had a series of acting deans, and each time the administration changed, it was really rough.

One time I remember, we went to a secret night meeting to which I was invited. There were about 10 of us. It was to remove one of the department heads. One of the people looked around and said, "I hate to be doing this, but I am glad to be one of the ones doing it." It can be pretty rough in politics sometimes.

Another time I was at a similar meeting to discuss who would be the new dean. I mentioned that I believed the only one who could handle the situation was Dr.

DeBakey. He sat there and contested a little, but then he accepted. How it was finally arranged I don't know, but within a couple of days he was dean. Then things became a great deal more stable.

By the time I got to Houston, surgery at Baylor was fairly well shifted from Hermann to Methodist, at least the private surgery. And, of course, when I got there, Ben Taub had not been built. We had the old Jefferson Davis Hospital. Our teaching service was over there.

19. Dr. Stanley Olson, M.D., dean of the medical school, is credited with solidifying the relationship between Baylor and the Methodist Hospital.

The relationship between Baylor and Methodist was a little strained over Pathology when I got there. Jack Abbott was the head of Pathology, and he was a very strong-willed person. There was no doubt that they wanted to integrate the two institutions, starting with Pathology as the first department. Dr. Olson tried to arrange it. I was not really enthusiastic about it. In the first place, Jack Abbott was fairly well en-trenched over there, and it was going to cause a lot of confusion in the community. In fact, after we really got serious about working on it, Jack wrote a letter to the College of American Pathologists saying that my behavior was unethical and that I should be removed from the college. Apparently they took this up at the national level—that I was encroaching on the private practice of pathology. I don't know how much of this really got out; I never did react to it one way or the other. One time Jack even jokingly threatened to kill me. But Jack and I were still friends.

In the end, they took Methodist away from me. In fact, Dr. Olson told me not to go over there anymore, even though I was the teaching head. He said, "They don't understand you. I'll take care of the policy over there." But I didn't like it there; attending the head-of-department meetings, I felt totally out of place. The only way I could make them happy was to fire Jack, and I wouldn't. I just never felt comfortable doing it. Jack was running that department as well as anyone else would. And the amount of money he made wasn't really that important to me. He made $100,000 dollars a year, and I made $25,000. If I'd wanted to make money, I wouldn't have been there.

—Bob O'Neal, M.D.

I Didn't Know

Bob O'Neal was wonderful, a very kind and a very gentle person. It was very easy to get along with him. I was invited to join the staff when I finished my pathology fellowship. By the time I was almost finished, in 1967, I was asked to join the Department. I remember him telling me, "Oh, I didn't know that you were so good." I thought it was very cute.

—Jochewed (Anita) Werch, M.D.

Experiments

My research really depended on other people. I depended a lot on other people. In fact, I think some of the best things we did were with the Department of Surgery, and it's a shame that, some of it, I didn't carry on with at the time. But I couldn't have done it without a good Department of Surgery that was willing to collaborate.

Dr. Halpert, over at the VA, was a really good, old German-type pathologist. He was the kind of man who, every time he arrived in the morning, he turned his calendar to the date. He was very meticulous. His name was Béla, and if I didn't put the little accent over the e, watch out. (Of course he would mess up my name a thousand ways.) But everything was so precise.

He had a technique for studying endothelial cells. It was an old technique, but it was very hard to do, very tedious and laborious. And when the surgeons got through with the experiment that we devised on these dogs, Halpert would take the specimen and examine it with these techniques. We also did electron microscopy and other stuff.

Halpert's work was just fascinating. We showed that you could suspend a little piece of Dacron in the aorta, and the cells would attach to it and grow. It would reconstitute the wall of the aorta just by being attached with little sutures. We should have carried on with that, because it was a startling thing. I think if we had followed through, we could have done a lot more with it.

For some reason—maybe because my father was a vet—I was in charge of procuring dogs for Dr. DeBakey to practice his heart surgery on. The problem was that the dogs from the pound were substandard. They had heartworms and other problems. So somehow we arranged for the prisoners in Huntsville to raise dogs. The murderers were the best with the dogs. Everybody else was a dishonest cheat. The best of all was a pharmacist who had killed his wife.

—*Bob O'Neal, M.D.*

Shared Interests

I was very delighted when O'Neal came, because we shared interests. So I had looked forward to working with him and did to some extent, but he didn't spend a great deal of time with us. So that was a great disappointment when he left. He was highly respected. ... He brought some additional stature.

—*Michael DeBakey, M.D.*

Troubles

Bob O'Neal came in with a strong reputation. He had national stature. Now shortly after his arrival, an important event occurred. Methodist Hospital decided that it wanted to change its relationship with the private pathologist in town who had provided the pathology services in the hospital, a man named Jack Abbott. The reason for the change had to do with economics. Methodist had said to Abbott and his group of pathologists that they wanted them to work on a more structured contract basis, which meant that they would not have the growth in income that they had been having. The pathologists stood their ground and turned down the deal. Consequently, they had to be replaced.

Methodist Hospital turned to Dr. O'Neal to replace them. He recruited people that he had known when he was in St. Louis. One was Sid Anderson, and one was Bob Fechner. It was a quantum change in the relationship between Baylor and Methodist. It was the first time Methodist Hospital actually had a full-time leader of the Department, of any department. So, I think that however that was done, whatever all the little nuances were, that was a great achievement. It didn't lead directly to the change in the affiliation agreement which took place in 1971, but it was a major step toward change in the relationship between Baylor and Methodist Hospital.

Dr. O'Neal was very busy trying to build the Department and its residency program. That was a time of great growth in medicine. He had a research program and founded some research activities at Baylor. He had a significant research program of his own, as I understood. And he was really one of the key people for change in the college.

He was a very, very, very dignified person, and he was extremely well-respected.

20. Michael DeBakey, M.D., was named dean of Baylor College of Medicine in 1968.

In 1966, the dean, Stanley Olson, left somewhat abruptly on a sabbatical for a year right at a time when no one could understand why in the world anybody would leave. He was having conflict in the community, with institutions, and with some of his own board members. Dr. DeBakey was asked in June of '68, I guess it was, to become vice president and dean at Baylor, still a part of Baylor University. The school was very troubled then. In 1968, I believe that there were seven vacant department chairs. It had to do with the struggle with the hospitals, and it had to do with finances; the school was losing money. It was growing, but it couldn't afford its growth. It's sort of like a business that has outstretched its resources. Desperate things needed to happen, and a lot of people got very discouraged over that. I suspect Bob O'Neal probably got discouraged about a lot of things. I don't think he left in a snit. I think he just left.

—*Bobby Alford, M.D.*

Time to Leave

So many things seemed to indicate to me that it was time to leave. I wasn't happy with the way Methodist was moving on. I had designed some research labs in the Brown building and participated in the grant writing. I even ordered the

21. Baylor College of Medicine's Cullen Building can be seen in the heart of the Texas Medical Center, in this aerial view taken in 1968.

equipment. And they decided to use that space for something else. That about did it. That's when I left. Maybe some people would say that my greatest accomplishment at Baylor was leaving.

—Bob O'Neal, M.D.

Between Chairs
1969-1972

The Phantom Chairman

And then there was Bill Roberts, the phantom chairman.

—Bob Fechner, M.D.

Appointments

There were some strange things that went on. Bob O'Neal left in '69. They asked me to be the acting chairman, and that was an unhappy situation for me, because I'm not mentally built to be an administrator. I thought I would try to hold things together until they chose somebody, which I hoped would be the next week. But that wasn't the way it worked out. Nine months later they still hadn't chosen anybody. Finally they did choose a cardiovascular pathologist at the NIH, Bill Roberts. That was good, because he was *the* cardiovascular pathologist at the time, one of the best-known, anyway. He was a nice person. He accepted, so then I was through. But a month later, he decided he wasn't coming, and I was reappointed. So that went on again.

Eventually they induced Jack Titus to come down. He came in 1972. When he came, then I was deposed. At that time, I was over at St. Luke's Hospital. I had my appointment over here, and I still had an office over here. But I got to a point where I decided, "I need to get out of this chairmanship." So I told the powers that be that I was going to leave. I got a position at St. Luke's, and I went over there. I was hoping to force them to get a chairman, which they did.

—*Harlan Spjut, M.D.*

Did He Get a Paycheck?

I knew Bill Roberts well. We had been friends, because of our fields of interest, and he had a very major, substantial career at the NIH. He is still there. He called me after he had been appointed and then resigned, and he said, "They are going to be looking around, and I'll bet they'll call you."

I said, "Well, I don't have any idea about that."

I was a competent general pathologist at Mayo, and he had become purely a cardiovascular pathologist. He thought I could speak with clinical colleagues in a different way than he could. He knew a lot of stuff, but I had some limited experience in managing people. I don't mean running a department, that's not true, but I was sort of No. 2 in one of the three departments of pathology at Mayo. I had run one of the training programs which were big in pathology. We had over 40 trainees of different kinds at one time. So, I had those experiences.

Bill took the job and quit before he ever got there. I don't even know if he ever got a paycheck.

—*Jack Titus, M.D.*

The Hardest Decision

Henry McIntosh was head of the selection committee for the chairman of Pathology. Henry, I'm sure, didn't know many pathologists, because he was a cardiologist, but he knew me because I was in cardiovascular disease. I would go to the American Heart Association meetings and the American College of Cardiology meeting, and he thought I was a decent guy that he could get along with. And I liked Henry a lot. He was killing himself working, but he was recruiting oodles of people. DeBakey had just gotten Baylor back on track financially. He got Baylor out from under Baylor University in 1969, and that was only three years before I'd been offered the job.

There were certain things, at least a little bit, that I was incredibly naïve about in 1972, especially financially. At NIH, where I was at the time, none of the laboratories had a budget. We just ordered anything we wanted, and it was either approved or disapproved from the top. So I didn't have any idea how much anything in my lab cost. And so, coming down here to set up a lab, I had to get sophisticated in finances. Budgets of hospitals—all that stuff—was brand-new to me.

And Baylor was the biggest pathology department probably anywhere in the country. You had Methodist Hospital, Ben Taub, the VA Hospital, the Children's Hospital (I think the departments there were under Baylor at that time). It was a huge operation. DeBakey would tell me, "Look, we want you to be chairman, but what we *really* want you to do is heart disease down here. You get somebody else to run that department." Well, the people in the Department were looking at me as a messiah.

Methodist Hospital would have been enough in and of itself, but there were all these other things. At the time, I had been dealing only in heart and lung pathology. I felt very comfortable in heart and lung, but I didn't feel comfortable with breast biopsies and bowel biopsies. I just didn't know much about it. I had gotten that out of my mind after passing the boards, and obviously, I'd have had to re-educate myself in those spheres that I'd neglected for 10 years. Too, I never had trained in clinical pathology. I didn't know a thing about clinical pathology. That bothered me. In other words, I would have been incredibly dependent on

22. William (Bill) Roberts, M.D., left, shown here with Tom Wheeler, M.D., in 2003, was "the phantom chairman" who never actually moved to Houston. His decision not to move to Baylor was the hardest of his life.

a lot of other people. I'd have to work hard to garner the respect of the other members of the Department.

Some article had come out in *The New England Journal of Medicine* about combining pathology departments and anatomy departments. And I thought, "Dear God, Pathology down here is enough." I mean, I was working pretty hard at that time. Henry McIntosh was getting to work at 5 o'clock, and DeBakey was getting to work at 5 o'clock. I worked pretty long, too, but I worked late. I didn't get to work at 5 in the morning, and I wondered how I was going to fit in, if that would be a problem.

I didn't hit it off very well with the head of Methodist Hospital. That was concerning me some. Ted Bowen. With DeBakey, I felt that my objectives and his objectives were the same, so I felt that I could get along with him, and I admired him enormously. Ted Bowen, I found him a bit tough, and I hadn't dealt with administrators before. Not that there's anything peculiar about them, I just hadn't dealt with the magnitude of the situation.

I'd have to meet in the morning at 7 o'clock or 6:30 with Ted Bowen and Mike DeBakey. Ted Bowen would sit at the head of the table, and I'd sit next to him, on Bowen's left, and DeBakey would sit across from me on Bowen's right. And it was clear to me where the money was at that time. It was in the hospital. And I wasn't getting along with Ted Bowen, I didn't think. I felt in parallel with DeBakey. I knew he was a tough guy, but his motives were great. He was trying to build a medical center, and he had wide vision. He was a wide researcher, and he was an organization builder. I consider DeBakey a great man. And he supported other people in the university who had nothing to do with cardiovascular surgery. DeBakey wanted a major medical center that was good at everything, not just cardiovascular disease, not just surgery.

I enjoyed Baylor, I enjoyed the atmosphere of Baylor, I loved the huge cardiovascular program, the magnitude of it, I loved the vigor of DeBakey, McIntosh, Harlan Spjut. He was a terrific surgical pathologist. He was not only a highly respected surgical pathologist, but he was a loved man in the environment. I thought he was just a terrific person in the Department. The other fellow that I liked a lot was the pulmonary pathologist who was at the VA Hospital, Don Greenberg. He had some health problems. But he wanted to come back to Baylor. And that's one thing I did in that short period of time. I got him back to Baylor. He was an academic person. He published. We were on the same wavelength.

Not coming to Baylor was the hardest decision of my life. Whether the right decision for me personally and professionally, we'll never know. I actually like the idea of being chairman of a department. This is an arrogant thing to say, but I thought I possessed some leadership abilities, and I thought those types of abilities were neglected in picking people.

I didn't have any money. I was a civil servant at NIH with four kids. How in the world would I send these kids to college? Baylor was dangling dollar bills in my face. I did like Houston very much, and I liked the atmosphere of Baylor, I liked the vigor of it. So it really appealed to me a lot. I think a lot, did I make the right decision? The chances of my becoming editor of *The American Journal of Cardiology* had I come to Baylor would have been much less, and I've enjoyed the editorship, but who knows?

Oh, another thing that appealed to me about this institution was that it was unassociated with a university. I guess that's good and bad. Baylor was independent. That appealed to me. In other words, your salary was not compared to a professor of English or a professor of history—not that that's bad, but I liked that. And that was unique in the nation at that time. Baylor was just big league, there was no doubt about it. DeBakey knew how to be big league.

At NIH, things were beautiful, but I had to work like the dickens to get heart specimens there. I mean, I was the cardiovascular pathologist for the whole city of Washington. I went to 12 hospitals a month, and one of them, Georgetown, every week. I was spending a huge amount of time just getting "the material" I needed, whereas at Baylor, it just fell in your lap.

DeBakey was just disgusted with me. I don't remember how I told him. I think I just called up and said, "I don't think I'm going to do this." I'd get on the airplane—I came down many times—and every time I'd get off the plane, I'd have a headache. (That's a bit of an exaggeration.)

When I decided not to come, I don't remember who asked me, but somebody asked me who I would suggest. And it was clear that DeBakey wanted a cardiovascular pathologist to be head of the Department. I thought of Jack Titus.

Jack Titus is a very smooth operator. I don't mean that in a critical way, but in a kind way. I knew that Titus could get along better with Ted Bowen than I did. DeBakey loved Titus, and I think that was a very fine relationship. I don't have any concept of how Titus actually hit it off with Ted Bowen, but I suspect it was good, because he's such a fine human being. He had his hands full, though.

I never really came down. I mean, I came down every other week almost, but I never moved. Actually, I bought a house in River Oaks. There was something in the contract that said that if I didn't do something in a month and a half, I could get out of it.

It's interesting, though, that I never really looked at another job after Baylor, after the first month of turning it down, anyway, until 20 years later. And 20 years later, I go to the other Baylor in Dallas, which was the original one, where the medical school here in Houston started.

—*Bill Roberts, M.D.*

Flapping in the Breeze

Bill Roberts was the greatest guy. He was a cardiac pathologist from the Armed Forces Institute of Pathology, but he'd come over to Johns Hopkins, where I was, and that's why I met him. In those days they only had anatomic pathology at

Hopkins. I was supposed to be chief resident. I think Roberts got down here and he was scared of DeBakey or scared of something, I don't know. He was intimidated. Maybe he didn't think he could live in Texas, or his wife couldn't live in Texas. But he recruited me down here, and I called Hopkins, and they got all angry that I wasn't coming back.

I love living in Houston. Bill Roberts seemed like he would be a wonderful chairman, but there I was flapping in the breeze with nobody to support me in the Department, because the person who had offered me the job was gone. And so you can imagine how happy I was when Titus was recruited in the first year of my return here, where I focused mainly on clinical pathology. Titus turned out to be the best thing that ever happened to my career.

—*David Yawn, M.D.*

Jack Titus, M.D., Ph.D.
W. L. Moody Jr. Professor and Chairman, Department of Pathology,
Baylor College of Medicine, 1972-1987

No Fooling Around

I was on staff at the Mayo Clinic. In those days, Mayo was an academic center, and we had a training program, but we did not have a medical school. One day I got a call from Dr. Henry McIntosh at Baylor. I knew him a little bit from national meetings, and I knew that the chairman of Pathology had stepped down. McIntosh has an oblique way of talking around the subject; you have to figure out what it is he is talking about. He said, "We're looking for a new chairman of our Pathology Department." He was chairman of Medicine. He said, "We can't seem to find the kind of people we want."

I said to him, "I know about you and that you do some credible research."

And he said, "We would like you to sit down and talk with us about what you would suggest for our situation." I honestly thought this would be kind of fun, so I agreed to go down. He said, "Well, it's hard to get everybody together and all, so we'll put you up for a couple of days."

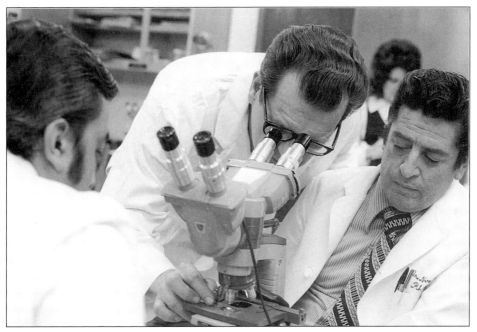

23. When Jack Titus, M.D., *center*, was offered the job as chair of the Department, the salary was almost twice what he had originally been told. Ted Bowen told him, "DeBakey and I know what we're doing. We decided you're the guy we want."

Actually it was my first formal trip to Baylor, but before that I had gone to meetings twice at M.D. Anderson. One time I presented a paper, so I knew the Medical Center that much, but it had been a long time before, seven years or something. So I said, "Sure." I was met at the airport and had a driver and all that. He took me to a damned nice hotel and made a big deal over a packet of stuff he gave me.

That was when I realized that this was a full-scale recruitment that would go on for about two and a half or three days. For my first visit to Houston. It started with breakfast with some people at 7 a.m. the next day, and it just went on until 10 p.m. or something, but I was doing that for three days.

It was interesting. I saw some interesting challenges. I'm nearly perfect, but not quite. The last time I tried to walk on water, I damned near drowned. (That's a well-known Titus-ism.) I thought I had some interesting things to tell them.

I went back home. I had already told them I would write a two-page summary of what I thought. A few weeks later, McIntosh—he's a wonderful guy—he

24. Jack Titus, M.D., front row, left, takes an annual photo with other Department members in 1975.

calls around, all around the place. He is originally from rural Florida. He's got a Southern accent still to this day. A brilliant man, truly a brilliant man. Henry called me and said they wanted me to come back for another visit.

I said, "Henry, I don't want to mislead anybody. I came as an adviser, and I'm sure there are a lot of things that are interesting and that we can talk about some more, but I don't want to kid you," and he said that's all right. So I went back.

The same interests were there a little more. I knew Baylor was still a relatively young medical school. I was trying to figure out whether they had the resources to do some things. It's hard to assess any place. Even places that are well-known are hard to assess, whether they have the resources to do something. So I went back once more, all in the course of the second visit with DeBakey and maybe Bobby Alford, chairman of ENT then, and some purely clinical types. I had two private conversations with DeBakey, and they each approached 10 to 12 minutes, which is very lengthy for him.

So they said, "We want you to bring your family down. We'll have just interviews for you, but let your family stay a couple of days and see Houston." It was in June. I will never forget this. It was a perfect Midwest June day. We got off the plane in Houston, and it was a typical June day in Houston. The temperature was 98, and the humidity was 220. My wife is very gentle and very easygoing, but later I found out that if she could have figured out a way, she would have turned around and gotten back on that airplane and just gone back home.

I must say they really took care of the family while I was interviewing. They had a chauffeur-driven car for her and the kids. They did everything. They took the kids to a ball game in the Astrodome. Our driver, our escort through all that, was a guy who was a senior resident at Methodist and was going on the administrative staff, Larry Mathes. He was president of Methodist for many years. To our younger kids, he was like another big brother. So it was a nice trip, and I had to really say something.

I had to go back for one more visit, a short one, and boy, DeBakey wanted to talk to me again. DeBakey asked me what I needed. He told me they wanted to do things, wanted to do what I wanted to do, and they would find the support to do it.

So I go back home, and I had to respond promptly. I thought about it, and my wife and I talked, and eventually I said yes. Within the next week, I got a letter from Ted Bowen at Methodist. It said, "Your initial annual salary will be n," which wasn't what they quoted me at all. It was almost twice as much as what they quoted me. I picked up the phone, and I got ahold of him, and I told him. He said, "We are aware of that."

I said, "Well, gee, I guess I just thought you ought to know, and you can send me a corrected letter."

He said, "Nope. DeBakey"—he always referred to him like that—"and I know what we're doing. We decided you're the guy we want, and we don't want to fool around with money or anything else."

—*Jack Titus, M.D.*

Very Desirable Characteristics

I had high hopes of working with Dr. Titus, because he was interested in the cardiovascular system. We did some work together, but again, he left before we could really get much done. While he was here, I must say I think he contributed a great deal to the leadership in the Department of Pathology, both in the hospital and at Baylor. He's a very able fellow and, you know, had very desirable characteristics in terms of investigation and research. I think we benefited from his presence, even though it wasn't a long one.

—*Michael DeBakey, M.D.*

Straddling

Dr. Titus was a distinguished cardiovascular pathologist.

He was a very genuine, pleasant, hard-working man but relaxed about things. Not relaxed about giving good service and so on, but not with the same kind of intensity of Spjut or McGavran. He's very good, and very intense, about cardiac disease and pathology.

He had a terrific problem because of the huge town-gown issue here at this Medical Center. He was able to straddle that and keep things going.

—*Milton Finegold, M.D.*

The Three A's

I am the first, as best I know, woman surgical pathologist here at The Methodist Hospital. I think there had been two women who preceded me here. One of them was Marion Worthington, a blood banker who left, and the other is Dr. Armstrong, a superb neuropathologist. So there was a woman here, but she did only neuropathology.

Dr. Titus was a general practitioner in a small town, and he had become a world-famous cardiopathologist. I think he was a superb leader, really, I think the Department grew significantly under his leadership, not that any of the chairmen haven't been good leaders, but he was especially focused on patient care.

I don't think that he and Dr. McGavran got along all that great on a day-to-day basis, but they shared an underlying desire to really serve patients well. That's true of all of our chairmen, but it's just more focused in Dr. Titus. Part of that may be because he was a hands-on country doctor.

When I started, he sat me down and said that to be successful didn't take brilliant feats, it really just took three things, three A's. Those were ability, availability, and affability. And you know, he's right. I have tried to convey that to people. Boy, if that isn't success in a nutshell. Not that you go out and purposely try to be successful, but again, it keeps you out of trouble, and as a side benefit, it brings success. Ultimately you want to serve patients well and do well. You are not going to do well if you can't communicate with other people, whether it's patients or other physicians or in the laboratory.

—*Mary Schwartz, M.D.*

Titus Sent Me

Titus and I got along well. He liked my ability to be versatile, which wasn't a good skill for academicians, because the way you get famous in academic medicine is by getting highly focused and specialized. So Titus liked that, and he would send me on any job nobody else wanted to do. For example, when Harvey Rosenberg left Texas Children's, he sent me to Texas Children's. He sent me to Ben Taub. When the blood bank in Methodist got into trouble with overwork—with only one pathologist who was greatly overworked—he sent me here. I was supposed to be here only for a few months to help out Dr. Worthington. For some reason, surprisingly, I changed from being an anatomic pathologist mainly to being a blood banker in the early '80s. And that's because Titus sent me all around. He helped me find the niche that I really liked. He was always accessible and such a friendly person.

—*David Yawn, M.D.*

Pay

When I got there, the job was about what I expected. Maybe a little bigger.

I think I brought some degree of unity to what were three separate departments. Is it perfect? No, but we got it on the road. And the biggest thing is, to put it bluntly, who pays you. I got the people off Methodist's own payroll and onto a Baylor payroll that came from Methodist. That's very different. Then I got the Children's people the same way. That was building some kind of unity. In reality, that took a lot of time and effort on my part, time just being around in those places.

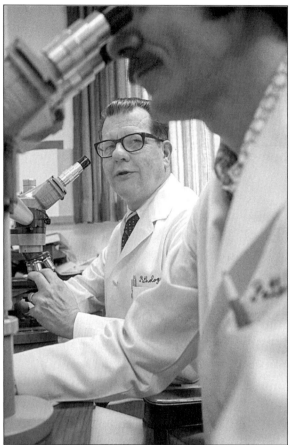

The key element was Methodist. I had an office there, a sort of cubbyhole. I had an office, a chairman suite, at Baylor. Then they later remodeled the Methodist office, and it was nice. (It's Tom Wheeler's office now. I am very proud of him. He was one of my best friends. He was one of our medical students, actually, at Baylor.) At any rate, I needed to show the residents and get the staff to know that at least I was around, I wasn't just somebody that showed up now and then as an academician. It was the same at Ben Taub. I had a dinky office over there. I wasn't there much, but I helped when I could.

What else did I do? I stayed out of jail. ... I canned a couple of people who were established faculty on the way to sexual-harassment com-

25. Jack Titus, M.D., sought to build unity among Baylor, Texas Children's Hospital, and Methodist. "What else did I do?" he asks. "I stayed out of jail."

plaints. I showed them greater career opportunities and said, "Better take them, friend." As a teacher, you have certain paternalistic responsibilities.

I was careful to do what Ted Bowen wanted done. He was a very powerful presence, and that was a source of much money for Baylor and everything else. Ted once paid me almost an ultimate compliment. Some fellows were talking about some plan and said, "What about collaborating with someone in Pathology?" and he said, "As long as Titus is here, I don't care what happens. He'll take care of it all."

I was able to recruit or was lucky enough to latch on to young people coming by. That's a big part of it. To get good people and to keep them, you had to pay them something, and that's where we could, to a degree, easily compete with most of the East Coast schools, because they pay embarrassing low salaries. They were losing people to places like Mayo, even in pathology and all. So I set off to do that. The American Association of Medical Colleges used to publish an annual survey of salaries for every specialty, along with the pay of the chairman of the department, and that of professors, associate professors, assistant professors, and entry levels. I learned that after two or three years, we were in the top five or six places in the nation. Well, if the people are good, then they are worth it.

—*Jack Titus, M.D.*

Special

I had been away on break or vacation and came back, walked into the Department, and ran into Dr. Wheeler in the hallway just as I was entering the Department. He was beaming. He said, "Guess what, we're going to start a cancer registry!" Back then, I didn't know what a cancer registry was, but we did start it. Then a year or so later, with the cancer program on a roll, I had an opportunity there for another management promotion to a director level and was going to have a conversation with the vice president. It was the Wednesday before Thanksgiving, in, gosh, probably 1984 or 1985. The meeting about moving out of Pathology and taking a position with the cancer program went on much longer than I thought it would, and it was the night before a holiday, so people were leaving early. I finally got back over to Pathology probably around 6 or 7 in the afternoon. I had a lot on my mind, trying to decide if I was going to take the position and leave Pathology, because work in Pathology really felt like home.

There was a hand-scrawled note taped to my phone where I couldn't miss it. It was from Dr. Titus wanting me to come see him. He had waited for me.

It was one more time that I was talking to Dr. Titus because I was at a fork in the road in my career. Jack Titus was almost a father figure. There was a lot of wisdom in what he said and the advice he gave me. He didn't want me to leave the

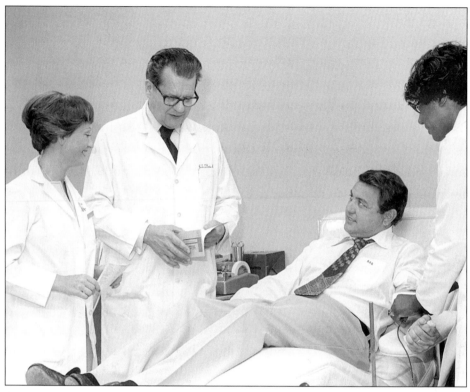

26. Anita Werch, M.D., and Jack Titus, M.D., left, visit a client in Ben Taub Hospital's new blood center on the day of its opening in 1976.

Department, and he didn't want me to take the position, but he also thought it was a good opportunity for me career-wise and a good opportunity to strengthen the bridge between Pathology and the development of the Cancer Center. You know, I had so much on my mind, and I felt so alone at that moment. It was pretty special that the chairman of the Department wanted to talk to me and waited for me. That's how caring he is.

—Judy Henry

Surprises

When I came back from a sabbatical, after seven months away, in January of '87, I met with Dr. Titus. I learned that he had decided to resign, but he hadn't told anybody until I got back so that I wouldn't be caught off guard. He was going to go back to Minnesota, where he would limit his activities to cardiovascular pathology. I was very disappointed for myself and the Department, in one sense. He was trustworthy in every way, it was a stable situation, and so forth. But I regarded it as an opportunity for the Department to make use of the resources of the general Texas Medical Center and the rest of the school in a way that it had not.

That's the big difference between before and after Lieberman. If you visit the second floor of the medical school building and see Dr. Lieberman's office and all the research labs down there, those weren't there before Lieberman.

—*Milton Finegold, M.D.*

Service and Research

Dr. Titus was a really nice man. When I first met him, I realized that he had a clean, down-home kind of way of talking and approaching things. My first impression was that this was some big ol' country boy, and I didn't know what he was doing here. But he was really good at getting people to do things and teaching. He was very calm about solving problems, and he brought a lot of good people here. He built the Department up quite a lot. I guess he didn't bring as much basic research that some think they needed. And after he had been here, I think it was his decision to leave. I think he was tired of being chairman. I can't imagine being chairman; I wouldn't like it at all.

So when he decided to leave, then they brought in somebody who was a little bit more basic research oriented. And that was Dr. Lieberman. At first, he actually needed to support service work more. It took him a little time to realize that he needs service work as well as research. I think everybody learns.

—*Edith Hawkins, M.D.*

Pact

Jack Titus and I had a pact: If one of us thought it was time for the other to go, we'd say so. But when he left, it wasn't because I told him it was time.

—*Bill Butler, M.D.*

Michael Lieberman, M.D., Ph.D.

W.L. Moody Jr. Professor and Chairman, Department of Pathology,
Baylor College of Medicine, 1988-present

Modified Push

Dr. Lieberman is a good organizer, and he's obviously interested in experimental pathology. That was his baby, so to speak, when he came down. That's why the Department got all that space going down this hallway. That was given to him as an inducement to come. So he's got a lot of active research going on down there. He fulfilled that, no doubt. The problem he met when he came here—and I'm not the only one who sees it this way—was that he was so involved in research, basic research, that he thought he could come here and say to somebody over at Methodist, "When are you going to get a research grant?" He never asked me that because I was too old. There were several people that sort of got pushed to get a research grant. The thing that he didn't quite realize—I know he does now—was that you can't really do a full-time service job at a big hospital like Methodist or Ben Taub or St. Luke's or Texas Children's and then also spend full time doing research. In other words, you have to have time if you're going to have a research grant and do research that will be of value. A lot of the people just said, "If he insists on that, I'm just going to leave." Over two or three years, he modified this push. There are people over at Methodist now who do have research grants. Tom Wheeler, for one, and Dr. Ayala received a big grant for research in prostate carcinoma. It has gotten to be where both things are going together, even at Methodist.

Over the years Methodist has developed a granting agency on their own. Every year they give a certain number of grants to people who work there. Things have really changed quite a bit. Part of this is due to the influence of Dr. Lieberman.

The other thing over the years is that he has allowed—or has at least become aware of—the importance of the service component of the hospital. After all, that's where the money comes from. It supports the salaries of many of the pathologists on the staff. He knew that when he came, but he didn't realize how important it was. You can't run a big department without money unless everybody has a grant.

He's been good. The real work has been through his organization. He knows what he wants, and he's a very particular person and has a nice way of saying things. He's very interested in student activities and building the residency program.

—Harlan Spjut, M.D.

Keys

A lot of credit goes to Jack Titus. He really was the first person to be a truly academic chairman here. It was during Jack's tenure that all the people at the various hospitals became full-time Baylor employees and got a check from Baylor. Jack developed a sense of the Department, and he recruited many of the people who are key in the Department today. Milt Finegold was recruited largely by Ralph Feigin, the current president, with the blessing and cooperation of Jack, but Jack found Tom Wheeler and Mary Schwartz as young trainees and promoted them early. He recruited Abe Ramzy. As a service institution, the Department was very well situated. Harlan was here. All those other people were here. Dina Mody had finished her training a few years earlier.

27. Michael Lieberman, M.D., Ph.D., brought a focus on basic research to the Department when he joined as chairman in 1988.

What the Department lacked was an academic mission and a commitment not only to basic research, but to investigation and academic pursuits in general. There was only one bona fide researcher here when I came, and that was Gretchen Darlington.

I was hired by Bill Butler, the then-president, and Bobby Alford, the executive vice president and dean, to build an academic program and build research here. It was very clear what my mandate was. The trick has been to convince the people who deliver services that I genuinely and truly value their services—because I do. I'm a physician before anything else, on the one hand. But on the other, to build a new program alongside of that, more new resources as a percent would go into the research and academics than into service. It wasn't because I valued research more; it was because there was a lot of remedial work to be done.

—*Michael Lieberman, M.D., Ph.D.*

Perfect Choice

I wasn't going to try to compete with other medical centers or pathology departments based on my skills as a basic researcher. When I decided to step down, I was delighted that Mike was looked at seriously, because he'd talked to me on the phone, and we got to be pretty good friends. He said, "What did you think?" and I said that we are in excellent shape, better than most departments anywhere, in terms of service. We are in pretty good shape in the teaching programs. What we need is basic research. What they need is to find a chairman to maintain what we've got—don't go changing it—and build the research, because the resources are there to do it. And Lieberman is a perfect choice. He didn't do everything perfectly, but, you know, neither do I. Sometimes you can't help it when you are doing good stuff.

—*Jack Titus, M.D.*

Flexing

When we first moved back to Houston from Austin in 1992, I had never even been to the Medical Center. All of my experience had been in the oil industry. I wanted to work in town, and I decided I didn't want to drive downtown, so I picked this area and thought it might be interesting. I had one contact at Baylor, who is no longer here, so I checked with her, and that's how I ended up here. This was 1992. I've spent my whole time here looking after—*chasing* after—Dr. Lieberman.

He crams so much into every minute of his life in the office and out of the office that it is just incredibly busy most of the time. He can't stand to have a spare minute that he is not being productive, so my life here is like that, also.

His mornings are mainly dedicated to his research unless he has meetings that he has to attend, and he doesn't set meetings himself in the mornings. The administrative stuff he pushes off to the afternoon or evenings. Just getting his day organized when I first get here is a big job, but he has a definite rhythm of the way he wants his day to go, so that's the way my day goes, too.

It's different from when I worked in the oil business. I don't know exactly how to describe it, except that he is very much in control. And I have always worked in the past for someone where I had a little bit of control. But I was able to flex into his style. Maybe because I am very laid-back and easygoing, and I just accept it. But it took about a year to get used to it. I kept thinking, "Am I going to be able to do this and keep up with this man?" But I did.

I like organization. When I first came, I thought I'd be able to whip things up in here, get things into shape for him, and I ordered all sorts of little organizer things—trays for his desk, to organize the stuff in his desk drawers. Everything is still in their original boxes from nine years ago, when I first came. I'm not allowed to touch.

—Sandy Oaks

Before You Do That

Every day is typical and no day is typical, but I have very few routines. I guess in terms of my own metabolism, I like to do the hard thinking and the hard work in the morning, so I tend to deal more with my research and with thorny conceptual problems then and tend to deal with meetings, when I have the opportunity to schedule them, usually in the afternoon. My goal has been to touch base with people frequently. If you have a relationship with people, when a crisis comes up, either between them and the Department or a crisis in which they can be helpful or valuable, then there is a relationship to build on. So I have put a lot of effort into personal relationships, even though I try not to manage everybody.

I don't believe in a completely flat organizational structure. There's a chief of each department, and I serve as chief of the research program. I spend a lot of time talking to Will Kyle about budgets and opportunities. There are only two commodities in this Department: One is money, and the other is space. In order to manage the Department, I need to use both to find and keep the best people.

I probably spend two or three nights a week out either for Baylor Pathology or for Baylor as a whole, running search committees for chairs, going to executive committee meetings, going to the Houston Society of Clinical Pathologists. I'm tired of two things: chicken served to me without the possibility of choice and salmon that I choose because of my cholesterol.

The other thing that my job requires—and it's not so different, in a way, from a busy surgical pathologist at Methodist—is that I have to be able and willing to do three or four things at once. To take a phone call, have someone in my office, and try to get something out the door on a deadline, because I don't have the luxury of scheduling everything, it just comes.

Incidentally, that puts a tremendous amount of pressure on Sandy, because even when I'm easy to get along with and not grumpy, which is not every day, the sheer pressure of my job flows to her, because I look to her to pick up the pieces. "Sandy, could you please get me an airline ticket to Washington, D.C.? I need to leave Friday afternoon before 2 o'clock. Sandy, before you do that, could you please call someone in the lab and get them to go to the library and Xerox something, and, by the way, before you do that, I need the document you're typing right away." I try to be understanding, and Sandy knows that it's not always me, but some days we're both frazzled.

I guess that's a typical day. Talk, talk, talk.

—*Michael Lieberman, M.D., Ph.D.*

Trails

Dr. Lieberman is not the tallest man in the world, and I always was amazed at how he can be out in front of you when you are walking from one place to another, even though I move at a pretty good pace. This guy can motor along pretty fast.

In recruiting mode, he thought it was very important to show me that

28. Michael Lieberman, M.D., Ph.D., says, "What has excited me most has been finding, recruiting, and empowering people. ... It's the things with the human touch to them, not the balance sheet."

Houston has all the amenities that Seattle does. I commuted to work on a bicycle there for 12 years. In Seattle, everybody commuted from wherever they lived. I remember when we first came here, of course it was in the middle of summer when I showed up. He made a point to take me walking all the way to the Braes Bayou Trail, which is quite a walk from where we are in the labs. He wanted to show me that this trail existed and that if you followed it all nine miles, you would end up out in the area where I was thinking of buying a house. I thought that was so curious, because it was quite an investment of time. It was hot and uncomfortable, and it wasn't necessary to actually go out to the trail, stand on it, and point down to the trail, but he thought that was necessary, so we did it. I ended up buying a house nine miles out on the trail, and I used my bike quite a bit in the beginning.

—*Mark Majesky, Ph.D.*

Contagion

Oh, Mike Lieberman. Bless his heart! He is such a wonderful person. Every time he comes over and asks for something, he says, "Oh, gee, I hope I'm not disturbing you" or, "Oh, I hope I'm not taking you away from something." He's just so considerate. Not many people at one level are considerate about what the rest of the staff members would think. Anytime they request something, it is never like, "Gee, I hope. ..." It's always a request. That just makes him so much more special.

The chairman has such energy that it is kind of contagious. When I see him, he is very cheerful. You never see him down or sad or anything. I take my cues from him sometimes. What I really like about him, too, is that he is quite a work-out-freak person. He likes to go to the gym every afternoon, and I have gotten back on that schedule again. So I see him and I say to myself, "Jeez, if he can do it, I can, too!" He has such an idea for what he wants the Department of Pathology to be that we all want to make it come true for him. I really feel that it all comes down from him.

—*Dilzi Mody*

Heart

What has excited me most about my job has been finding, recruiting, and empowering people. The really gratifying things have been to find and attract the very best young people and get them started in diagnostic careers or research careers and to recognize senior people, by, for example, creating five new endowed chairs since I've been here. It's the things with the human touch to them, not the balance sheet or whether we're in positive cash flow with respect to the school, or even my own scientific accomplishment. There are good people here, and what we have to model is a workplace where we all care about each other, and we're going to pinch-hit for each other, and we're going to value each other, because institutions by definition don't have a heart. They are corporations.

—*Michael Lieberman, M.D., Ph.D.*

Protection

I wake up thinking about science. I am looking at the same project I began, and I am going deeper and deeper into it. A lot of people look at things superficially, and they look at a lot of different things. So I wake up thinking about the project, and hopefully during my sleep maybe I've thought of something. I drive

29. Department of Pathology leaders in 2003 are, *front row, left to right,* J. Clay Goodman, M.D., Walter H. Moursund Chair; Michael W. Lieberman, M.D., Ph.D., W.L. Moody Jr. Chair and Chairman; Mary R. Schwartz, M.D., Robert O'Neal Chair; Thomas M. Wheeler, M.D., Harlan J. Spjut Chair and Associate Chair for Clinical Affairs; *back row, left to right,* Martin M. Matzuk, M.D., Ph.D., Stuart A. Wallace Chair; Michael M. Ittmann, M.D., Ph.D., William D. Tiggert Chair; Thomas A. Cooper, M.D., S. Donald Greenberg Chair; James M. Musser, M.D., Ph.D., James R. Davis Chair and Associate Chair for Research and Academic Affairs; James R. Davis, Ph.D. Associate Professor; and Harlan J. Spjut, M.D., Irene Fulbright Trust Foundation Chair.

to work, and when I get here, I have to answer the telephone and all of my e-mail messages and interact with people in the laboratory. I am always working on a manuscript and thinking about writing a new grant. I try to refocus my thoughts and my people in certain areas. You come up with certain models, and you test the models, and then you realize how you set up certain people doing experiments, and then you realize that the model was wrong. You are trying to do your best to make sure your people are not going down the wrong trail. I want to make sure that my people have publications and have a career. You could focus on something and end up with nothing; it is very simple. The scientific community is not very kind. So I try to help out people who have helped me.

Dr. Lieberman has been very helpful. I am the leader of my field now, studying glycoprotein quality control using alpha$_1$-antitrypsin deficiency as a model, but I would never have been there if he had not helped me, because it was very hard to get funding at first. Although he never gave me lots of money, he gave me enough to survive until I could finally make it on my own.

I was the first person hired for the research area. I told all of the people who interviewed after me that Mike would protect you. I was just telling a graduate student something I once read: You do not necessarily have to be real smart as long as you have some people who are willing to protect you when you are young. Then you can find your way. That is one thing I can say that Dr. Lieberman has done—he has helped initiate a lot of people's careers.

—Rick Sifers, Ph.D.

Fun

I view leadership as piecework. As every situation arose, I tried to do the best thing for the Department. It's actually not hard. If you keep in mind that your role is to do the best you can for the Department and the people in it, and not to do the best you can for yourself, then it's easy. My goal is to build a great department, and the fun is in the doing. Nobody is going to remember anyone's name in the 27th century, so what does it matter whether you're remembered for 20 or 30 years? When I'm dead, it's not going to be any fun to be recognized. It's fun doing things now.

—Michael Lieberman, M.D., Ph.D.

More Than Description

Dr. Lieberman has perhaps had a more permanent impact than the other chairs, not only from the standpoint of Pathology but also from a standpoint of Baylor as a whole. He has given great leadership to the Department, and I would say greatly enhanced its activities in support of the clinical departments. He played a very good role in maintaining the dynamics of pathology as more than just a descriptive discipline, one that you might say provides a great opportunity for investigation. He's introduced a very important research concept into the Department, which I think has been a great contribution.

—Michael DeBakey, M.D.

30. The current leadership of Baylor College of Medicine: *left to right*, Peter G. Traber, M.D., president and CEO; Ralph D. Feigin, M.D., former president, chair of the Department of Pediatrics, and physician-in-chief of Texas Children's; Michael E. DeBakey, M.D., chancellor emeritus; and William T. Butler, M.D., chancellor.

Outstanding

I have known Mike since the day he arrived. I was on the search committee that helped identify him and bring him here. Mike has done an outstanding job as chair of the Pathology Department. He continues to build on the strength that Jack Titus had created. He has brought in a lot of research expertise, and I think he runs an outstanding department.

—Ralph Feigin, M.D.

To Be Human Is to Trust

I had one very unhappy experience as chair here. That was when two members of the Department sought to undercut the Department and use the Department's business and finances for their own profit and well-being. It was particularly painful because I was very close to both these people as individuals, and it shook my confidence in human nature. There is no choice other than trust in spite of the possibility of violation of trust, because you can't be human if you don't trust. So, that was probably my worst time at Baylor.

There was another time that was bad for a slightly different reason. For about 10 years, I was chairman of Baylor's Committee on Scientific Integrity. I had one particularly difficult investigation that lasted almost a year. I was spending 20 hours a week doing it as well as everything else I was doing. It took several years to dig out from under that, because I just didn't have the time or the energy to run the Department on the one hand and on the other to do justice to this process.

—*Michael Lieberman, M.D., Ph.D.*

How Do You Do That?

I was going to avoid admitting that I have seen the chairman naked.

It all started several years ago. I worked for UT. I came here in 1988. I followed a friend whom I had worked with in San Marcos and in San Antonio to UT. When I was being good and exercising at lunch, we would go work out. I knew Mike Lieberman from there, but I don't think I knew for a long time that he was chairman of the Department of Pathology at Baylor.

Rick Gaines was a mutual acquaintance of ours and a friend of mine from UT. We were pretty routine customers at lunch time. We had many conversations about the state of health care, billing, and HMOs and who the villains were in this era of managed care. That's how I first got to know Mike.

I don't know how many years after having met him and talked with him there at the Knight Road workout facility, he stopped me and said that he had a vacancy in his Department. The administrator had left. Would I help him find someone? I said, sure, I would definitely try.

That is what I started out to do. I spoke with a few friends, who were happy where they were. In all candor, there were not a lot of people that I was comfortable recommending who had academic health-care experience. After a month maybe or so, I finally realized that this was an opportunity for me. Maybe I would be the person.

I don't know how that idea got broached. I don't know if that was Mike's intent

31. Both men of multiple interests, Tom Wheeler, M.D., left, and Mike Lieberman, M.D., Ph.D., take pride in a good hunting day.

all along. We talked, and I said that I would give him a résumé and be willing to meet with the people he wanted me to meet. We'd see how it would go. Things worked out very well. It really has been a great move for me.

I heard a quote coming in to work the other day. I can't remember who was being quoted, but her comment was that leadership was the ability to build community. This is where Mike is just outstanding. I know he is an outstanding scientist, although you may not want him signing out your slides. He hasn't been practicing pathology as a clinician in a long time.

He has Marty Matzuk, for example, on the research side and Mary Schwartz on the clinical side. It is such a diverse group of people, and Mike has to be the chairman for all of them. How do you do that? I think you do it with caring, credibility, and a lot of hard work. Those are the components of building that community. Almost everybody has a sense of belonging, I think. Mike creates that by knowing people's names and knowing people's issues and attending to them and being available to them. He is a great person to work for and with, because he gives you the feeling that you are working with him, not for him.

He has been willing to trust me to create a certain management structure. He clearly recognizes his position in that structure. It facilitates getting good information and having good communication with the people he needs, so that, ultimately, better departmental decisions are made. He fosters a lot of meaningful things in the Department. I am really appreciative of that.

—*Will Kyle*

Hiding and Poetry

I've been hiding over here at Ben Taub for many, many years.

Mike Lieberman is very distinguished. He's a well-known poet. I have all of his books right here.

—*Han-Seob Kim, M.D.*

A New Side

I knew Mike was into the poetry thing. When I went to hear him do a reading here at Baylor, I saw a side of him that, even though I worked with him for years, I never saw before. It was very enlightening. I really enjoyed it. Even though we joke and laugh and we are of the same age group—we love the same old songs from the '40s and so forth—you know, still that was a side of him I had not really seen very much.

—*Sandy Oaks*

The Secret

I still don't know how he just gets things done that require 26 hours per day, yet he accomplishes them in eight or 10 hours. He is the head of a big department. However, he knows exactly what's going on in his lab. When you are working at the bench in his lab, Dr. Lieberman will visit and stay with you at least a few minutes, twice a day, asking about your research. He's very interested in your results. He makes suggestions, and when some experiment doesn't work for some reason, he gives you good advice, despite the fact that I'm guessing that he has not worked directly in the lab for at least 15 years. Yet he knows the methodology very well, and he is very well informed. He starts trying to rule out possible reasons for your failed experiment.

He is hyperactive. He wants things to get done as soon as possible always, and I think that's the secret of why he accomplishes a lot. By the same token, he is very thoughtful with everybody. He's a good chairman. The amazing thing is that he is also a poet. That's another life. It's interesting that you can be so energetic. I think that's the secret to a successful life.

—*Roberto Barrios, M.D.*

CHAPTER THREE

TEACHERS AND STUDENTS

At the beginning of this history, medical students studied pathology in the makeshift quarters of an old Sears store. There was no established residency program for them when they finished. At the end of this history, medical students study pathology in air-conditioned lecture halls. Bobby Alford, the current dean and vice president of Baylor College of Medicine, wondered whether the students still use microscopes in lectures. The answer is no: Slides are projected. And now there are medical students, physician's assistants, medical technologists, graduate students, residents, fellows, and post-docs who study and learn in the halls of Baylor and its affiliated hospitals.

If technology has revolutionized education in many ways, there is one idea that remains the same: Good teaching is about people spending time with other people, encouraging and challenging them.

32. Baylor University College of Medicine students, Houston campus, pose for their annual photo circa 1943.

Dead Ernest

In 1944, every morning about 7:30, the members of the Army Specialized Training Program and the Navy V-12 Program who were students at Baylor University College of Medicine would line up in formation on the parking lot of the old Sears and Roebuck store on Buffalo Drive (now Allen Parkway). After making sure that we were all accounted for, squads were dismissed to begin classes. World War II was in progress, and a new class of medical students arrived to begin their studies every nine months. I started my medical studies, along with the fellows in the military service and a few other civilians in a class of 84 students, in late March of 1944. Our class graduated in May of 1947.

The laboratories and classrooms in the Sears building were made of fiberboard partitions about eight feet high and were far from soundproof. In fact, some of the professors used to shout at each other across them, as the ceilings in the building were at least 18 feet high. The building was not air-conditioned, and there were only high windows through which one could see only the sky.

Courses in gross and microscopic anatomy, embryology, and biochemistry occupied most of our time the first nine months that we were there. Pathology, physiology, parasitology, laboratory diagnosis, physical diagnosis, and microbiology were added when we began the curriculum for the second year's courses. One of my most vivid memories of those days was the long hot summer afternoons in the gross anatomy lab dissecting our cadaver, whom we had named Ernest. We thought ourselves clever to be working in Dead Ernest, that is, until Fridays came and we had an oral exam by one or more of the anatomy professors.

The laboratory for the pathology class consisted primarily of the study of 400 microscopic slides that illustrated one or more of the processes that had been presented in lecture. But did we have a lovely binocular microscope through which to view these slides? *No!* We sat on a hard four-legged stool and peered through a rented monocular microscope. Sometimes we would also have the opportunity to review with a faculty member some of the preserved and bottled museum specimens illustrating these processes. These specimens were really quite good, but I could not always correlate the specimen with clinical symptoms.

One member of the faculty would be in each of the four labs with us and

33. Baylor's new Houston campus was in a former Sears warehouse. The building still stands on the corner of Montrose Boulevard and Allen Parkway.

34. Paul Wheeler, M.D., guided many of Baylor's medical students toward careers in pathology.

35. Joyce Davis in the mid-1940s, as a student at Baylor University College of Medicine in Houston.

would answer our questions or help us to find the lesion if we were having trouble doing so.

I recall that several of us were able to see an autopsy at the Jefferson Davis Hospital during the year. The patient had died of a myocardial infarct, and his heart had ruptured through the infarct.

At the end of our second-year curriculum, I was offered a job as night technician in the laboratory at the old Methodist Hospital on Rosalie Street. In addition to learning and applying the things that I had learned, I would be compensated by a room in the ladies' quarters on the floor of the Methodist annex building and my board, plus $50 a month. I was responsible for doing admission laboratory work each evening as well as any emergency lab studies during the night. It was mostly routine CBC and urine analysis.

Some of the best sessions in lab were when Dr. Paul Wheeler was our instructor. He would sometimes sit on the lab bench and tell of patients who had lesions or diseases similar to what we were studying. These accounts were usually taken from his experiences at St. Louis City Hospital. As an internship adviser, he made it possible for a number of Baylor graduates to go to St. Louis to intern.

He was also a friend to the four women in our class. He and his wife, Pinkie, had two of us at a time to their house for Sunday brunch during the year. It was the first time that I had ever tasted pickled herring. He advised me and Phil Davis, the classmate I married between our junior and senior years, to marry then instead of waiting till we graduated. He pronounced that just-married interns were not worth shooting. He would not allow us to apply for internships in the same hospital. I think that he wanted each of us to stand on our own merits, without depending on one another throughout the day.

About the women in the class: Two were older and were nurses. The other two were about the age of 20 when we began medical school. All four of us graduated with our class, although only 72 of those who began with us graduated when we did. Some of the others flunked out, and a few had to repeat a year.

One of the other memorable exercises during our junior and senior (nine-month) "years" was the 5 o'clock Friday afternoon Clinicopathological Conference (CPC), usually led by Dr. Greene, head of the Department of Internal Medicine. We students had to study the clinical history given to us early each week and submit a written diagnosis at the beginning of the conference. Dr. Greene would often begin by reading the first line of the clinical history and then calling on one of us to say what it made us think of. Other questions were interspersed throughout the hour. A few other clinicians were usually also in attendance and contributed to the discussion. In the last five or 10 minutes of the hour, Dr. Wallace or one of the other pathologists would present the diagnosis. We were pleased if the diagnosis which we had submitted was the correct one.

Phil and I became good friends and friendly competitors regarding our academic records during the latter part of the first year. We had our first date on VJ day, August 15, 1945. Two weeks later we became engaged, and we were married in Bay City, Texas, on March 17, 1946, right after we had taken 14 final examinations and Phil had been discharged from the Army. We had three weeks' time to marry, work a week at The Methodist Hospital, and then ride the train to St. Louis to interview for internships before beginning our senior year.

Our graduation celebrations included a banquet and a senior play. It took the form of a CPC. The actual ceremony and awarding of our degrees was held in the old Second Baptist Church at Milam and McGowan streets. Then came the three days of State Board examinations that were held in Fort Worth in June. Finally we were off to St. Louis in the 1935 two-door black Chevrolet sedan that we had bought from Phil's sister and her husband for $350 at the beginning of our senior year. We slept on the side of the road for the two nights on the way, once at the edge of a cemetery in Missouri.

Many years later, starting in 1961, I was in charge of the student teaching program at Baylor. I am not exactly sure how my involvement in the program began.

Dr. Bob Bucci and I began by being responsible for selecting the gross specimens—thick specimens that you could hold in your hand for the teaching lab—and museum specimens that would be used in the laboratory sessions with the students. We continued to sort them and file them. Ultimately the responsibility of preparing the teaching schedule devolved to me.

When Dr. O'Neal came, he allowed me to have the opportunity to organize the schedule and list the lecturers and arrange for the whole program. He encouraged me a lot in that. He encouraged me in areas of research as well.

I sought to involve the clinical faculty with special interest or expert knowledge to lecture to the students and to instruct in the laboratories. To provide some continuity for the students, I attended all of the lectures. It also allowed me some control over whom I would ask to lecture the next year. I became part of the Curriculum Committee at Baylor, and we tried an integrated system of giving examinations and a coordinated schedule, so that hopefully the students could relate the various topics being studied to one another. We would give one big exam at the end of the quarter with one question that would be graded by each department. For example, one question that I think we asked that each of us graded was "Discuss jaundice." Later we began to use multiple-choice questions in evaluating the students.

I gave open-book practicals as far as the microscopic exams were concerned. You don't make a diagnosis when you are out in practice just by looking at the slide without going to the books, so you should be able to look at the information when you are taking the exam.

One time a group of five students came to me and said they really didn't enjoy the lectures and they would be responsible for their own learning from the book. They would take exams just like everyone else, and they would be in laboratory sessions, because you can't learn all of your laboratory stuff without being there. Four of the five were above 90 at the end of the quarter or semester or whatever we were using at that time. I learned different people learn in different ways, and what you need to do is try to provide different opportunities for students to learn.

That is the way you begin to evolve in the teaching program.

We also began a series of electives in pathology for the students in their last two years of medical schooling. The course in pathology doesn't give the student any

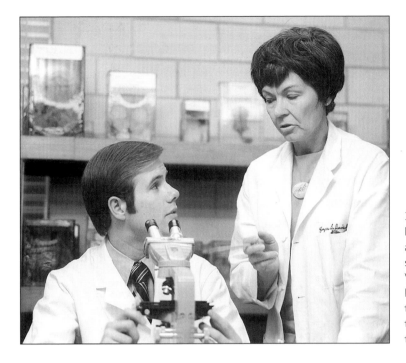

36. Joyce Davis, M.D., discusses a slide with student Thomas Ward Neal. Davis did much to modernize the teaching in the Department.

contact or idea of what the *practice* of pathology really is. So having the opportunity to be in the hospital to see what a pathologist does, how he interacts with other physicians and so on, is a good thing for students. It gives them another option. Plus they know how to utilize the pathologist in their hospital for whatever type of specialty they choose to take.

—*Joyce Davis, M.D.*

Pertinence

In the late '60s, there were all sorts of changes. The students were rebelling. They wanted everything to be pertinent. There were a lot of revisions in the school curriculum at that time. One thing they did was to try to integrate the teaching. At the same time Internal Medicine was teaching arthritis, the pathologist might be talking about arthritis. Or when liver diseases were covered by the hepatologist, Internal Medicine would be talking about the clinical aspects, along with whoever is giving the lectures on liver disease in Pathology. It sounds good, but the thing that happened is that everybody thinks their component is most important. So if you integrate things in an hour or two hours, the Internal Medicine guy just talks forever and ever, and the pathology guy gets maybe the last 10 minutes or so. That's what happens; it's just inevitable.

—*Harlan Spjut, M.D.*

You Name It

I did teaching for the med technology school, starting in the late 1960s. Until four years ago, we had a school of medical technology, and I taught all of the courses. I did the lecturing part, cytology, hematology, blood staining, you name it. You know, some of those first students that I taught in 1967 retired about two or three years ago.

—*Anita Werch, M.D.*

An Evolving Thing

A little over a year ago, Dr. Lieberman asked me to be the faculty director of the medical student pathology course. It is a difficult job, in and of itself, and the time commitment varies. During the course it is more intense, and we have specific preparations. A fair amount of it is administrative—not anything that anyone I know of, probably, particularly enjoys. The actual teaching is kind of fun, and so is interacting with students, but planning who is going to teach this part and who is going to teach that part, making up the tests, and all of that stuff is not necessarily all that enjoyable.

Quite frankly, I didn't know how to do things the best way, and it has certainly been an evolving thing over the last, well, over a year. I have to say honestly that a fair number of people see it as just something that sucks up your time with no benefit. It doesn't generate any money for the Department.

I take care of the odds and ends, and the headaches, and the people bitching—people bitch, and I think they always will. Both residents that we have help us teach, as well as faculty. I think I am enough of a co-dependent/enabler type that I hope I keep enough people happy, and they think it is going reasonably OK.

—*Chris Finch, M.D.*

Fifteen Minutes

I use a lot of photographs for my lectures with medical students, of flowers and scenery and things like that. They help make the lecture much more interesting.

Some students have commented that they are surprised by my timing, because every 15 minutes, I put on the light or show a picture which is not related to what I am talking about, or it's related but it's not scientific. A flower or some strange thing wakes them up.

When I go to church, I listen to the minister preach, and if it takes more than 15 minutes, you notice that the people start looking around. So the attention of people cannot be held more than 15 minutes without a break. If you want to deliver a message, you need to deliver it in 15 minutes, stop, and wake them up. All our lectures are usually in semi-darkness showing slides, so we need to stop, put on the light or ask them to walk, or something like that.

I get a lot of teaching awards. It's interesting how I always get good feedback from these students, and it is infectious. When you get good feedback, it makes you want to do more. You want to excel.

—*Abe Ramzy, M.D.*

A New Way of Thinking

You know, when you have been in this business for a long time, it is very hard to think with a fresh perspective. Well, then, here comes a medical student with a new way of thinking. He just really floors you. You think, "Wow, this guy is amazing." What constitutes the joy of teaching is the student himself.

You see, if you don't have students, it's stale. What you have for him is stale. It is just from books and whatnot, but he comes up with fresh ideas. My goodness, these guys are so bright, it is incredible. They floor me all the time by their thought process.

I also, of course, have daily dealings with our medical technologists here, and I hope it is a learning/teaching process each time.

I love teaching. I am not so sure that the students would say, "Yeah, he loves

37. Students gather to study during a regular Friday afternoon slide conference in the early 1950s. Stuart Wallace, M.D., observes the class participants from his post in the corner of the room.

teaching, and it comes across that way," but that is probably the reason why I stayed in academics. I enjoy teaching residents and medical students. That is why I take care of a teaching program for the physician's assistants at Baylor on behalf of the Department of Pathology. I am very proud of that, because I am the only one doing it, and I've been doing it single-handedly all these years. I also enjoy teaching the residents, and they have been very appreciative of my efforts, as well as the efforts of the Department as a whole.

—*Gene Bañez, M.D.*

Rotations

My family and I returned to Houston in August 1953. I asked Dr. Wallace if I could come to work at Baylor part time to keep my hand in medicine. He agreed, and I worked at tasks related to the teaching program. Then I began to go to Jefferson Davis Hospital, where I did autopsies. At the time the residents were doing over 300 autopsies per year. One day I was told that it was time for me to rotate onto the Surgical Pathology service. So I did, and ultimately I also rotated through Microbiology, Biochemistry, and Hematology. We had no formal instruction in these laboratories but worked with the technologists, finally doing what they did to a limited extent except in Hematology, where we were responsible for preparing the bone-marrow reports.

By 1958, Dr. Wallace agreed to support my application to take the American Board of Pathology Specialty Examination in anatomic pathology. Dr. Ella Sheehan and I flew the milk run in a prop plane to Chicago, where we took and passed that examination. Two of our fellow residents who also passed the examination at that time were Drs. Arch Brown and Frank Chapman. In 1960, we were prepared to pass the American Board Exam in clinical pathology. We did so and were very pleased.

One of the things that helped us greatly in preparing for the anatomic path exam was the 3 o'clock Friday afternoon slide conference at Baylor.

—*Joyce Davis, M.D.*

Routine

We didn't have nearly as big a faculty as we have now, and there were only a few residents when I was a resident. I remember when I first came back from Johns Hopkins, the only two residents at Methodist were me and Don Weilbaecher, and we literally did everything. We kind of changed around from working up surgicals and autopsies and reports and so forth. And when I was in Clinical Pathology here, we also had very few residents. Maybe there were three or four total. I remember that heavy workload.

Of course, we didn't do as much then, either, as we do now. We didn't have as many diverse things. Molecular biology was non-existent, and we focused on routine chemistries and clinical pathology, very routine things in blood banking and very routine things in anatomic pathology.

—*David Yawn, M.D.*

Personalities

I finished my last year of residency here. And Dr. Rosenberg offered me a job. Actually, he didn't offer me a job, and he didn't offer me a job, and he didn't offer me a job. I kept on waiting around, and he never said anything. It kept getting closer and closer to the end of the year, but I knew that Dr. Titus would find someplace for me. I had to stay here because my husband and family were here, and I couldn't go anywhere else. I wanted to be here.

38. Edith Hawkins, M.D., oversaw the Department at Texas Children's Hospital with David Yawn, M.D., after Harvey Rosenberg, M.D., and other pathologists left.

So finally in April, I went to Dr. Rosenberg, and I asked him about whether he would have a job for me. He said, "Oh, I thought you knew you were going to be here." I don't know how he thought I knew.

And then they took his contract away from him. And so he left, and most everyone else left the Department, except for me. I didn't leave because I didn't have any other place to go. I couldn't unless I broke my family up. Then Dr. David Yawn came over here, and he and I ran the lab for a year. And that was probably the single most extensive learning experience I ever had. I learned more in that single year than I did in any other year. I probably never would have gotten where I have gotten if I hadn't had that year.

The one thing it taught me was that I didn't want to do administration. The major disadvantage was to make sure that the people were doing what they were supposed to, doing what you wanted them to, and not what you didn't—just keeping people working together and appropriately and so forth. We had some personalities. I didn't like that part of it.

But working with Dr. Yawn was a pleasure. He is certainly a personality. He is very, very smart and dedicated.

He's also really funny. One story about him: While he was working here, he got about a hundred eggs and hatched baby turkeys. And he had these hundred baby turkeys in his garage here in Houston. After a while the turkeys got too big for his garage, so he packed them all off and took them to his farm in East Texas. By that time they had imprinted and become very people-oriented. And they followed people around the farm. Wherever you went, these turkeys would follow you. One day all of the people at the farm had left, and the turkeys got lonesome. They went over to the next farm and surrounded the farmer on his truck bed. He wasn't too thrilled when that happened.

And that was typical of the things that David would do. But he is a very smart man, and he has been a real addition to this department.

—Edith Hawkins, M.D.

A Family Thing

If you ask me what is my most important achievement, I would say the stimulation and training of my fellows and the residents. I look at my fellows as sons and daughters.

The important part of this is that I'm part of the team. I feel very strongly about the need not to focus on myself and promoting my career, but on promoting the careers of the people who work under me. When I was an assistant professor, I needed to think about how to move up, but I moved up with the help of the people who worked under me, with me, and above me.

I have an accordion file here which contains pictures of the babies of my former fellows. Here's a picture of somebody just having her baby, and there is the husband. They don't send this to just anybody. So, I have a whole bunch of these pictures here. You know, I am part of their life, and they keep me informed. When they do something good, they always send me something about it. It's a family kind of thing.

—Abe Ramzy, M.D.

Rewards

Research laboratories are very informal places. People wear cutoff jeans. One of my students—in fact a fellow who just graduated—wore a ponytail, a baseball cap, cutoff blue jeans, and boots. Nobody worried about that, but at the hospital there was a sense that you might run into a patient at any point, and you had to "look the part"—whatever the part was. Our lab was always told to "stay indoors" when important visitors were coming through, to wear our lab coats, hoping they could cover the skin.

We had to adapt a bit to the hospital setting, but of course the students had all their training in classes, and their classmates were over here at Baylor, and much of that environment was carried back into my laboratory. Some of the situations could be a little bit amusing. We had students who were sometimes way ahead of things and other students questioning whether they really wanted to go through this or not.

Being a Ph.D. candidate is kind of a lonely thing. You may have enough classmates in your course work that you can say, well, I'm doing about as well as everybody else, but when you get into the laboratory, the project is your own. You have no one to compare yourself with, because what you're doing is so different. It is often hard for the student to sort out variables.

We have had situations where students ultimately just decide that this isn't their thing, and after being in a lab for a year or so, that is a loss. Then you have other students who come through and love it. One of my students graduated in less than four years, which is kind of a record. Just seeing the different ways in which they respond to the frustrations of problem solving—which is what research is— and how excited they get over finding some little bit of new data is a reward.

I think physicians are often rewarded, especially if they deal face-to-face with patients, by the good that they do the individual, and that is an immediate and obvious sort of reward. In research, you can go a long time before you find something new that you understand well enough to know that it is significant.

I always worried about the students who decide at some point that they don't want to do this when they had gone through most of the hard part. They had taken the courses. They had gone through the qualifying exam, and they had done six months of research and somewhere felt that something went wrong, it wasn't working out right, and they didn't know what the answer was anymore. Sometimes they didn't know what the question was anymore, and that was really upsetting. I would keep saying, "Oh, jeez, you made it through the hard part. Now the fun part is starting, when you get to try different things." But it is all in your outlook, I guess.

39. Gretchen Darlington, Ph.D., often reflects on her work history "in terms of the students that I have had in the lab."

I had one student who was very quiet, but a very bright young woman who breezed through her course work and qualifying exam and got onto a project and then just before she graduated, she became pregnant with her first child. We were trying to get her papers and her vita written up, so she would bring the baby in, and either she or I would walk around the conference room with the baby while the other person was writing the report. The baby was quite happy, and I didn't mind it at all. I hadn't been able to carry babies around for a long time. My student is actually doing very well now.

I think about my work history very often in terms of the students that I have had in the lab. Part of that is because they really were the driving force for much of the data that was generated. Post-doctoral fellows who work in the lab often bring new insights into things, a kernel of an idea, and they develop the research program beyond that.

It is nice to look back on the people who have graduated and who have gone on to do well. Teaching is a very demanding career, but at the end of it, teachers should be very proud of what they do. I really admire the people who are in high schools and colleges, who have an impact on a lot of people. Here we are doing it slowly, one at a time.

—*Gretchen Darlington, Ph.D.*

Amplification

Probably the single event that was most rewarding for me just happened a few months ago. I was one of five people who were being considered for this Dresden Award in graduate student teaching that's voted on by the graduate students. Then it got narrowed down to two of us, and I was one of the two finalists.

So there's a college-wide meeting for the awards ceremony with 400 people in the auditorium. I found out that I won this award for graduate teaching. You know, it's actually very important to me. I spend a lot of effort teaching, and I think it's very, very important to do.

If you can train 20 or 30 good people over the course of your career, and they go on and make a significant contribution, then that's really an amplification of what any one individual can do. Maybe I'll have 10 or 20 important papers in my life, but if I have trained 20 good people, then there are 200 good papers that might come from them. Teaching has a potentially much greater impact than one individual in their own lab.

—*Graeme Mardon, Ph.D.*

Coattails

I really do enjoy training graduate students. It is very rewarding. I have kept in close contact with all the students who have left, and I enjoy watching their careers develop.

It's funny, because when I first started the lab, I felt the last thing I needed was a bunch of graduate students who didn't know anything about how to do science. What I thought I really needed was a contingent of really good post-docs. So I started out with a couple of post-docs that caused me nothing but trouble and nothing but headaches. They were not motivated, not interested, and just a real difficult problem from the day they showed up. I began to realize that as a young—beginning—faculty member, you're not going to get the best post-docs that are out there. There are a lot bigger, more established mentors and principal investigators for them to work with, but that didn't occur to me in the beginning. I had to learn that lesson the hard way.

The students, however, come in and are very eager to learn. They're open-minded, and yet they're not going to question too much what you ask them to do. It's really great when it starts to click for them, when they leave your coattails and begin to start having ideas of their own. When they run their own experiments—even if they might be flawed at first—watching them start being successful in that, it's really great.

—*Mark Majesky, Ph.D.*

To Go Out

I basically ran the residency program for 11 years, which is, I think, a record. Most people do it for three or four years at a time. I continued to function as a clinically oriented practicing pathologist. When I look back on how I did it, I'm not sure how.

I made it a 24-hour-a-day job, and I took it home with me at night, on weekends, on vacation. I lived it. You can talk to my husband. He was about ready to strangle me, because I couldn't leave it alone. I think that I gave it my all. I have stepped down, but I am still very involved, and there is not a day that goes by that I'm still not called with some question.

How do you train residents so that they are safe to go out and serve a patient well? They come in knowing stuff from med school and at varying other levels, and you foster them and nurture them and hope they can fly. That is a challenge. Certainly pathology has its share of challenges, for whatever reason. Pathology is a very varied field with lots of diverse opportunities, but it is not entirely an attractive field to people who went to medical school to work with patients. How do you attract people into a specialty that you know offers a lot of things, that you know there is a need for? The population is growing and graying. How do you attract the next generation when nobody seems interested and you know there is going to be a need for it?

I hope I have taught the residents an approach to what is important in life and what is not important. I always want to remember, "What is the question being asked? What is the impact of my diagnosis?" Get to the nitty-gritty of it and save the esoteric for conferences. Figure out what it is the doc needs to know to take care of the patient. I hope that I have conveyed that to the people I have trained, about being relevant and appropriate and direct.

I am known to grumble a lot, not in any destructive way, but just about generally feeling overwhelmed and not able to keep up. And, you know, I wouldn't give pathology up. It's almost all been great. Trying to teach residents to learn and mature—it's what parents feel like when they see their kids go off to college or get married, with great pain but yet a great sense of pride. I have that feeling every year, so that has been terribly satisfying.

—*Mary Schwartz, M.D.*

More Than Being Chief Resident

Mary Schwartz and me, we go back. Mary was my chief resident when I started out. Once I went to drop a book off at the library, but somehow that book-return bin had been moved, so I hopped out of my car, and I ran inside to return the book. While I was there, I went to do something else, and in all that, maybe it took a little longer than I thought.

I didn't see the tow truck. I was still too new in the country. And as I walked out, I saw them towing my car away. So I'm running after them, shouting, "Wait, wait, you can't tow my car away" as Mary was walking into the library. So then we hopped in her car, and we chased the tow truck. It was like 7:28 in the evening, and they towed it to the Brown lot. When we got there, we said, "Well, this is our car, we have been following it."

The driver said, "Oh, well, you've got to pay." I forget what it was, maybe $58. So between the two of us we counted out every dollar and every penny, and we came up with the money to rescue my car.

So Mary was great. She was the chief resident, and she taught you all the stuff, but it was more than just being chief resident. She rescued my car with me. That was really great. I think, overall, the camaraderie still exists among the residents.

—*Dina Mody, M.D.*

40. Mary Schwartz, M.D., admired by students for her strong work ethic, confers with Edward Tuttle, M.D.

Twenty Beats Per Minute

There is no single anecdote that would begin to capture the impact that Mary Schwartz has had on my training in pathology at Baylor. Very early in one's tenure as a resident, you begin to hear the stories about how she handles unruly surgeons, her high expectations of everyone from chairman to tech, and how she shepherds residents towards a better understanding of how the job is done. You hear about her wit and her razor-sharp mind. And you hear about her surgical pathology skills. And you think, "C'mon, how good can she be?" Then, the following things happen:

1. You have to ferry about a million tough skin, gyn, breast, GI, GU, endocrine, and soft tissue cases to her office, since all the experts in the Department want her opinion, too.

2. You knock on her door after peeking through the holes in the mini-blinds, and she's in there, glasses off, phone on the right shoulder, resident in the hot seat, a secretary standing in front of her desk. She's dictating into the phone like an auctioneer, knocking out the 43rd case of the day, and motioning to the secretary to give her the paperwork. The secretary comes out, and you wait the requisite 20

seconds or so, then knock. You don't hear the first "Come in" because of the din in her office, but the second ushers you in. Now you just have a dumb personal issue to ask about, but she drops everything, sends off the other resident, and focuses on your question.

3. You're giving grand rounds, and she appears at 12:25 p.m. Your pulse quickens a good 20 beats per minute, and you complete your lecture. Dr. Schwartz then asks you a question about something you covered before she got there, just to make sure the residents got it as a teaching point.

4. You sit on a committee with her. Curriculum, resident issues, whatever. From her voiced concerns to her suggestions for the group, the things she brings to the table show the level of personal commitment to the program that she has made.

5. You're a first-year on your first Frozens day with Dr. Schwartz. Of course, you get a specimen from one of the prominent Fondren-Brown boys, who think you can get a diagnosis in two to three minutes, max. They break scrub and come to the Frozen lab to breathe down your neck. The slide comes out, and Dr. Schwartz calls you over, reviews the slide, calls for a recut. All this with the surgeon breathing down *her* neck. She runs the entire differential diagnosis (keeping in mind that she knows *exactly* the personality of the surgeon and how he/she's going to react to the diagnosis rendered). She *handles* this surgeon. All this without breaking a sweat. The surgeon returns to the OR, satisfied with his/her answer. You've been handed an experience that you hope, someday, you'll be emulating.

6. You are three hospitals away working on a complex specimen, and you think, "If I were grossing this for Dr. Schwartz (since it's entirely possible she'll see it in consultation), how would I do this *exactly right*?"

7. Friday morning, Unknown Conference. Dr. Schwartz's day. Attendance is high. ... When you're a first-year, her calling on you is an unnerving experience, till you realize that she's doing this for you. You struggle through the differential; she's coaching you all the way. When you're an upper-level, it's worse, because you desperately want to show her you've learned something; you don't want to disappoint. Like all great teachers, she brings this out in you. You can't help it.

What did I learn from Dr. Schwartz? Scholarship. Compassion. Professionalism. A strong work ethic. I hope someday I'm half (or some fraction thereof) the pathologist she is.

—*Rob Edwards, M.D., Ph.D.*

Inspired Ideas

My very first rotation residency just happened to be here at Ben Taub, and of course any first-year resident who hasn't done an autopsy by himself or herself is nervous about that and about being on call the first time. The two dieners here at that time, Ricky Evans and Leroy Stewart, were both extremely experienced. They could, either one of them, do an autopsy quicker, easier, and more accurately by themselves than a first-year pathology resident and probably an upper-level resident.

I remember a weekend when I was on call, and Ricky Evans called me at home and said, "Doc, there are three autopsies." So I got here, and I don't even remember which staff I was with. It was someone who is no longer here, and he didn't come down and help, which is honestly not too unusual. So I'm just thinking I'm going to be here all day and all night, because I'm so new at this that I'll be so slow. And Ricky, he said, "Oh, don't worry, it will be OK." He had been dealing with residents for years and years.

As it turned out, he found a problem with the consent form on one of the cases himself. So he got rid of one. This sounds really bad—us trying to get rid of doing autopsies. ... Then I was looking through one chart and getting ready to do it, and in the meantime he was just kind of looking at the other chart. I don't know how he did it, but he found in the nurse's notes some allusion to the boyfriend beating up the deceased. In that kind of scenario, where the person then dies, there is a question about homicide, so we ended up talking to the staff, and then the medical examiner, and that case was sent to the medical examiner. Then with the one we were left with, Ricky was extremely helpful, and we got done very quickly. He is quite the guy.

He oftentimes comes up with these inspired ideas to facilitate the autopsy. I can remember one I had, again, during my very first rotation here in the first three months of residency. It was a case where there was a question of GI bleeding, and so we were looking and didn't see anything. We got to the stomach, and it was full of clotted blood. He suggested we tie off both ends of the stomach and fill it with formalin. He said, "Then, if there is a bleeding site, we can see it much easier." He was right. It was very clear then. So he helped me enormously in many ways over the years. Plus he is always pleasant and charming. I hope he doesn't ever plan to retire.

I was doing an upper-level surg-path rotation here at Ben Taub. I was with my close friend, Jennifer. She took a job elsewhere now, and I really miss her a lot. Anyway, she and I worked here together for surg-path rotations, and we were the two upper-levels. The third person was a first-year.

Most of the time there were four people for surg-path. For that three-month rotation, there were three of us, and the first-year student was very unhappy with life in general. She ended up leaving Baylor and going elsewhere. So she was not the easiest person to be on a team with, and it was really a miserable three months. Really miserable.

Jennifer and I were here routinely from 7 in the morning until 8 or 9 at night, day in and day out. I know other people have worse rotations, and people stay all night in other services, but this was miserable enough. The first-year called in sick frequently, or she would be so disturbed and upset. Before she finished her work for the day, we were often soft-hearted enough to say, "Why don't you just go home, ride your horse"—she had a horse here—"go ride your horse, and we'll finish up." In some respects it was easier than to have her here. We were counting down the days.

Our last day was right at the end of December. I don't know if it was New Year's Eve or just before New Year's Eve, but our last day was extremely miserable. I remember we were grossing, trying to get everything done for the next group of people coming in. It was about 9 o'clock, and we were grossing these awful, disgusting specimens. One happened to be a colectomy on some poor patient who had ischemic bowel, essentially dead bowel, and I don't know how long the patient had been in this condition before they operated, but it was essentially rotting. So it was in a huge container, all this bowel, and it was one of the worst smells that I can recall from residency. It was so disgusting, and so huge. We were putting out big plastic bags, the big red biohazard bags, spreading them out on the floor to deal with it, because we couldn't get it all up on the grossing tray. It was just a nightmare.

We finally got done that day. It was our last day here. Jennifer and I were walking out the back stairs of Ben Taub, where there is parking for two administrators, and nobody else could park there. Jennifer's husband would typically pick her up there. He would stay in the car in case he had to move it. Then I would walk past them to get to the parking garage, where I'd parked.

So this night, it's dark, it's late, and we are exhausted but happy the rotation was over. We walk down the stairs, we open the door, and there is Greg in the car as usual, and Jennifer opens the door. He pops open a bottle of champagne. In the CD player is the Alleluia Chorus. And he has three glasses, and we each have a little sip of champagne. I'm sure there is a camera right there at the back door for security purposes. I'm sure someone got all that on tape.

—*Chris Finch, M.D.*

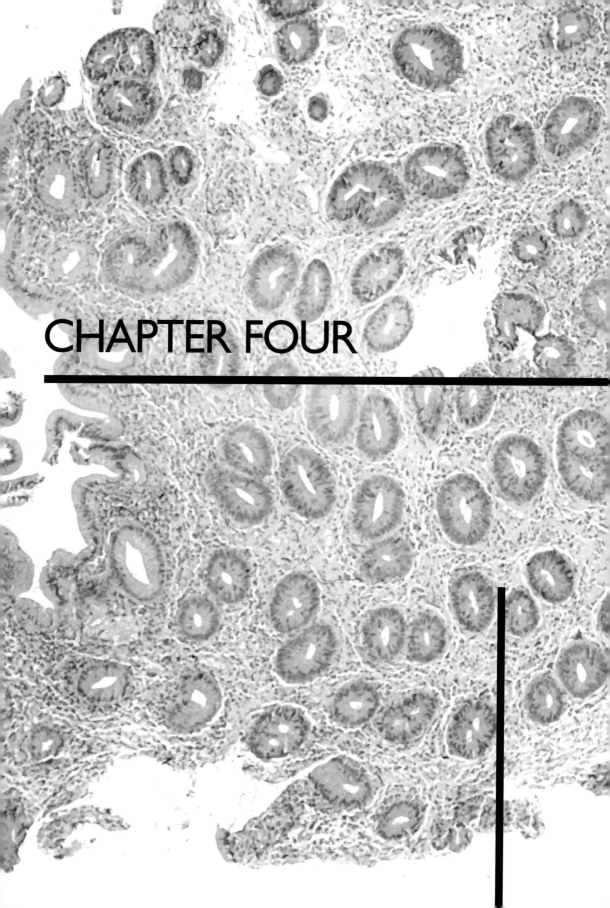

CHAPTER FOUR

THE DOCTORS' DOCTORS

If the popular image of the pathologist is someone who sits in a musty office filled with icky things floating in formaldehyde while he drinks ancient coffee, takes an occasional leisurely look at a slide, and hides from humanity, the reality is markedly different.

Pathologists don't have time for such leisure, and they couldn't be effective doctors if they were recluses. Every pathologist I interviewed discussed the acute responsibility he or she felt for making the proper diagnosis. The pathologist's work is constant pressure.

Rudy, What Do I Do?

Being a pathologist has made me realize how lucky we are as human beings to be able to get up every morning, do what we do, go to bed, and get up the next day again. It is so important to keep ourselves healthy, because you never know when it's going to be your turn. What pathologists do can, from one day to the next, change people's lives irreversibly. And oftentimes, the general public doesn't know that, because we have always told other people we are the doctors' doctors.

The surgeon, the internist, all those people get the credit because they're on the front lines, but obviously they don't make the diagnosis. That really comes into play when you do a frozen section. We tell the surgeons, "Well, this is what it is," and then based on that, it can alter the way they do the surgery and ultimately what they end up doing to the patient.

I don't know how many times I have been called into the operating room, when the patient's asleep, obviously, and doesn't know what's going on. The surgeon will ask me, "Rudy, what do I do? Should I take more tissue? You tell me—what do I do?" At that moment in time, I have the responsibility for that patient's life.

I have a letter from one patient that I have kept in my files to remind me of the importance of what we do. Oftentimes we are disconnected—which is good in some ways, because it gives you more objectivity. It would be hard to take care of a human being and then have to do a biopsy when you've established a patient-doctor relationship, and then you have to make a diagnosis of malignancy. But by the same token, you have to realize what you see under the microscope is connected directly to a human being.

Anyway, this patient was diagnosed with breast cancer, and she came to my office. I didn't make the diagnosis—one of my colleagues did—but she wanted to sit down and look at our slides. She's a very intelligent woman. So I explained to her how we do it and what it means. She wrote me a letter and thanked me for what I did. Every so often I pull the letter out and read it, not because I want to hear what she said about me, but because I want to constantly remind myself that a human being's life is in my hands.

—*Rudy Laucirica, M.D.*

People Skills

In some respects it takes a lot more skill to interact with other clinicians than with patients. We're their consultants. The surgeon is like my patient, that's why the pathologist is called the "doctors' doctor." I tell the surgeon, "This is what you need to do, this is the severity of it, go get me this, get me that, come back to me." If you're talking to a patient with a third-grade education, you may not have to

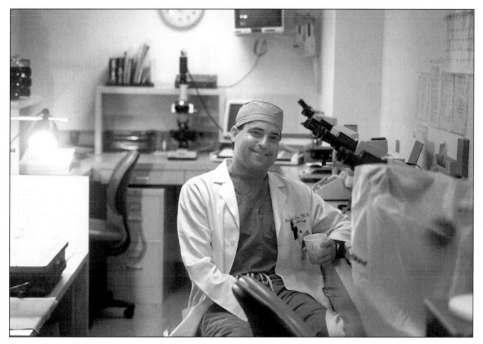

41. Rudy Laucirica, M.D., says the Department is "like the United Nations" because it is so diverse.

have as great people skills, because they just want you to tell them what to do, and they'll do it or they won't. Peers don't really know what you do or the subtleties of what you do, and interacting with them requires people skills actually more than one would think.

I've done well in pathology. I went a lot farther than I would have in a field like medicine, where a fifth of the doctors are internal medicine doctors. You have a big field of competition to be the top guy at the hospital, whereas pathology has a lot less people. One to 2 percent of doctors are pathologists; it's very small.

All the people who work in the lab are hospital employees, but I'm the medical director at Methodist. Dr. Lieberman is the medical director in terms of inspection purposes, and for what is listed as the true boss. He delegates to me as the deputy chief to run the day-to-day service. As such, all these 250 hospital employees who work in the lab report to me as the medical director. So I have to be able to effectively deal with them and recognize their needs, from the people that scrub the glassware to the other pathologists, a whole spectrum of people. Unless you can do that, you won't be that effective.

I had left shortly after Dr. Lieberman came. That was 1989, around June. I came back in October of 1991. I left as head of Anatomic Pathology at Methodist. The chairman was trying to recruit someone to be in the office that I'm in now. He had a number of people come through. Some people wanted the job, but weren't really thought to be good candidates, and other people were good candidates but for one reason or another turned it down. After a period of two years, they had not recruited the deputy chief of service. Then the chairman had Dr. Cagle take me to dinner one night. He said, "Why don't you go back and talk to the chairman?" I still did academic stuff when I was in private practice. I thought, well, there was no harm in talking. He offered me the job to be deputy chief. He said, "You can come over there, you can be in my office"—which is my office now—"you can run the day-to-day operations" and that sort of thing.

It takes getting used to when you come back as a boss. Things are different. You tell a joke to the residents or something, and they don't know whether to laugh, because "It's Dr. Wheeler." I left younger, I came back older, I came back in a higher position, and I noticed a difference immediately. I wanted to come back and have it just exactly like it was. It never is. I remember fussing one time about something up in the frozen-section lab—I wasn't fussing any more than I ever did—but Dr. Lechago came to me a day or two later and said, "Why were you so pissed off in the lab on Monday?"

I said, "What are you talking about?"

He said, "You were raising a stink up there." Everybody in the lab was talking about it, and it filtered up through the hierarchy of the technicians, over to some of the pathologists. Then my buddy comes and tells me, "You blew up in the lab."

I said, "I was just acting like I always do."

He said, "You have to remember, you're 'Dr. Wheeler' now, deputy chief of service. When you say something, people stop and listen. It's not like old times."

I rarely get upset, at least at work, and I wasn't really upset. But I was saying, "We should really change this, we've been doing it this way, it's prone to mistakes, why haven't we done this yet?"

Dr. Lechago told me a story about when he was head at the VA Hospital. He went to the lab and asked somebody, "How are you doing today?" And the guy got paranoid, like, "Shouldn't I be doing fine?" and "Why are you coming through

42. Lee Tuttle, M.D., left, shares a laugh with Tom Wheeler, M.D. "Not only do [pathologists] have to deal effectively with ... other pathologists, but with clinicians and surgeons, and they have to be able to project an image of confidence," says Wheeler.

and asking me this?" Even in daily, casual conversation, when you have a different position of authority, it becomes quite different in how people perceive you.

We have a culture of cooperation, teamwork, at least in our department at Methodist. I can't speak for the whole Department, which encompasses a lot of different hospitals. We tend to hire people we know we can get along with and work effectively with. It doesn't matter how good someone is—if they cause discord in the Department, it's not worth it. In the interview process, we take that into account. Because not only do they have to deal effectively with us as the other pathologists, but with clinicians and surgeons, and they have to be able to project an image of confidence. When you tell a surgeon someone has breast cancer, go take her breast off, if the surgeon finds out a week later that it was the wrong call. ... He has to have supreme confidence that the pathologist is right.

—*Tom Wheeler, M.D.*

A Shock

When I first got here, I guess that was two years ago, I had never really thought about doctors or hospitals very much, you know. What they actually do. I went to a surgery, and I saw how the doctors were really playing God almost, standing over a body there with its torso open. It hit me really hard that my dad and every other doctor who works here are responsible for the lives of a lot of people. There are a lot of people who put trust in them. It was scary at first, and it hit me really strong; it was kind of a shock. But I got used to it, and I had a different viewpoint from then on about what goes on around here.

—Dayton Wheeler

Do No Harm

43. Like all other pathologists, Bhuvaneswari Krishnan, M.B., B.S., feels an enormous sense of responsibility to "do no harm."

Pathology offers a good lifestyle. You don't have too many calls. It's not odd hours, and you're not working long hours. And for women with a family, it is really helpful. That's why you see a lot of women. Pathologists are all interested in a lot of things in life; it's not just medicine. Most of them are more artistically oriented, which probably is because pathology is to some extent appreciating histology.

Fear is always there. You constantly remind yourself, "Do no harm" all the time, especially when you're on the faculty. The first year was really rough. You are always worried, because during the residency you had no responsibility, and suddenly you hold a lot of responsibility. At that time, the person who helped me out a lot was another pathologist who is not here now, George Saleh. I used to consult him a lot, so when he, too, agreed, I got a lot of mental support that I was going on the right track. And so the first year was rough for me, but because he was there, it was really helpful. And now since I'm seeing more and more cases, now I feel confident, and I'm doing so many things that I feel confident to handle.

—Bhuvaneswari Krishnan, M.B., B.S.

Every Day

Really as a woman I didn't have an issue in this department, which I did have in medical school and I did have in private practice. I started on the faculty pretty young, and I know that was an issue for some other faculty, but it really wasn't an issue. I guess the challenge is always, how do you learn everything that you are supposed to? I still haven't figured that one out. You cannot learn everything, but how do you keep learning to keep up with all the stuff that fits around you? I mean, you can't not make a mistake. You sure don't want to, but you know you will.

Dr. Ramzy has a famous saying: "The only pathologists or other physicians who don't make mistakes are the ones who don't practice." You just try to undo whatever you can and not let the guilt overwhelm you. Taking responsibility is not an issue. Every day I say, "Please, God, don't let me miss a melanoma"—because if it is melanoma, they should have a bigger incision. If they don't, the melanoma could recur, and they could die. You are just overwhelmed by the amount of work that you are doing, so you are flying through the stuff the same way you'd fly through a bunch of patients in an office. You think, "My God, I have got to slow down, what if I miss the wrong cancer?" It is a challenge, to get done what you do, and still serve patients—and hopefully "do no harm" along the way.

—Mary Schwartz, M.D.

The Whole System

Pathologists tend to be compulsive, detailed people who really care about the product they deliver. They really don't want to deliver a faulty product. I don't think any physician does, but with a pathologist, you are *it* for the whole hospital. One physician makes a mistake, and he or she affects only one patient. You make a mistake in clinical labs or in the blood bank, and it is systemic, it goes through the whole system.

—Michael Lieberman, M.D., Ph.D.

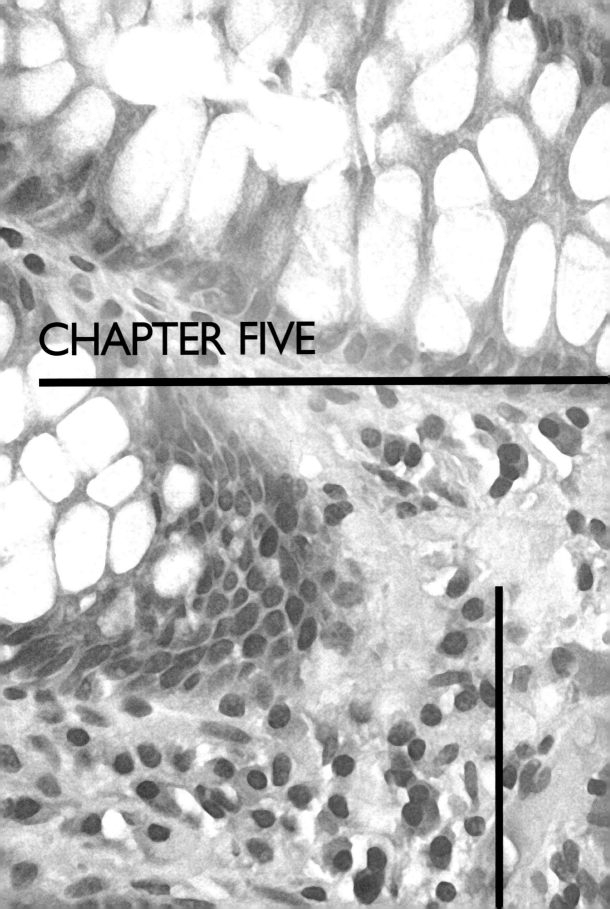

CHAPTER FIVE

LARGER THAN LIFE

In the course of researching this book, I encountered some stories—and some characters—over and over again. These are the legends in the Department. Of course, stories that are told and retold also reflect the values of their culture.

What kinds of stories does the Department of Pathology value? In the Harlan Spjut stories, modesty and integrity. In the David Yawn stories, independence and creativity. In the Malcolm McGavran stories, directness and fearsome intelligence. The people who become legends in the Department live life on their own terms.

Harlan J. Spjut, M.D.
Dear Bob

When I was offered the job as chair at Baylor and I'd accepted, Dr. Ackerman, who was the head of surgical pathology at Wash U, came over to me one day and said, "You know you need someone in Surgical Pathology down there. I want you to take Harlan Spjut." I said, "OK, that sounds good to me." So I got down there. Practically just as soon as I walked in, I had to do several things—get a place on the budget, talk to the dean, go to the faculty and get an appointment for Harlan as a professor. Then I wrote him a letter and offered him the job. He wrote back a classic letter:

Dear Bob,

I accept.

Harlan

So that's the way that happened. Ackerman came to me and said he thought Harlan should come with me.

—*Bob O'Neal, M.D.*

Extreme Modesty

One of the attractions for me in coming here was Dr. Spjut. Everybody in the whole world of pathology knew of Dr. Spjut. I had never met him before visiting, but once I did, I understood his charismatic qualities. Of course I knew about his scholarly work.

One of the things about any profession, of course, is mentorship. Dr. Spjut was the first pupil of what may be regarded as the first surgical pathologist in the world, Dr. Lauren Ackerman. Ackerman started working at Washington University at a time when surgical pathology probably was not even a part of the pathology department. Pathologists were just there to do autopsies and teach. The surgeons hired their own pathologists to help them understand surgical cases that were taking place while the patients were still alive. That was a big transition that took place around, I guess, the beginning of the '30s.

Arthur P. Stout and Dr. Ackerman in St. Louis were the fathers of this field of pathology. And Spjut was the first student of Ackerman's. He was the distinguished surgical pathologist in this city, and he'd won every award that Texas pathology can give to one of its own, because he was responsible for training so many of the people who came to Houston to learn how to become pathologists. He followed Dr. Ackerman's system of doing it, which was to demand a lot of himself and therefore set a tone for all of the pupils.

And Spjut, of course, was best known for everything in surgical pathology, but especially bone tumors and then tumor pathology in general. That's the main role of the surgical pathologist. "Is it a tumor, and, if so, what kind?"—those are the two questions always being asked. And then, if it isn't a tumor, what is it, and what can we do about it? But mainly, solve that problem. Tumor pathology in general is his forte. He's written I don't know how many papers and book chapters. He's done it all with extreme modesty.

To this day—and I don't know how old he is now, but I bet 80 is pretty close, plus or minus a couple of years—to this day, when we have a regular conference where the residents present, he will be one of the most faithful attendees, and he will ask the most difficult questions, even though it may be a first-year resident just starting out. He'll ask them something, and they'd better darn well know their stuff. He's not doing it maliciously or viciously, but because it's an important or interesting question that occurred to him, and if it occurred to him, being an old geezer, then the young guys just in training ought to be darn well prepared to answer it, or at least have thought

44. Harlan Spjut, M.D., a legend in the field of surgical pathology, is known for his modesty and his kindness.

about it. So he hasn't changed, from what I can see. Well, he hasn't changed in the 22 years that I've known him. Physically he looks exactly the same. My goodness, he's incredible.

So all of us hope we are going to be like him when we get to that age, and I hoped that I was going to be like him when I first came here in my 40s. Now that I'm in my 60s, I still want to be like him.

—*Milton Finegold, M.D.*

Take It Easy

I studied at Wash U and Dr. Lauren Ackerman—who was internationally famous in pathology—was there. He lived into his 80s. Malcolm McGavran and

Walter Bauer, his young lieutenants, were there, too. Altogether there was an air of "This is the way it is, by God."

I graduated from medical school in '60. I went into the pathology program there at Wash U. I'd done a post-sophomore summer project with Bob O'Neal and liked him. That first year of my residency, I first heard about Harlan Spjut. Lauren Ackerman, who was not given to timid statements, said Spjut was the best surgical pathologist in America.

So when the job at Methodist opened up, especially since it was oriented towards clinical aspects, I took it. I didn't want to be a rat doctor, the way I'd have to be if I stayed at Wash U. Under Spjut, plus O'Neal, it was very realistically oriented. It was about as ideal as it gets.

I went to Methodist in '65, after Methodist had been wrenched away from Jack Abbott. The most exciting thing from '65 to '71 or so was the change in the Pathology Department at Methodist. Here was a department that had previously been nonacademic, and it became academic. I started teaching conferences for residents and kept those going. I made contributions to the resident training program. It was the job I was supposed to do, but at the same time, there was the excitement of trying to mix the daily work of surgical pathology, plus writing papers. I was slow to get into paper writing. Spjut used to beat on me. He said it every 10 days. He wore me down. And once I started, I saw that it was great. That was one of the major things he did. He was so powerfully influential, but he was quiet in his reminding. Still, if he brings it up every couple of weeks, you get tired of hearing the message.

After he stimulated me to begin writing papers, I did write some of at least minor importance. They included several papers on breast cancer that were minor milestones. For several years, it has been interesting to see how they are no longer quoted. They have been incorporated into standard background information that "everyone knows." I am sure that only a few people understand that even the most standard information was once a "new" idea. There were many conversations with Spjut at the time I wrote these papers, and in large part they were written because I did not know the answer and, far more importantly, Spjut did not have an answer.

John Overstreet, the chief of surgery at Methodist, said to Spjut early on, during the first month or two, "You all [Baylor] have managed to run off Jack Abbott, and now we've got these two kids [me and Sid Anderson] here." But we were a couple of young brats who actually knew a lot, more than the previous private-practice folks, and he came around after a few years. Spjut would have been saying, "Take it easy, I'm behind them. I'm looking over their shoulders." He was there every afternoon, but he also left me alone. He struck a good balance. He could really balance his experience and expertise. He's an extraordinary person and a story unto himself. Everybody would say that.

—*Bob Fechner, M.D.*

Thank Goodness

Harlan's been a mentor and close friend of mine now for probably 30 years. I have known him since I was in medical school. When you talk about brilliance, integrity and gentility, he has all of those. Most of us don't have all of those, me especially. McGavran didn't have gentility, but Spjut had all of those and still has. He still actively works in our Department, thank goodness.

There's nothing that's comical or catchy about Spjut, because he is so even-tempered and so genteel, really. I have used that word several times talking about him, but that's because he is a perfect gentleman, he's a perfect scholar, and he's also unlike many people who become famous like he did, especially for his knowledge of malignant and benign bone tumors. He never became egotistical. Pathologists are probably not perceived as being egotistical the way surgeons are, but we are, believe me. We are very egotistical. Harlan Spjut truly is not. He's always predictable, always steady, and always there if you need him for any problem, whether it be a personal problem or a scientific problem.

—*David Yawn, M.D.*

The Whole Book

Oh, my God, he is so cool. Calm. Oh, incredible all the time. Calm in every situation. The thing about it is, when I was a resident under him, he may not have had the force of Dr. McGavran or even Dr. Fechner to cause the terror, but you know what? When he was talking to you, it was like, this guy is laid-back, all right, fine, but after he was gone, you think about what he said, and you say, "Oh, my God, he was really saying something to me personally. I was so stupid that I missed it." That is how you felt, so small after he was gone, because he would say these nice things without sounding personal about it.

Dr. Spjut is probably the kindest, most gentle person I have ever met in this Department. I think that more than 90 percent of people would say the same thing. I have never seen a more humble person. See, he has the license not to be humble because of his accomplishments, so his humility is even more meaningful in my mind. I cannot believe how gentle he is with everybody. I cannot think of anybody he doesn't treat fairly and gently.

He could fill this whole volume about Baylor and the Department. He could single-handedly fill the whole book. But I think that his humility and his gentleness are what make him even more effective as a pathologist. Sometimes I think we react negatively to people who are too haughty and too loud, even if they are saying the truth. Somehow it becomes marred because it is just too jarring.

Dr. Spjut is my model. He is so humane. He is a *physician*.

—*Gene Bañez, M.D.*

Always Some Challenge

A time I found very challenging was in 1995, when we started the outreach program at Baylor with the orthopedic hospital and the ob/gyn contract. Initially the idea was to have the program at Methodist, but there were some politics involved, so we had to do it at Baylor. And Baylor had this medical student lab that had medical student types of things, like rat brains. We had to get that lab up to speed. I really had to fight a lot of battles to get that lab up to speed. And I think now it's a success story. The person who really helped me out, aside from my colleagues here, Mary Schwartz and Tom Wheeler, was Dr. Spjut.

Dr. Spjut had never learned how to use a computer ever before, but he was a trooper. In one month he learned two computer systems and two dictation systems. The first was a Columbia HCA Meditech system. I mean, that's like the Big Bertha of computers. I said, "Dr. Spjut, there is no way around it."

He said, "What if I hit the wrong key and the thing just catches fire or something?"

I said, "Don't worry."

And he learned. He used to dictate on tapes or write down those things. We didn't have the Dictaphone system which now everyone uses, but at that time we were the first ones to use it. So it was Dr. Spjut and me.

There were days when I would get really frustrated. He would tell me, "Oh, Dina, don't worry. The long-term results will be great. You'll be happy you did this." He was so great.

—*Dina Mody, M.D.*

The Anonymous Award

I've mud-wrestled with Harlan on a couple of issues, and I must say it's a little bit like Jacob wrestling with the angel of the Lord Almighty. He came away with a broken hip and didn't prevail, but I, I won. I won hands-down on one issue, and on the other I fought him to a draw.

45. "Every year I go to Dr. Spjut, and I try to raise his salary," says chairman Michael Lieberman, M.D., Ph.D., right. "He tells me that he really is not doing much and doesn't need the money and that I shouldn't raise his salary, but every year I go ahead and do it anyway."

First, the fight to the draw. Harlan very generously and semi-anonymously donated $25,000 to the Department to set up a prize for the best research done by an investigator. I came to Harlan, and I said, "Harlan, I really want to thank you for your generosity and your thoughtfulness in doing this. We haven't had a way to recognize our faculty, and you've recognized this early, and it's really wonderful." And then I said, "I think it's only fitting that we call it the Harlan Spjut Award or the Spjut Family Award or some designation that pleases you. After all, it's your gift. ..." So I went on in this vein.

Finally Harlan said, "We're not putting my name or anything about this on the award. This is to be entirely anonymous."

I said, "Harlan, I can't call it the Anonymous Award." I thought for a second. "Who would you like to honor?"

He said, "Well, if I can have anybody I'd want to honor, let's honor Bob O'Neal. We have the Titus conference room and the Wallace conference room over at the hospital. Bob's not been honored."

And I said, "Harlan, I'm willing to put O'Neal's name on it if we could put your name on it, too."

So Harlan said, "Well, no," and we went back and forth.

Finally I convinced him, and I said, "That's great! Let's call it the Spjut-O'Neal Award."

Harlan said, "Absolutely not. I agree to have my name on it, but we're going to call it the O'Neal-Spjut Award."

So I feel like I fought him to a draw on that one. The next problem came when I wanted to set up an endowed chair and honor Harlan. And I went to Harlan, and I said, "Harlan, you have served this Department more loyally and with more distinction than almost anyone I know. I want to set up a chair in your honor."

Harlan said, "I really like the idea of the chair, but you can't honor me."

I said, "Well, why not?"

He said, "Well, for a couple of reasons. First, I haven't done anything."

I reminded him that he served twice as interim chair of the Department, that he is indisputably the best diagnostician in greater Houston and nationally one of the most recognized diagnosticians.

He said, "No, no, you can't, you can't honor me, because that's just nothing. That's just what I do every day. Besides I hardly belong, I hardly deserved admission to medical school. I sort of got in on a fluke, and I didn't do very well, and I ended up in pathology." He mumbled on for a few minutes, and then he said, "You just can't honor me. I just don't deserve any of this."

I said, "Harlan, I really think your accomplishments are quite substantial." He demurred once again. I said, "Harlan, let me ask you a question. Michael DeBakey and Ralph Feigin have whole buildings named after them. Don't you think we could honor you with just a professorship?"

He looked at me. He said, "Well, if you put it that way, OK."

Every year I go to Dr. Spjut, and I try to raise his salary. He tells me that he really is not doing much and doesn't need the money and that I shouldn't raise his salary, but every year I go ahead and do it anyway.

—*Michael Lieberman, M.D., Ph.D.*

Malcolm McGavran, M.D.
McGavran Shows Up

In January of 1972, Jack Titus arrived. Now, it doesn't snow often in Houston, but in January 1972, on that day, it snowed, so of course we said he'd brought it with him from Minnesota. Then it snowed twice more in 10 days.

I liked Titus a lot. He's extremely personable and takes an interest in the people he encounters. I admire and respect him. But Sid Anderson viewed Titus as a threat to his position as head of the lab. The way it was structured, Titus was over the lab at Methodist in a way that was much more close than it had been under O'Neal.

Anderson felt more and more threatened. In '74 he decided to go into private practice, and he was never heard from again. He didn't go to any meetings or national conferences. Mike Farr and Richard Gray were two former Baylor residents who went with him, and they weren't ever heard from again, either.

When Anderson was getting ready to leave, I thought it would be a burden on me. I didn't like Houston. I left because Houston was a terrible place to live, but not a day goes by when I don't think fondly of Methodist. But I couldn't stand the climate, the growth rate, the traffic, the crime, the background noise. I'd grown up in a four-season climate. Virginia, in my opinion, has one of the best four-season climates.

A job opened up at the University of Virginia. It wasn't a great job, but it satisfied my longing to get out of Houston. Plus I was concerned about what would happen when Anderson left.

Titus got McGavran to replace me. He was a graduate of Wash U, and he was there when Spjut was. (And Walter Bauer, too, but he doesn't enter into the story of Baylor.) McGavran and Bauer with the young stars—they were very influential in surgical pathology. They'd worked with Ackerman.

Around that time, McGavran developed diabetes, and he became very angry. He was one of the most intelligent people I've ever met, but he couldn't cope with his own problem. He couldn't stand people who did stupid things. He went off to the University of Pennsylvania at Hershey in, maybe, '67, and he did a good job there of getting the program off the ground, but he tired of it after several years. When I was getting ready to leave, and since he knew Spjut, he looked into coming down. His title would be director of Anatomical Pathology, whereas my title had been director of Surgical Pathology. He came down in '75 in July, I think.

I took the University of Virginia job starting April 1, 1975. I sold my house, loaded up everything. After a couple of weeks, I came to my senses. Titus had said all along that the job wasn't the world's greatest idea. So I got there, and I saw it wasn't a good idea, and I called up Titus and said, "Can I come back?" Titus said, "Give me a day or two." He needed to check with the dean. It all worked out. I came back after being away four weeks to the day. And that was because Titus was a good guy. He said, "In three years, nobody will remember you ever did this."

I never had any problems with McGavran, who had come in July. We got along because I had such a respect for him and didn't take his outbursts personally.

After I'd been back at Baylor for three years, the University of Virginia made some immense changes, and I went back there in '78. Titus was very supportive of me. ... I can't say enough about that. And that's how McGavran showed up.

—*Bob Fechner, M.D.*

He Thought in Incredible Ways

Malcolm McGavran was another Wash U graduate who followed shortly after Dr. Spjut in the Ackerman training program. Malcolm had a much more in-depth scientific approach to pathology from a research point of view. He thought in incredible ways about implications of what you've observed and what might be ways of studying it further. That was not Dr. Spjut's particular way of doing it. He is a superb diagnostician and sees what's crucial and knows what to look for, and that's what he does. He doesn't pretend to do otherwise. McGavran never pretended anything, either, but his interest was far more intellectually exciting, in terms of the biology and the implications. He asked: How can we study it? How can we learn more about it?

He was in charge of the residency training program, and he was just absolutely magnificent. Again, incredibly demanding. He tended to be far more challenging in an overt way. Spjut would ask a challenging question, but it wouldn't come across as, "I'm going to pin you to the wall," whereas Malcolm intimidated a lot of the residents, particularly if they were weaker and scared. Of course, some people, when they get scared, just clam up and can't learn anything. He encouraged scholarship at a very high level, but he also drove away people by virtue of his intensity. But he asked as much of himself as of anyone—really, more of himself than others.

For me he was a great asset. But I knew him from the same time that I knew Feigin, and since he'd been recruited only a few years before me, I thought that if those guys could thrive in this environment, then much can be done.

—*Milton Finegold, M.D.*

Basic Philosophy

Dr. McGavran was a man who was loved, feared, revered, hated, you name it. He just struck strong emotions in people and had a very interesting background. He was born to American missionaries—actually born in India and raised in India. He spoke fluent Hindi.

Dr. McGavran spent really significant years at Wash U and worked with a pathologist by the name of Walter Bauer. They really did outstanding work in head and neck pathology and the biology of head and neck cancer, cancer of the voice box and laryngeal cancer, where metastases go and where on the larynx it goes and what different types of tumors did. They found diseases that we now just take for granted. He wrote chapters in the textbook that covered survival rates and surgical pathology, and it was used for years.

I had no intention of coming to Houston, this godforsaken place. I had grown up on Hawaii, and I had been to Stanford, and somehow I had moved to the

Midwest, which I had also thought was a mistake, but Wash U was a great medical school. I had personal reasons for wanting to stay in certain places. I came down here on a lark because Dr. Bauer told me I just had to go see his friend, Malcolm.

A lot happened on the day I visited. I met David Yawn. He was a pathologist *who took care of patients*. He was at Ben Taub in those days and was just intimately involved with care of patients. Unlike residents whom I had seen in other programs, he was dynamic, interesting, and so different from the myth about pathologists as this introverted group who did not like to get along.

Dr. McGavran was known to terrify people on interviews. I did not know this, but I knew it afterward. He would ask people for the vascular supply of the stomach, things like that. But he was very kind to me, and so he played a major role in my decision to come here.

He was a severe diabetic, but he knew about the consequences of diabetes and the damage it can cause to the brain, heart, kidneys, and eyes, and so he regimented his glucose extremely tightly, to the point that he was often hypoglycemic and passed out. I would keep glucose in my desk, which no one else wanted to give him, and the family would keep glucagon so they would not have to put anything into his veins. When he died, he'd managed to make it into his 60s with a couple of MIs—but not congestive heart failure—with his vision intact and his kidneys intact, so there had to be something to this incredible type of control. Certainly that type of control accounted for some of his bizarre behavior. He was always sort of—some people thought—bizarre, but he was extra bizarre when his sugar was off. He'd say totally off-the-wall stuff. So that is how some people remember him.

He had a passion for learning. He was an anatomic pathologist, but I would come into his office, and he would be reading some journal of microbiology. He was always reading something beyond what the confines were. I like reading medicine, but he would bring books for me to read like Primo Levi. He was interested in art and wanted to know what I thought about it. He was really a Renaissance man, and most people didn't see that side of him.

He was incredibly devoted to residents, to nurturing them, to challenging them, but a lot of people didn't see past that eccentricity, if you will. I think that a lot of my basic philosophy really comes from him. His underlying philosophy was to do what was in the patient's interest. As eccentric as he was, I think he really had a concept of the total patient.

This is the overriding philosophy that I have tried to convey to the residents. I have trained them to "do the patient no harm." Always do what is in the patient's best interest. It is a valuable lesson. You would think it is intrinsic in us, but it is not. I don't care what you are, whether you are a pathologist or surgeon or psychiatrist, just "do the patient no harm."

Of course, he was also involved with the clinical pathology conferences. In these conferences, we went over X-rays and clinical presentations and pathology. It really stressed to residents the importance of looking at the total patient. You can't just look at the blood smear or tube of blood or chemical analysis or tissue. Some of us would see this as intrinsic, but you would be surprised at how many people don't. I think he had a major impact on, not only me, but on many of the pathologists here, such as Dr. Wheeler. All of us were affected across the country and, really, around the world.

46. Malcolm McGavran, M.D., was known for his intensity, intellectual prowess, and challenging manner of teaching.

He wasn't even satisfied with human pathology. His wife, Ursula, had worked with the St. Louis Zoo, and she was active here in the Houston Zoo. He had a picture in his office of an autopsy he had performed on an elephant. ... And the residents were all challenged not only to know human pathology but also animal pathology.

We have a program where we take people who have finished at least two years of medical school at Baylor and give them an opportunity to spend a year in Pathology, where they can function as a resident. One of these fellows, at the end of her year, thanked me for pushing her past what she thought she was capable of. And I thought, "My God, I have become Dr. McGavran." She was very appreciative and must have struggled along the way as I had pushed them, but I certainly don't believe in fear. I don't even think that was Dr. McGavran's intention.

He just looked ominous, and he probably had some personality traits, and some of the time, he was acting bizarre.

Most people don't realize what they are capable of, and they need to be challenged to see what they are, but certainly not with fear. I hope I haven't done that. I guess in some ways you learn what not to do.

—*Mary Schwartz, M.D.*

Very Successful

The Unknown Slide Conference used to take place on Friday afternoons when we were residents here, but now it is Friday morning for our new residents. It was very scary, because you go to a meeting place with your own scope, and each person would be given the same set of slides, and you go over those, study those yourselves individually, and then come up with a diagnosis, cold. It is very difficult to come up with a diagnosis when you don't know much about the patient. Sometimes you don't even know where the tissue is coming from. It is totally cold.

These conferences are led by faculty members, and they used to have what we called "terror faculty members." One of them was Dr. McGavran; another one was Dr. Fechner. The ones who are not as terrorizing were, for example, Dr. Spjut, who is very, very soft-spoken, and maybe Dr. Greenberg. But it was always scary when you had Dr. McGavran.

I consider him a classic pathologist—extremely bright, extremely bright. I think his method of teaching was maybe old style, in that he tried to scare you, and he was very successful most of the time. He was very, very successful.

The thing about Dr. McGavran is that he never kept any grudge in his mind. It was always for the moment, but later on it was like nothing happened, even if he got mad at you. For example, if you gave him a slide that he did not like in terms of quality, he would throw it in the trash and say ... he wouldn't say four-letter words, but he would say well-chosen words for you, so you would know that he was very displeased with what you had done. Then later on you'd come up with something better, and then he would praise you, and that's it. It was always an intense experience being with Dr. McGavran. You always had to be on your toes.

But I felt like he was like my father, in a sense, because he was always demanding the best of me. He was like a strict father, and yet you knew that he did not hate you, or he did not harbor any ill feelings toward you. Therefore, when I went to him, even if I was scared for the moment, I wasn't really scared. A lot of people were. A lot of people were afraid to go to his office, literally afraid. I wasn't, because I felt that even if he gets mad at me now, well, he doesn't get mad at me for a long time, and he likes me because he is trying to teach me. He would have been a nice one to emulate as a teacher, but it is not my personality. It just won't come out right. It just won't.

He was a short person, totally bald and really stern-looking, but, oh, he had a good heart. He even sang tenor in choir.

You could strike up a conversation with him about classical music. He knew his tenors and all that. That made him very human. You look at him, and he is huge in pathology, right? But when you start talking about these other non-pathology things, it brings him down to human stature, a human scale.

—*Gene Bañez, M.D.*

The Art of the Interview

I interviewed for Pathology, but I didn't choose to go to Baylor. Dr. McGavran, he had these little glasses and a little top hat. He would look over at you. He said to me, "I'm the head of the residency program, and I keep my residents in line. Now, look over there on my door." He had this bullwhip on the door. He said, "That's how I whip them into shape."

I said, "Oh." Then I was telling him that I enjoy art.

He said, "Oh, art." He took out a picture of a fetus with three heads, and he said, "Isn't it interesting how medicine is like Picasso?" He ultimately took out some electron micrograph pictures and was asking me what they were. Nobody else tested me that way in my interview.

When I came back to interview for the position as faculty, I talked with Dr. McGavran again. He said, "I want you to tell me how many types of amyloid there are," and I thought, "Oh, my." I said, "Twenty, 30, and a new one every day." He laughed. He liked that answer. So he was just the same back then as he was when I interviewed, but he was an individual, quite an individual, colorful.

—*Linda Green, M.D.*

A Loving Heart

He was a character and a wonderful person, a very smart man. He was very demanding. When you were signing out cases with him, or when he reviewed gross autopsy findings with you, or if you were doing work at the microscope with him, he was hard to please.

He had very brittle diabetes. He went into cardiac arrest—literally—in my office two or three times. Fortunately, with my internal medicine background, I could resuscitate him. I kept dextrose in my desk. The thing I admired about him the most was that he never let his very severe, brittle diabetes and his cardiovascular disease later in life—which was associated with that—bother him. I know he was the most courageous and tough person. A lot of people didn't like him, because if he thought you were an idiot, he would tell you that to your face. On another level, he had a very loving heart, as did his wife. Here you have this real tough guy, and you went to his house, and they had a colony of about 40 cats in their back yard that Ursula, his wife, had given shelter to because they had feline leukemia. They couldn't run wild, so his whole back yard was converted to a huge cage. He also had all these dogs that he loved. One of them was a pit bull that looked like Winston Churchill. One day he called me because the dog had been sitting in a lawn chair by the pool and tumbled over into the pool, dead. At first they thought he had drowned, but the dog had had a heart attack and fell into the pool.

So he had a great love for animals as well as for people, but he didn't tolerate any lack of enthusiasm among the residents or young faculty. I knew him both as a resident and young faculty. He was very intolerant of any mistakes, or any evidence that he thought represented laziness or the inability to work hard, but he didn't ask you to work nearly as hard as he worked.

He had a whip on the back of his door that we residents gave him. That was one of the roast-type gifts that he got during one of the residents' dinners. I remember that it was presented to him as a token of his behavior, a symbol of his behavior toward the residents. But I must say, most of us, except for a rare few whom he had fired, most of us loved him.

He was one of my favorite people.

—*David Yawn, M.D.*

Ferenc Gyorkey, M.D.
Living and Breathing

Dr. Gyorkey was the chief of service at the VA, long ago, for 20-some years. He was from Hungary, and his wife was his technologist in the electron microscopy lab. They were such dedicated people that they lived and breathed biology and electron microscopy. He had such a desire and love for EM that even when he was diagnosed with multiple myeloma and he was going through his chemotherapy and his treatments, he still would have them bring him here every day. Even when he was extremely ill, he would have some-

47. Ferenc Gyorkey, M.D., chief of service at the VA, was at the microscope until the day he died.

one get him out of bed, put him in a wheelchair, and bring him here. He was at the microscope until the day he died. So he was extremely dedicated, and his wife also was very dedicated. Unfortunately, she developed colon cancer and died. They endowed a chair at M.D. Anderson Cancer Center, so they made use of their money in that way for other individuals.

—*Linda Green, M.D.*

Colorful

Dr. Gyorkey made so many things peculiar.

I was told that Dr. Gyorkey would come to my desk and look at all my stuff during the night. I had nothing to hide, so it wasn't really a big deal to me, but I thought it was such a peculiar story. We made a lot of jokes. We would put hairs on papers or across a desk drawer to see if they'd been moved.

He would be particularly apprehensive if we ever got any mail from Baylor, and so those envelopes would tend to be opened. I wouldn't get anything that was a big deal from Baylor, nothing secret. However, one time, I don't know why, he stuck a piece of scotch tape over the flap to pretend that he didn't open it, but he left a fingerprint. We didn't know for sure that it was Dr. Gyorkey, but we all thought it was him. So I blew up this fingerprint, and I pretended that I was going to take it to the FBI, because that was a federal offense, opening mail. I used to keep the picture of his fingerprint in back of my desk.

—*Jill Clarridge, Ph.D.*

S. Donald Greenberg, M.D.
Mainstay

Don Greenberg's father was an ear-nose-throat man in Beaumont, and he was really proud of Don. Don was an honor student all the way through school. And then when Don finished medical school as an honor student at Baylor, he went up to Chicago to train in ENT. His first big surgery was a radical neck resection. The patient died on the table, and he went into a depression. That is why he went into pathology, because he said he couldn't face anything like it again. And what that really had to do with it, I don't know. A lot of surgeons can just walk out of there and say, well, it was a bad day. Still, he concentrated on ENT pathology. So that was his connection to his father.

When I came to Baylor, he was still in ENT pathology. I was interested in the lung and not in ENT at all. So I said, "Don, you know, the lung is right there. There isn't a quarter of an inch between them. They do work together as a unit, and what affects one affects the other." I said, "You've come halfway." He accepted that and went after the lung. It ended up most of his work was with the lung, only he still had this little feeling about ENT. But he had a very close working relationship with the pulmonary disease section in the Department of Medicine, and they did some really good stuff. In some of the other places I've been, I have tried to do some of the things that Don and I had done. I really didn't realize how *very* important he was. He just kept after things until they were accomplished. Don was a mainstay of our department, especially as far as research goes.

48. Phil Cagle, M.D., left, recognized Don Greenberg, M.D., center, as his "academic father" and sent him a Father's Day card every year. Carlos Bedrossian, M.D., joins them at a conference.

Don had such a hard time with what is now called bipolar illness. When he was in his manic phase, he would just get so much done that he would finally go over the top and take on too many projects. I told him one time that he was heading for trouble if he didn't settle down and do the projects that he'd already got started. He started crying and said he just had to do it. Sometimes he could barely speak. It would take him five minutes to get from my office door over to me.

—*Bob O'Neal, M.D.*

Fathers

During the '60s and '70s, Don Greenberg became an international figure in lung pathology. He pioneered a lot of things. He was present for a lot of the early developments in pulmonary medicine, and therefore he wrote a lot of the original pathology on those things. He was involved in the very beginning in recognizing occupational medical diseases and in the early litigation. Greenberg also trained a lot of people who went on to become well-known lung pathologists in their own right, people like Victor Roggli, who's at Duke; Armando Fraire, who's at the University of Massachusetts; and Carlos Bedrossian, who's now at Northwestern and who is primarily known for pulmonary cytology. Again, this is a field that Dr. Greenberg helped to really establish in its early days. There are others who are well-known lung pathologists whom he helped train in their formative years, even if they weren't his fellows. He was an influence on people like Dr. David Dail at Virginia Mason.

49. Donald Greenberg, M.D., was known for his intense passion for research.

When I began my pathology residency, I did not know that I would go into lung pathology. I knew that I wanted to do academic pathology, and I knew that I would find an area of special interest, but I think that while Dr. Greenberg was not the only person who influenced me along those lines, he was, of course, the world-famous lung pathologist here.

He gave me my first really big project. I had done some case reports in lung pathology with Claire Langston over at TCH and with Dr. Greenberg. He had a project on so-called scar cancers in the lung that had been begun by Dr. Steve Cole, who is the medical examiner in Grand Rapids, Michigan. He was a resident here. Steve had not completely finished that project. I ended up inheriting it, and it was the first really big lung project that I did. It's still quoted today.

I think that when Dr. Greenberg realized that I was going to carry through with things, he and I developed a relationship then. I was constantly doing projects with him, visiting with him. He had a great deal of interest in things like American history, Texas history, the Civil War, things like that. We spent a lot of time actually just discussing those types of things. He really became my academic father, and because of that, I would send him a card on Father's Day. I sent one to my biological father and one to Dr. Greenberg as my academic father.

—*Phil Cagle, M.D.*

A Perfectionist

Don Greenberg and I did a lot with the ENT Department under Bobby Alford. The interest stems back to St. Louis, where McGavran was a pioneer of

ENT pathology. Everybody thought that because I came from Wash U, too, I must know a lot about it. I was too dumb to say I didn't know much.

Greenberg was a great guy. I liked him a lot. He had the strongest handshake of anyone I ever knew. It was painful. He showed a lot of patience for accumulating details and studying them. He was really a perfectionist. By contrast, I was always wanting to write something up and get on to something else.

I shared a hotel room with him once for a meeting in Chicago. One morning, when I was half awake, I heard a terrible gasping noise. Was Don having a heart attack? But he'd gotten up, and he was on the floor doing exercises. He was always in excellent physical condition. He was just on his 5,000th sit-up.

—*Bob Fechner, M.D.*

Intense

Dr. Greenberg, what a character he was. He was so intense and intent about everything he did. He was interested in the lung and smoking and cancer. If you made the mistake of asking him one question about that subject, you better be prepared to sit down and listen for at least half an hour.

So we would sit down, and he would explain to me in detail about what all these things meant. He would become very emotional about things, and he would cry about the fact that people don't know about smoking, and he wished they would know more and be more educated about how bad it is, and so on. I remember one time, one of our people here, a secretary, asked him about the oat cell carcinoma. She'd heard or read about it in one of our reports. Dr. Greenberg sat her down and literally talked to her for 30 minutes about oat cell carcinoma. That is how intense and earnest he was about his interests in this subject.

—*Gene Bañez, M.D.*

Harvey Rosenberg, M.D.
Very Scary

Oh, my God, what a character Harvey Rosenberg was. Very scary. He had a sign on his desk that said, "Don't." Every time we got together to sign off cases,

50. Harvey Rosenberg, M.D., had a sign on his desk that said, "Don't."

he would bring that sign with him. It meant: Whatever you are thinking, just don't. So the clinicians who would come and do the cases would not talk. That was Dr. Rosenberg.

There is another pathologist by the name of Dr. Robert Fechner, who is now at the University of Virginia, I think. Oh, my God, he was a terror, too! He was at The Methodist Hospital. He was brilliant. Brilliant. In the beginning of my rotation there, he said, "Bañez, I am going to turn a pancake out of you." I don't know what that meant. Maybe just squeeze me really hard to get the best out of me?

I was always scared of him, but my gosh that man has such stature in pathology and such brilliance.

—*Gene Bañez, M.D.*

Robert Fechner, M.D.
A Good Team

Robert Fechner was a very quiet and reserved pathologist who, like McGavran, was brilliant. He had an ability to recognize patterns of disease. He also was very impatient. He was very refined and gentlemanly.

I remember when he told me he bought a house in River Oaks, which is a very expensive part of Houston to live in. I said, "Well, now you've got azaleas—you have the luxury of azaleas."

He pulled his glasses down and said, "David, in River Oaks, azaleas aren't a luxury, they're a necessity." Besides his very quiet personality, he had a very dry and funny sense of humor.

—*David Yawn, M.D.*

Barbara Shurberg
Speak Up

Barbara Shurberg was my administrative assistant for some years. She knew everybody and everything that was going on. She is one of those women who

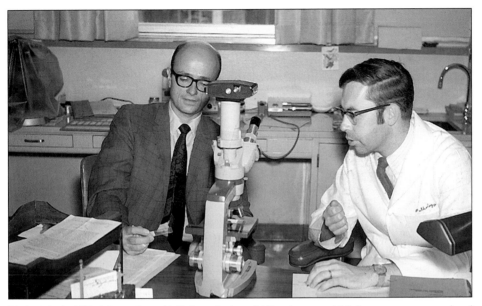

51. Lee Tuttle, M.D., left, confers with Robert Fechner, M.D., who was widely known as a reserved and gentle, impatient and brilliant man.

could speak up to people and tell them what she thought, even Michael DeBakey.

Once Ted Bowen was making rounds, which he did, and he came by my Methodist office. He said, "Where's Titus?" to Barbara.

She said, "He's not here, Mr. Bowen."

He said, "I can see that. Well, hell, if he got up in the morning and got down here, I'd see him."

And she said, "Well, Mr. Bowen, he's here, and he's been here long before you got here. If you got around earlier, you would have seen him."

One of Bowen's administrative assistants later told her that he'd damned near fainted when she said that, but Ted thought it was funny.

—Jack Titus, M.D.

David Yawn, M.D.
What You See

David Yawn had a sports jacket—maybe he got it at Goodwill or something—and he wore it with totally unmatched pants, some kind of a shirt that didn't fit very well, and sometimes a tie that was 100 years old and looked it. He didn't really tie it right. He just made a knot close to his neck. That's the way he looked. Barbara Shurberg got to know him and told him he had to get some decent clothes. Then she said to him once, "You know, David, I work here in the chairman's office, and when it is time for you to get your paycheck, I am going to hold on to it. You come by and see me to get it, and we are going to go get you a decent suit!"

52. David Yawn, M.D., is known by former chair Jack Titus, M.D., as a man who "can literally do everything."

He is one of the most capable people we have ever had. He went off to do the tail end of his residency at some second-rate place back East called Johns Hopkins. They tried to recruit him, but he ended up back here.

He can literally do everything. He was, I guess, mostly interested in surgical path. But we needed some help in blood banking, so he helped out, and pretty soon he was the best blood banker in Houston. But he is able to keep up his skills in all other kinds of fields. Everybody loved David in those days, and they still do.

As a blood banker, he would interface some with patients deliberately. The blood bank at Methodist is called the Eileen Murphree McMillin Blood Center. The Murphrees are a wealthy Houston family. Their daughter had leukemia and finally died of it. David was one of the principal caregivers, and they wanted to do something to honor him, so they built this new blood center there.

David Yawn is a genius. He really is, I think. If there is a paper published in something-or-other research journal of some screwball thing in molecular pathology, he has read it, understands it, and remembers it. He always seems to know everything.

David is "what you see is exactly what you get." He is just like an old East Texas boy. You have to look to be sure he is not going barefoot or something.

—Jack Titus, M.D.

Milton Finegold, M.D.
Quite Extraordinary

I first met Dr. Finegold in 1965 when I was inducted into the military service and I was assigned to the U.S. Army Medical Research Institute of Infectious Diseases and assigned to Fort Dietrich. I was, at that time, assigned to work on the defensive aspects of biological warfare. We were given a little house on the Army post at Fort Dietrich, and Dr. Finegold and his family were two houses down. Milton had also been inducted into the military service, and he was working on other aspects of this problem.

So our families became very close during those two years in the military service. In fact, our two eldest children were about the same age, and each of our wives had our second children while we were in the military service.

I subsequently moved to Houston in 1977 to take the chairmanship of the Pediatrics Department at Baylor and the position of physician and chief at Texas Children's.

One of the first things I encountered when I got to Texas Children's was a pathology department that needed a lot of attention, so I contacted Milton and asked if he would be willing to be considered to come down here as the chief of Pediatric Pathology. After making a few visits, he ultimately agreed to come. He arrived, I believe, in 1979, about two years after I came.

He has proceeded to build an outstanding Pathology Department at Texas Children's, with broad representation of a large group of pediatric pathologists. They have special expertise in areas like kidney disease, represented by Edith Hawkins; and pulmonary disease, where he recruited Claire Langston; and bone marrow problems, where he recruited people like Vicky Gresick.

Over the years, he's added people that direct the clinical pathology lab, like Greg Buffone, and a variety of people who have worked in microbiology and serology, and people in pediatric neuropathology like Dawna Armstrong and Hannes Vogel. So he has built a wonderful department that has served to help support the growth of Texas Children's, which over the last 25 years has been quite extraordinary.

The hospital has gone from 158 to 468 beds and has gone from about 5,000 admissions a year to 21,000. It has gone from 8,200 outpatient visits a year to 496,000. It has gone from about 9,200 emergency room visits in 1977 to 73,000 last year. That gives you the magnitude of the kind of patients that need to be supported by Pathology.

—Ralph Feigin, M.D.

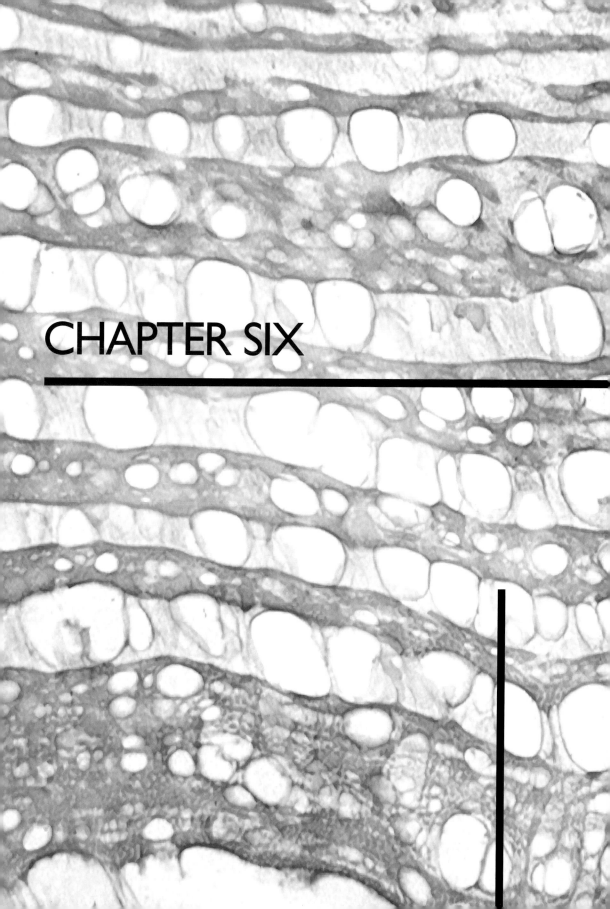

CHAPTER SIX

IN THE LAB

Early on in the process of researching this book, I had the privilege of touring Mike Lieberman's and Milton Finegold's lab facilities. While I've certainly loved listening to people's stories, there was something about seeing the lab coats, the mysterious and intriguing machines for doing such things as impregnating tissue with wax, and the people focused on their tasks—not to mention smelling that lab smell—that made the Department much more real to me.

Alas, there will be no scratch-'n'-sniff patch in this book, but I hope this chapter captures a bit of the tremendous variety of work that goes on in Department of Pathology laboratories.

Pink

When I came from Boston in 1967, the laboratory at Ben Taub was quite primitive, very basic. I was able to help in developing an entire clinical laboratory, in introducing and helping set up things like hemoglobin electrophoresis. It's incredible. Now they say, "How could you work without that?" Serum electrophoresis, again, they say, "How could you diagnose myeloma and many other diseases without having that?" Everywhere there was a need. I also developed a number of the hematologic procedures that are being used nowadays, like improved tests for coagulation.

Dr. Jarvis was by himself in this area. It would take three weeks to a month to get a diagnosis from him, so I started getting all of these biopsies. I started getting more and more and more work. It was a busy time, and it was a lot of fun to be able to implement and develop and apply what I had learned in Boston, and to improve the level of quality of the laboratory here.

I had done studies on frozen blood, and I said, "Look, we have a lot of difficulties in providing enough blood for the emergency room and trauma cases at Ben Taub." There were times—even Dr. Maddox, our chief of surgery, can remember—when we would only have enough red blood cells so the blood would look pink, but we wouldn't have enough to make it red. So I said, "Why don't we use frozen cells? Then when we have an opportunity, when we have a lot of blood, we can freeze it."

Even though I was a newcomer, they decided to buy the whole system based on my recommendations. The system of freezing RBCs, this was the first hospital to have this system in Houston. At that time, elsewhere in town, they were freezing with liquid nitrogen in platelet studies, but we were the first ones to do red-cell freezing at Ben Taub. It was 1969. We did it here, and it was just wonderful. It was a thrill, you know?

—*Anita Werch, M.D.*

Quality

Those were lean times in the '60s. We did not have a sufficient number of people to cover the lab 24 hours a day, and it was becoming increasingly necessary. For years we would cover the lab with part-time people or people that we could train to do a few things. They would work the way a fireman does: If there is a fire, they go to the fire; if there is nothing going on, they sleep or wash their car or do whatever they do. That was the nature of that kind of life, and the same was

53. Anita Werch, M.D., pioneered the use of frozen red blood cells after she arrived at Ben Taub in 1967.

true about the hospital in those days. We would hire dental students—not so much medical students, because they were too busy. Dental students were mature people who had some scientific background.

But as time moved on, and as the need for laboratory work became more and more essential, that old method wasn't working. We began to train our own. We tried to be selective of individuals whom we would train. This was over and above our regular training program.

There has always been a school of medical technology at The Methodist Hospital. This year, I think they only have four students. Back then we had 12, although Methodist was approved for 18. We always had a class of 12 that we would train to become medical technologists, who would then become certified after passing an appropriate examination. Those types of people were in short supply; there were new training programs and new levels created.

There was an MLT (medical laboratory technician) program—that program is still in existence. LT—laboratory technician—that was the lowest level, for high school graduates. The MLT was an associate degree program, and the MT (medical technology) program requires a college degree. The LT program was phased out 10 years ago. But the MT and the MLT program are still in existence. And the MT for many years now has a subspecialty program; you could be an MT with a specialty in chemistry, blood banking, or hematology, or whatever. And those were special people; those were few and far between.

We began to try and fill the slots, especially after-hours, weekends and nights, with people that we had trained ourselves. We would only select individuals who were basically two years into their college work and therefore had some degree of maturity and some degree of education. We did pick out a few high school graduates who had been working in the lab as aides, who were familiar with the operation and had shown an interest and devotion to patient care. One of them is still working there. I ran into her within the last year.

One of the great satisfactions to me was the quality of people we had in clinical chemistry. We had minimal turnover, comparatively speaking. At one time we had as many as eight people, and they had to be subspecialists in chemistry. So we had highly qualified people working there just within the chemistry area. And that was always very gratifying to me, because I think that it set the example and the standard for other areas as well.

Now there are so many people involved with paperwork. You are taking people away from patient care, whether it is in the laboratory or at the nursing level, and having them do paperwork. And so the number of people has expanded, and yet the number of people in the labs has decreased.

—Phil Migliore, M.D.

Thirty

There was a local physician here who was Amish—that is just an aside, but it is an interesting thing—who got a Ph.D. in microbiology from Yale in '39. At that time, there was a raging controversy regarding the stability of bacterial spores.

A prior experiment had been done by drying spore-forming bacteria on a piece of filter paper and just hanging it up. It had proved that spores are bacteria, which is in essence a survival mechanism somewhat analogous to a seed of a plant. The difference is that seeds of plants are reproductive mechanisms, in the sense that a plant produces multiple seeds, but a bacterium only produces one spore. So it is not really reproduction so much as it is survival. The controversy was whether or not in water, or an aqueous environment, spores lived as long as they do in dry environments. So this guy in 1939 put a bunch of bacteria—*Clostridia*—in an aqueous culture medium, grew them up, sealed them, and kept them until 1969. In the meantime he didn't even practice microbiology. He had gone on to be an internist who was practicing here. He showed up in my office one day and asked if I would get these things out and see if they are still viable. And so I got them out. I think that he had about 30 different strains, and we were able to make all of them but one grow after 30 years.

—*Jamie Davis, Ph.D.*

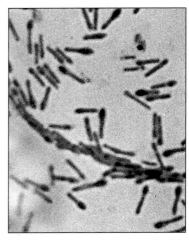

54. Clostridia bacteria were revived in the lab after 30 years in storage.

Sandwiches and Specimens

I did not even know what histology was when I came to work here. It was August 18, 1975. I had been working at a blood and plasma donation center, and I just got fed up with that kind of work and the people that I had to deal with. I started going through the newspaper, and I saw that there was an opening for a lab aide at Baylor. I applied for it, and after a couple of days they called me.

I started off making coffee and whatever it was, doing the runs between here and Methodist. There were not nearly as many runs as there are today. I probably had to go about three times at the most. We did not have the workload that we have today; mostly it was research. When I started, we were not even doing kidney biopsies. We had one surgical group, and that was Dr. Raymond Kaufman's practice. Everything else was research.

After about nine to 10 months, I was doing some of the technical work. I really felt comfortable doing it, and I loved it. There were three technicians. They asked me if I wanted to become a histologist, and I said, "Yeah." I started studying. As a matter of fact, Frances Miller sort of tutored me. She is no longer here.

I had watched the histologist sit there and cut—turn that wheel—and it looked so easy, and I thought, "I can do that." Well, when I finally got my opportunity to sit down and turn that wheel, it wasn't quite so easy. It took a lot of practice. It takes a lot of practice. It takes years of practice to just sit down and cut a block without any difficulties.

Different tissue cuts different ways. Breast cuts horribly, and uterus, that kind of tissue is very difficult to cut, so it takes a lot of practice. But it is quite rewarding when you see the work at the end. It is quite rewarding.

The next year I took the histology exam, and I made the second-highest score, even though all the other students had been to a certified school. I felt real good about that. That did a lot for my ego.

55. Tissue specimens are dissected, and representative samples are submitted for microscopic examination.

So I have been learning ever since. I have been in it for 25 years now, almost 26 years, and you always learn something from somebody else. It is a continuous learning process.

We used to sit down right at the same table that we gross specimens on and have our lunch. We would move them to the side, spray the table down, and bring in our lunch.

We never had any gruesome mistakes, but there were people who smoked, and you just smoked right in the lab. The guys would sit around on a can of xylene and fire up their cigarettes. Or they'd have a specimen in one hand and a sandwich in the other hand.

In maybe 1979 or 1980, we started doing immunofluorescence on kidneys. I set that lab up and organized it to do the immunofluorescence, but there have been a lot of changes. The equipment used to be big and bulky. Things have now trimmed down. Everything is slim-lined. Knives used to be 10 inches long; now they are disposable knives that are 3 inches long or 2½ inches long. As the years go on, the stains themselves and what the pathologists were looking for has changed. There used to be an H&E, which is a routine stain, and maybe the doctor would ask for a PAS or trichrome if they are going to look at the muscle fiber. But now it's gone into a lot more detail, a lot more detail.

The biggest challenge is to take a difficult case and make decent slides from a

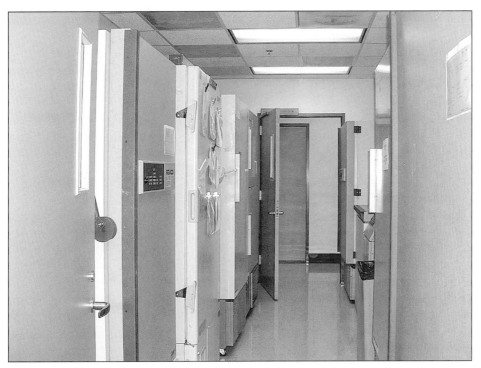

56. Multiple freezers are used in the Department to store research samples at -80 degrees.

crummy piece of tissue—maybe something that some nurse has left lying out on the counter that is half-dried. You have to make magic. It's satisfying when you think of what you started with, and you look at your completed work. It is a good feeling to know that you are doing this for a person, to know that that could be my mother or my sister or my good friend. You want this to look right, because you just know that it is a human being.

—Grace Hamilton

Who Do They Know?

If you wanted to ask the population of Houston about TCH from the point of view of the laboratory—and they are always doing surveys like this—no one knows the pathologists, or maybe they do, rarely, if they have a rare tumor. Who do they know? They know the people who take the blood.

—Milton Finegold, M.D.

57. The Automatic Clinical Analyzer, new to the lab in the mid-1970s, was able to do individual tests on demand that had previously been done manually or semi-manually.

Performance

I started here in 1975. I've noticed a lot of changes. When I first started here, we only had seven phlebotomists, and now we have 37 on the day shift. And first we only had eight floors. Now we have 20-something floors. We had to write everything out. Now we have computers. I really like that.

We have changed our name. First we used to be blood collectors. Then we were phlebotomists, and now we are called processing technicians, because we do a lot of things now. First of all, we used to only draw blood, that was all. But now we process the blood. We even have a place to spin the blood, a centrifuge. We do everything.

You have to love kids. I like working here and being an actor. That's what you are. You are like, "Good morning, how are you, Mom?" You make the mom feel comfortable and get her ready to be able to trust you. Well, she will always be upset about the baby, but she will be more cooperative. Even if they get hostile, you still have to be like, "OK"—just be nice and gentle.

You can't bring your feelings here. Because you are dealing with the kids, and kids can sense when you come into the room, if you are not all that sweet, if you come in with an attitude, it seems like they just know. So you have to like acting.

—*Faye Jones*

One Time

I am very patient with kids. Some of the kids, you really have to really get down to their level. You have to think like they do. One time, I had a patient at the Feigin Center. It took me 2½ hours to get this patient to draw blood. She was a 15-year-old. I promised her everything under the sun, and she wouldn't do it. I'd take her out to eat, to the movies, whatever—she wouldn't do it. Finally, she broke down and did it. I ended up taking her out to eat. I took her out to eat, and she and my daughter got along pretty good.

—*Yolanda White*

Three Things

Here are the three best things that have happened.

When I came here from New York, I had not done research for several years because I was running the laboratories at Bellevue—which was a very big municipal hospital—for three years. In that three-year period, it was all I could do to stay alive. And I was, in fact, on sabbatical in 1976, learning to retool in research, when I was asked to run the hospital lab at Bellevue. So when I came down here, I was going to use the resources that TCH had promised to try to build a research department.

Dr. Tom Caskey, who is one of the principals in the Human Genome Project, was the director of genetics at Baylor at the time I came. He has the best ability to pick out talented young people of anyone I've ever known. This is where Titus did not work well. But Lieberman has been very good, very cost-effective. Everyone that Mike recruited for research has done very well, getting their own grants and being very meticulous. That's very hard to do and a really great achievement.

Caskey was like that. He built a terrific genetics department just as the genetics revolution was taking place. It was up to me to design how it was going to work here at Texas Children's. And I negotiated with the executive director of the hospital and the chairman of the board so that they would put money into research at my discretion. And as we were involved with money, we would be repaying them with overhead from grants and so on.

So I got a call from Dr. Caskey, saying he knew I was very interested in liver disease in children, which often results from an abnormality in the genome. Would I be in the market for a scientist to work on these kinds of problems? He had just gotten a call from someone he didn't know, but who knew of him, asking if there were any opportunities here at Baylor for somebody interested in gene expression in malignancy. I replied that yes, absolutely, I was interested.

At that time, I didn't have any research space. I had commitments for it, but I didn't actually have any. But as soon as I had a person, then I would design a lab for that person. So he put me in touch with Dr. Gretchen Darlington. Dr. Darlington was a graduate of the University of Michigan and a Ph.D. She went to Yale Medical School for a post-doctorate fellowship. Then she was recruited to head up the section of somatic cell regeneration in Cornell Medical School in the Department of Medicine because the chairman was a geneticist, which was, at that time, quite rare. When he retired, his successor said that he had no interest in genetics and needed no genetics in the department—talk about not smart! So that's why she made the call. When I got the call, I said, "Oh, fantastic, give me the number!" Gretchen came down for a visit. She liked what she saw and joined us.

That was the single best thing that happened. It suddenly changed our department from a group that did only service work with no research. Within two years of coming here, I had a distinguished young scientist who was really well-recognized working on issues that I cared about personally. She was completely responsible for supporting herself financially in terms of NIH grants. We put money in so she could hire a post-doc and so forth, but she took care of herself from then on until the time she left. And the reason she came was that she knew if, for some reason, a grant did not get picked or refunded right away, we would support her. That's what the hospital provided.

For me personally that was the single biggest and momentous thing. And it was accidental, mind you, because I would never have found her, and she would have never found me.

The second thing was that she had a big role to play at Baylor. The distances aren't far, but any distance is meaningful. Gretchen was willing to make that effort, to go over to Baylor, and she became the director of one of the graduate programs there. So she was there a lot. Whereas I was mostly here, except for teaching and conferences and seminars. Her presence there acted as a big liaison to research and other goings-on at Baylor.

In 1980, the first paper in *Science* appeared in which mice were made transgenic—that is, you could take a human gene and put it into a mouse. And there was at Baylor at that time a physician in cell biology—Savio Woo—who was studying proteins made by the liver. He started with proteins that controlled blood coagulation and moved into other proteins which involved liver disease.

I was teaching people who did adult and pediatric hepatology and gastroenterology, regardless of whether it was here or at Methodist. And whenever someone came here to train in those areas, I would teach them pathology as part of their training. So I got to meet these people. And one of those people, Joyce Carlson, had been part of the team that had discovered a lot about a particular protein that was mutated in liver disease and caused cirrhosis, called alpha$_1$-antitrypsin. As soon as this paper appeared in *Science,* we wanted to see if we could make this disease of human children by putting the abnormal human gene into the mice.

And Savio Woo and Gretchen had both worked on alpha$_1$-antitrypsin. And so when Dr. Carlson wanted to work on this, she went to Savio, who was interested in these types of proteins and had that gene. She asked to put it into mice and said that if we do, we need a pathologist to tell us what mischief we have caused.

Since Joyce had been one of my pupils, she came to me. And that was the second-biggest thing that ever happened. First it was Darlington, and then through that contact, Woo and Carlson. And so when the first mice came out with this disease, one of my fellows who was working here, Dr. Rogers, and I were the pathologists on that project. Our work was published in the very fine *Journal of Clinical Investigation.* It helped us solve some of the unanswered questions about how that disease occurs.

That is still ongoing work. Dr. Rick Sifers in our department was a graduate student with Dr. Woo; he and I still collaborate. We are running a course together. So that has been a wonderful phenomenon that has kept on going, never stopped since 1983 or '84.

After that, because of Woo being such an ambitious and aggressive guy, we had this going with the models, and he put in a program project grant study with all those different metabolic diseases using mouse models, and I was a part of that program. Well, pretty soon I became known as the mouse pathologist. And every time anybody in any department had a mouse model where they didn't know exactly what they were looking at, they would come to me to ask me to look at it. I didn't do all the work myself. If it involved a lung, I would ask Dr. Langston; if it involved a brain, Dr. Armstrong, etc.

But I was involved in a lot of this stuff, and part of it was, again, related to the initial pact I had with the hospital, which was that I had the discretionary money and resources to use when the opportunity arose.

That is the biggest part of my life here, and the joy of it. Administrations have come and gone, and TCH separated from St Luke's, etc., etc., but the original ground rules for having Baylor Pathology come here have not changed. So we have Baylor people working in our lab as well as TCH people, side by side. It has allowed me to recruit people of a very high level to come work here.

One day I got a phone call—this is No. 3 but in the same tract—from a Ph.D. scientist whom I knew at a distance. Lutz Birnbaumer was his name. He was in the Department of Cell Biology, but he is really a physiologist. He had come here in the early '70s to Cell Biology, Dr. O'Malley's department. As a signal transduction expert, he worked on a class of proteins called G proteins. These proteins are very much involved in hormone signaling. He could get into the nucleus of those cells and change the genetic expression of those cells, and then they make thyroid hormone or adrenal steroids or estrogens or whatever. The signaling that takes place at the border of those recipient cells is based on G protein. They are the mediators for the outside signal to get to the inside of the cell, to set into motion all of the new gene expression that has to occur, whether it is simply making more of what you were making before or changing what you made. So he was a G protein expert.

Birnbaumer had taken transgenic mouse technology to try to find out which of the different functions different G proteins had. He picked one of them out, and he knocked out the mouse gene with a mutated version of that to see what happened. Many of the mice stopped growing, stopped gaining weight, had very swollen abdomens, and their large intestine looked very inflamed and swollen.

He called me and said that he had these mice that he had made some histologic sections on, and he thought they might have Hirschsprung's disease (which is a disease in which the nerve cells that we need to get normal peristalsis and contraction of the intestines are not functioning). Because he thought that the G proteins are involved in signal transduction, it must be involved in the nervous system. It was just a wild guess by a physiologist who had no idea about the human disease.

Right over there, he and the post-doctoral fellow gave me a tray of slides. When I looked at a slide, the first thing I said was that this is not Hirschsprung's disease, but this looks like something that is really interesting. This looks like ulcerative colitis, a very common and important disease.

I said, let's look at it further, and let's look at the other mice, and is there other tissue, or is it only here, or elsewhere? Pretty much only there. And I said, "Hey, what about cancer?" Because mice get cancer the same way that humans do. We got together, and we all started looking at these things.

We published our first paper in '95 in *Nature*. It was like a rocket going off. This is the single best model still to this day. And we don't know what it is doing. We know that humans with ulcerative colitis do not have mutations in this gene. So that is not a simple answer. It is not easy to say that it is a genetic disease at all.

That was the No. 3 most exciting thing for me.

—*Milton Finegold, M.D.*

Leaps and Bounds

My work has focused primarily on gene expression studies, with the liver being the major organ that I have worked with over the years, for a variety of reasons. Part of the work that I think interested Milton dealt with subculture models, which were used to examine gene expression patterns that might be characteristic of the liver *in vivo*. It is a little harder to do those studies *in vivo*. I was looking at the time at the inflammatory response elicited by cytokines, which can change a whole pattern of gene expression in response to the infection and other tissue damage.

A number of those studies could be informatively done in subculture and not so easily done *in vivo*, so he was interested in someone who could culture hepatocytes. He had an interest in liver disease as well. There is research that I do in my own lab that really developed more into using mouse models as the technology became available to make specific mutations in the mouse as a whole organism. Then we carried out some studies where we made a mutation in those genes, which was very critical for liver differentiation.

We have gone from tissue culture and studies using cell lines into studies using mammals. We are now using a variety of mouse models to test the genes and their effect on the organism as a whole.

At Texas Children's, there were no other individuals there who were carrying out basic research, so it was a time, when I first got there, of trying to communicate and educate people about the kind of questions that I was asking and then be educated by them about what their clinical issues and questions were. Many of them were carrying out clinical research, which often has a very different focus. There was a challenge both to try to integrate and benefit people around me in whatever way I could and also to broaden the local people at Texas Children's, to communicate with Baylor and begin to understand all the expertise that is here and how we might mutually take advantage of one another's interests.

One way I found I could do that was to accept the invitation to form the graduate Program in Molecular Genetics when that first became a department at Baylor. That enabled me to work with the faculty who were being recruited to Genetics and the people who gained secondary appointments. Setting up that program and working with the students who came in was very, very rewarding. It gave me good contacts with many people who contributed to the training effort, because we had to organize courses, teach them, recruit students. It was very demanding, but as I say, very rewarding.

Now the program is huge. It has just grown by leaps and bounds. The faculty of Molecular Genetics is the fastest-growing faculty in the school. I don't know the numbers in their department at this point, but it is a very dynamic group. I have enjoyed having a secondary appointment in that department and maintaining contacts with the faculty there, although I find at the Christmas party I know fewer and fewer people.

It was such a good time to be involved with people in genetics. My Ph.D. was in genetics, so that was a natural interface. The genetics at Baylor is unequaled. I am biased, perhaps, but just the quality of the people, the breadth of the research, the quality of the research is just astounding. It has been a delight.

—*Gretchen Darlington, Ph.D.*

A Door

It was an exciting time when we first made the transgenic mice. They were the first transgenic mice made that expressed the alpha$_1$-antitrypsin gene. We were the first ones to look at feature-specific expression for that protein. It was exciting to be the first ones in the world to identify the oligosaccharides that are placed on proteins.

It was our work that showed the function of oligosaccharide, not just that it is there. It was frustrating to me that some of my early work was, well, not necessarily stolen, but used by some other laboratories at different institutions, which aided their career.

It turned out to be really great, though, because then they opened up an avenue for me. A lot of their models were based on my data, and they have a volume industry. So what looked to be really bad turns out to be really good. What looked like a dead end to me turned out to be a door for my career. You just have to be persistent. You cannot give up.

I was not going to let a bunch of people make choices for me. Life is all about how you choose to react to things, it really is, and so that is your choice, that is your freedom. No one can take that from you. A successful life and career is really based on how you choose to respond to things like that. So I stayed in there, even through the tough and difficult times.

I finally got to the point where I could focus and really test my hypotheses and come up with some interesting models, which are now accepted by the industry, as to why oligosaccharides exist on proteins, that they are really used as a marker.

58. "What looked like a dead end to me turned out to be a door for my career," says Rick Sifers, Ph.D. "A successful life and career is really based on how you choose to respond to things like that."

They help the protein to fold, which is called conformation. That gives it activity. Then there is a quality-control pathway in the secretory mechanism whereby proteins, if they do not fold correctly—that is, if they are nonfunctional—are not allowed to be secreted. And the way the protein sees that is by other proteins recognizing the other protein as being misfolded, but the way they are tagged to be degraded is through the oligosaccharide, and we identify the tag.

—*Rick Sifers, Ph.D.*

Quite a Lot of Work

I am back and forth between Texas Children's and Baylor. Bobbie Antalffy is in charge of that lab for me. She does neurohistopathology, and she's a rare person. I actually met her in Toronto when I worked at the Hospital for Sick Children. She was working there. She's Australian, and she moved to Texas, and I thought, "Where is Texas?" and then I ended up coming.

In that lab we study the nervous system, and other systems as well, for many of the mutant animals that are models for human disease. And that's quite a lot of work. There are probably about 20 investigators who use that facility, so it's very interesting. I have met a lot of interesting researchers.

And then I have two or three main research interests myself. One is in perivascular perinatal brain injury, and Dr. Mizauguchi is with me now. She is a pediatric neurologist who has a Ph.D. and is very interested in cerebral palsy and brain injuries. This is the second time she has been here studying human disease and the various factors involved in brain injury. And then another research interest I have has evolved out of epilepsy.

Dr. Grossman is head of neurosurgery here. He's been really my best friend and, I think, my greatest ally at Baylor. He allowed me to establish the lab initially to study epilepsy. We developed a very good epilepsy center here, so that I work with human tissue primarily, and in that study I've gotten a fantastic person in Dr. Zhu, who is a neurosurgeon. Bobbie and he and I do the epilepsy work, and then the other interest that I have in research is a disease called Rett Syndrome.

Rett Syndrome is a form of mental retardation in girls. Now we know it's in boys, too, but it was described by an Austrian pediatric neurologist who had a room full of children with neurologic disorders. One day he saw three of these little girls sitting together, all doing the same thing, and he realized that there were similarities. It's been studied really intensively in all parts of the world, and there is very active research at Baylor. Dr. Zoghbi is the principal investigator now. She's also the principal investigator for the Mental Retardation Clinic.

She actually found the gene for Rett Syndrome a year ago. So it's very exciting now, studying this. The syndrome is relatively rare, but in terms of people with mental retardation, it has been very difficult to understand. The brains look normal, except that they are small, so it's a real challenge to try and figure out why they're not functioning.

So those are the things I spend most of my time doing. I'm on Study Section for the NIH, and that takes time. I'm involved with the Autism Tissue Committee for the National Autism Society. ... And then I'm on the Neuropathology Committee for the American College of Pathologists.

It was really a choice I made to concentrate on research. There were things I wanted to finish. I'm 65, so I'm on borrowed time.

—Dawna Armstrong, M.D.

A Climbing Vine

"Hycel" is an acronym for Hormone Chemistry Laboratories HCL—which also ended up being the ticker when the company went public on the American Stock Exchange, HCL. Hycel was founded by my father, John Joseph Moran, in the mid-'50s.

My father came to Houston from Phoenix. He was asked to come here to be the Harris County toxicologist. This is circa 1952. He was the Harris County toxicologist for a fair number of years. Then he started doing other research, actually at first in our house on Byron Street in West University. Hycel was very much a biochemical and instrumentation research company. The first test developed would have been the PBI—protein-bound iodine—the very first standardized thyroid test. Gosh, going on from there, there were a host of cholesterol tests, uric acid, a very wide variety of blood-chemistry tests, and then in the mid-'60s, Hycel developed the first discrete multi-channel, multi-test clinical analyzer, the Hycel Mark X, which ran 10 blood-serum tests per sample, 40 samples per hour, and things pretty well went from there. There was expansion into flow cytometry and then into blood-cell and platelet counters and the side area of that, industrial applications for particulate counters and solutions. Hycel went on to become one of the premier blood-chemistry instrumentation firms in the world.

The Moran Foundation was originally created in 1968. It began life as a private foundation with a tremendous capitalization of $5,000. Of course, you have to realize that in 1968, $5,000 was actually a reasonable amount of money. The foundation transitioned into a medical foundation, I want to say, circa 1971. That is essentially where it really took shape as we know it today.

There was the wish to foster research by new and younger investigators who would not ordinarily have these opportunities as early as they might, just simply because of the realities involved with the politics of grant-making from both the private sector and from the governmental sector, coupled with the realities of the politics involved in academia.

On December 21st, 1972, a resolution was adopted by the board of trustees

59. Hycel multi-test clinical analyzers introduced by John J. Moran, center, brought greater automation to the lab and drew the attention of KTRK-TV reporter Sondra Feldman and other members of the media.

authorizing the foundation to become affiliated with Baylor College of Medicine, and Leon Jaworski was elected as a member of the board of trustees of the foundation as the representative for Baylor. Leon stuck around through November of 1973. And that was effectively where the relationship with Baylor began, so we are at 30 years now.

The foundation has pretty much worked exclusively with the Department of Pathology. There is an annual call for papers, call for research. This is reviewed by the foundation's scientific advisory committee, which is basically peer review from within the Department of submitted proposals. So there is a very good structure that essentially lets anyone submit and be reviewed academically without any outside influences. Basically we just fling them a whole bunch of cash and go, "Here, spend this, do something with it," and they, over the course of the past 29 years, have done some absolutely amazing work, a lot of which has gone on to further funding and studies from CDC and NIH, and a tremendous number of papers have been published. Sometimes there are more strong proposals than we actually have funding for, and I'm trying to rectify that.

I have been responsible for the management of the foundation since 1996, and we have grown appreciably in that term and hope to continue to. Baylor Med School is making a tremendous effort to grow in stature relative to other schools around the country, and I think we'll be a part of that.

It's interesting to see the growth as the situation where success begets success. More people have come in from the outside providing grants and funding, and the Department of Pathology gets carried along with that. We were very happy to see that. Sure, there are much, much, much bigger sources of funding than us, but having been there for so long, having been one of the seeds that bred the success, the seed goes on to develop and grow into a climbing vine. And to that end, it attracts more and better people, attracts larger funding, which attracts more people, and round and round and round.

—*John A. Moran*

Reactions

John J. Moran was born and raised in Detroit. His mother was French, his father was American, and he was perfectly bilingual. He was in World War II. He was very much an entrepreneur and realized the way chemistry was done in the early '50s was largely one reaction at a time, test tube by test tube, and that the future was going to be automation. He conceived of and then designed one of the first automated chemistry instruments and started Hycel. And of course it was enormously successful.

There are 90 faculty members in this Department, not all of whom feel that I recognize their unique talents and contributions as completely as I should. It has to be that way. One of the things I've done to protect the Department from the vagaries of my judgments is to take the Moran Foundation money that we get every year and not distribute it myself, but set up a committee independent of me to distribute it. Because I want people to feel that they have access to research monies in spite of what my personal opinion might be of their research, that they have an opportunity to have a jury of their peers make a decision about the value of their research.

—*Michael Lieberman, M.D., Ph.D.*

Changing Directions

There are a lot of struggles that you have to overcome, especially as a young person trying to get your career started. First of all, there is a funding hurdle that you have to get through. I scrimped by, and it turned out not to be too much of a problem to begin with. The next set of problems comes in actually running the lab and dealing with people in the lab, because no matter how many times people tell you that everybody is different, you don't know what that means, as the person directing other people to do science, until you actually live through it.

If you have an idea, you've been translating that idea into data through your own hands. Now you have an idea and it gets translated into data through other people's hands, and there are an enormous number of difficult steps. I think that most post-docs, as they start their faculty position, have to learn about that. It does govern the rate of progress of the lab, how well you do that. Everybody requires a different way of mentoring, of guiding and disciplining, of encouraging and so forth, so that's probably, I would say, the biggest challenge that I have had in learning how to run a lab.

As a research scientist, the most satisfying times to me are when things work in the lab in ways that you had hoped they would. I took a risk about five years ago in changing the direction of my research, from projects that were funded which were going along OK, but I didn't see that they had a really great future. I had been growing as a scientist and began to realize that there were other things that I was more interested in. They would, however, require quite a bit of work to get started in the lab.

I think probably the happiest time has been as we began this new direction, which is what we're doing now—the study of coronary vessel development in the embryo. We began to see the fruits of the labor in the time we spent developing model systems, developing assays, reagents, and so forth, to make this research program actually work. When that actually began to pay off, we were able to get successful results from my experiment and were able to publish papers in very good journals. Students were happy; I was happy. It was a great time. So that was probably the most satisfying time as I look back on it.

Probably the most important lesson I have learned in the last 10 years as a scientist is how to focus. I came here doing too many different things at the beginning, which a lot of young people do, and realized that a jack of all trades is master of none. What I really needed to do is learn how to focus, in combination with putting together the direction that we have in current development. I have a very clear set of objectives. I know where I want to go next and where I want to go next after that. So that's really great. I'm just looking forward to putting ideas into action as quickly as possible.

—*Mark Majesky, Ph.D.*

Ah Hah

In the late '80s, I realized that morphology alone—just to look at structures in the microscope—was very important, but it had its limitations if you wanted to do research. At that time, molecular biology was growing at exponential speed, so I decided to take a sabbatical year in order to learn some molecular biology, and that's how I came and met Dr. Michael Lieberman. I have been working in his lab since 1990.

For many years, as a pathologist, I had just looked at slides. Suddenly I went back to the bench and started using pipettes and petri dishes. It was a very interesting experience just to use my hands again, and to hold meetings with Dr. Lieberman, planning experiments. It's really a different perspective. Diagnostic pathologists, surgical pathologists, are really observers. They record what they see, either for diagnostic purposes or for research, but in a lab dealing with molecular biology and what people call basic research, you are really experimenting and designing things and just watching carefully for results. You might expect one result and get an entirely different result, but it's a result. Then the idea is to explain why you got that result. So I have done an entirely different type of work. I enjoyed it very much, so much that I decided to stay, and I've been here for 11 years already.

When you get some clear-cut results, you go home and you say, "Boy, this is it! I, I really don't even care about my salary—this is so rewarding, and I'm so happy." That has happened to us in the lab several times. Not often. Occasionally you see some unpredictable results that open the doors to other research projects. That happens.

Several of the models of the transgenic mice that are in Dr. Lieberman's lab were really a surprise to us. When I started working in his lab, we were working with the mouse model that was configured in a way that it carried a human gene for a malignant tumor. Everybody expected that the mice would develop a malignant tumor, which didn't happen. The mice developed a kidney lesion, which

60. Roberto Barrios, M.D., savors doing both diagnostic pathology and basic research.

consists of multiple cysts of different sizes and shapes, resembling polycystic kidney disease of the human. That was a surprise, but then we started going back and trying to explain why. And we think that we found an explanation. The gene induced proliferation in the kidney. The oncogene was hooked to a so-called promoter that is expressed in the kidney, and that gene induced proliferation of epithelial cells, and that's how the cysts formed. That was probably one of the "ah hah" days or weeks that I remember as rewarding.

—*Roberto Barrios, M.D.*

Best Investment

When I got here, obviously I didn't have my Texas medical license. And that takes a very long time, I found out, so I had to wait. We knew that I was going to have at least three months, so Dr. Lieberman gave me 10,000 bucks and put me in contact with David Rowley, a researcher, and said, "Let's see what you can do."

And I think that's been his best investment. I only used $2,000, and I brought him about a million bucks in grants. So I can't complain about that. I'm trying to be a viable clinician at Methodist, which requires a lot of energy and a lot of input, and at the same time, I'm trying to be a somewhat decent researcher in

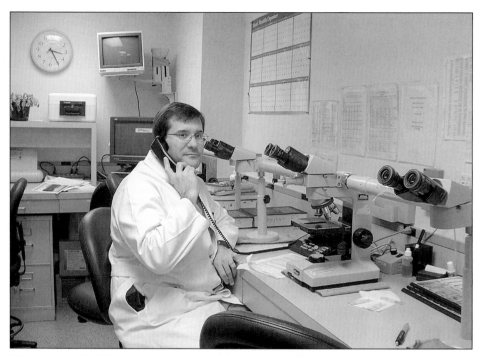

61. Gustavo Ayala, M.D., takes pride in transforming about $2,000 worth of seed money into about $1 million in grants for his research.

translational research. It's a lot of work. Not to toot my own horn, but I'm proud of what has happened in the past three years.

—Gustavo Ayala, M.D.

Worldwide Stomachs

I spent a lot of time in nice places, talking, around the world. As long as *Helicobacter* lasts, I will last on the international circuit, but *Helicobacter* is towards the end of its career. Because the pharmaceutical industry had invested a lot of money, Dr. David Graham and I have spent a good six or seven years lavishly treated by the international circuit, traveling the world, getting to see beautiful places. We had things to say and also were getting decent funding for our work. And now it's drying up, because there's nothing more to say. There are lots of scientific questions that are valuable from the viewpoint of living well.

After working on the *Strongyloides*—a worm, a parasite—I started to work on

Helicobacter. It's been 10 years now. I work on the interaction between *Helicobacter* and the gastric mucosa to discover what causes different types of gastritis to develop and one specific type to increase the chance of getting gastric cancer. For most of these years, we worked on people, and we collected epidemiological data in lots of patients from various parts of the world, comparing the results between different populations to see if we could identify trends.

Now, for the past two years, we have also developed an animal model. It's called the Mongolian gerbil. It's a little gerbil that can be infected with *Helicobacter*, human *Helicobacter*, with very similar results to what happens in people. It started in Japan years ago, and for some reason we always ignored it here. Then about two years ago, some of us got on the bandwagon—with great difficulty at first, because the American gerbils apparently are different.

And now I have a research group for the cardia portion of the stomach, the interface between the esophagus and the stomach. It became a trendy thing to study because it's where, in the West, cancer of the stomach is shifting. It's going from the distal portion of the stomach, where it has almost disappeared. Now more Western, usually white, relatively well-off people develop cancer of the cardia. It may be related to reflux, but it is unclear how. Some people think it's related to the disappearance of *Helicobacter* from these populations.

So I have put together a group of, so far, 14 gastroenterologists and some pathologists in countries where the cardia is held in transition. With people from Brazil, Israel, some parts of Italy, some parts of the United States, in transitional populations, we want to see if we can catch the cardia when changes happen.

We get to know a lot of interesting people. Since I usually talk to each of them in their language, I get my kicks for linguistics satisfied.

—*Robert Genta, M.D.*

If It Comes

One of my most satisfying times was when I published three papers in one issue of *Nature*. I think that also my first paper in *Nature* was very, very significant for me. It was an article in 1992. I always thought that that would be the best I would ever do, because an article in *Nature* is about as good as you can do. I think that also seeing my students defending their theses is also a great time for me. I have been pretty lucky to have some talented people come through my laboratory.

In my research, I hope we can identify a novel target for contraceptive development. Most of our work is on the ovary, but we have several interesting target proteins that could be targets for contraceptives right now. We define function by using the mouse as our model, so we generate knockout mice. If the mice are fertile in the absence of the protein, well, that is not a good contraceptive, right? But if the mice are infertile, then that would suggest that perhaps if we had a drug that inhibited the activity of this protein, that would be a great contraceptive. So enzymes are good targets. That's one major thing that we strive for in our research. If it comes, that is great. If it doesn't, we have a lot of funding along the way.

—*Martin (Marty) Matzuk, M.D., Ph.D.*

Conservation

One of my greatest contributions to the Department was relaxing the dress code. You expect the clinicians to wear suits and ties all the time. They don't have a lot of choices, I understand, but over here in basic research, most of the people were dressed rather formally every day.

I've always been a blue jeans and T-shirt kind of guy, and I wasn't really about to change that. I didn't think I needed to, from all the other places I had been. Shortly after I got here, and as the weeks went by, I was looking around and seeing all these people who looked really formally dressed every single day.

I went to Mike Lieberman and said, "Is there some kind of dress code that I don't know about?"

He kind of grinned and said, "Absolutely not. I wish I could dress like you every day, but I can't do it." So I didn't pay much attention. But then, during the next few months, you could see the creep of my dress code influencing many of the other faculty within the Department. I think I helped liberate some people from the M.D. coats that had been constraining them.

So I think it's more relaxed here. It was a good thing.

There have been lots of little mini-successes and many huge failures. We have

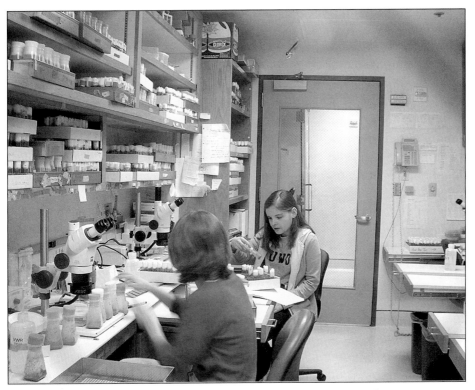

62. Researchers in Graeme Mardon's lab study the molecular genetics of eye performance.

not yet, for example, done anything completely stupid where, you know, we'd say, "What were we thinking about? We should never have done this. The whole thing is a disaster because we didn't think clearly." Fortunately we have avoided that, so the things that have been disappointing are just the way it is. And I feel very fortunate with funding. I haven't had any major grant applications rejected yet.

The first two weeks of November last year were really hard because I had three grant deadlines, three lectures to teach, three trips out of town, and something like three talks to give in a two- or three-week period. It was extremely high pressure, and I don't want to go through that too often. So, you know, I can't really complain about it too much. If you're in academic science and you don't like high pressure, you're in the wrong job.

Our main focus is to try and understand molecular genetics of eye performance, so we are working on a group of genes that are necessary for eye development in *Drosophila*. If you take the genes away, the flies have no eyes.

The first striking discovery in the last six or seven years concerning this group of genes is that they're all highly conserved in humans, and some of them are also required for normal eye development in humans. So it looks like the genetic pathway controlling the eye development has been conserved for more than 500 million years. I was a little bit surprised. When I first started at Baylor, that was not known.

Shortly after I got here, it started to become clear that this group of genes was also going to be required and performed really similar roles in eye development in mice. So I was already committed to working on the same gene in mice, but it just got more exciting because the conservation became more and more clear the first few years that I was here. Later we found out that not only was the gene required for eye development, but it is also sufficient for eye development, which means that if you turn these genes on during development in places where they are normally not expressed, you can get ectopic eyes forming in those tissues. You can get flies that have eyes coming off their legs or their wings or all kinds of strange places on their bodies. Turning on just one gene or a combination of these genes is sufficient to initiate the entire program of eye development, which has got to involve several thousand genes that are interacting very high up in this pathway, but sufficient to make a compound eye.

Other researchers have found that these same genes or at least some of them are also sufficient to initiate eye development in vertebrates. If you turn on these genes—there's a large number of these genes—you can also get ectopic eye development in vertebrates.

That's really the major focus of what we've been doing for the last several years, the first five years that I was at Baylor. Now we're working on the homologs of these genes in mice and knocking them out and seeing what they're doing, which has been somewhat disappointing—but probably because these genes are a part of multi-gene families, and so you can't just knock out one. You've got to knock out all of them to see phenotypes, and so we're in the middle of doing that.

In addition to studying eye development, we're studying neural degeneration. So we study how neural development occurs in the first place and then what the mechanisms are for degeneration of those neurons later in development.

—*Graeme Mardon, Ph.D.*

Gentle, Slow-moving

Just recently we have had a barrage of little, tiny bugs that I thought were gnats flying around, and they had been bothering Dr. Lieberman—and me, too. He said they were *Drosophila* and maybe I should call Graeme, you know, and see if something is loose. So I did, and he asked me to describe them, and I said, "They are little gnat-like bugs just darting around here and there."

And he said, "Do they have red eyes? If they don't have red eyes, they are not mine." He said, "If they are darting around very quickly, they are not mine, either. My *Drosophila* are very gentle, slow-moving flies."

So I thought, "OK, if you could tell from that they are not yours, I won't blame you."

—Sandy Oaks

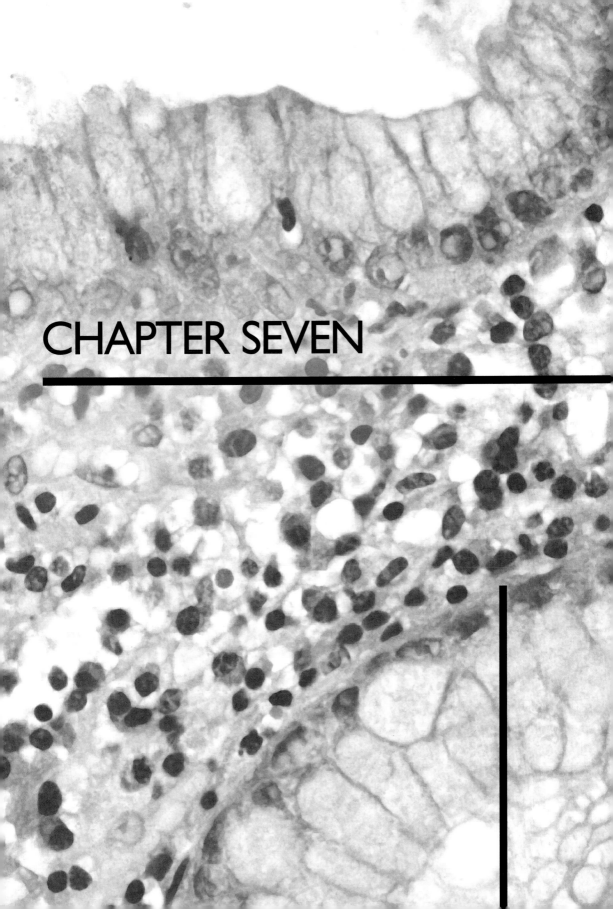

CHAPTER SEVEN

THE BUSINESS OF PATHOLOGY

In Stuart Wallace's day, the business of pathology was a straightforward matter. His annual reports in the '40s listed the faculty and staff, clinical and research activities, and the budget. They rarely exceeded four typewritten pages.

Now the Department employs 329 people, and there is an entire administrative staff to make sure that business runs as smoothly as possible. At least two of its members have MBAs. The Department has gone through the Medicare revolution and the managed-care revolution.

For all of the challenges brought about by this complexity, the Department continues to grow, especially with the expansion of services into area hospitals through Community Pathology Associates. Michael Lieberman has proven to be a gifted entrepreneur.

63. Milton Finegold, M.D., prepares for an Internet consultation with a colleague in Oregon about an experimental model of human disease in mice. They are trying new therapies to treat metabolic disease of the liver, which, if successful, may be considered for human cases. Using software and digital cameras, collaborators around the world can view samples together and discuss them online.

Portions

At the time that I started in pathology, medicine had very little business-like quality to it, in any specialty. None of us were motivated to become a physician by the idea of the income that we would generate. We were probably aware of the fact that it was a good profession, and you would never suffer financially. As long as you could do your job, you would be OK. And of course all the physicians in New York who had cars drove Buicks, and that was better than Fords or Chevrolets, so obviously they had more money. But nobody I knew ever entered medicine for the money—or, nobody that I cared to know. And none of my classmates, to my knowledge, many of whom became very wealthy, ever really thought about it.

When I entered into pathology, in addition to all the scientific and medical advances that we had to learn and cope with, we subsequently had to learn about business matters.

From my point of view, this was partly because of being in charge and managing the laboratories. Until I did that, I never cared a bit about it. I cared about getting grants and running a lab and hiring technicians and so forth, but I never even thought about funding the delivery of health care until I became a lab director.

Now initially, everything was paid to the hospitals, and the hospitals billed, and we just did our job. We had salaries—from the university, in my case, or from the hospital, whatever. In the days before Baylor took over Texas Children's, the pathologists who worked here had a contract with the hospital, whatever the terms were. It was at that time a percentage of the gross billings. Whatever they billed in lab tests, they got some fraction of that. They could spend it any way they wanted.

Well, when Baylor came in here, my background was not very strong, because I had only worked at Bellevue Hospital in New York, which is a city hospital. And I was in charge of preparing budgets, but I had absolutely no control over how the money was allocated or spent or how it was divided. I was never educated about the money side of things until I came here.

And here, of course, it was very business-like. My first meetings with the vice president of the hospital taught me about what their expectations were, taught me that there was money to be made by the hospital from the laboratories and that they would be willing to support the scholarly work of the pathologists. When they invited Baylor in, they understood that it was a *quid pro quo*. People who want to work under those conditions would need time and support to get their research and writing done, and they would pay for that.

The hospital had been doing pretty well at the time that Medicare and Medicaid came in, which was the '70s. They were earning money for the delivery of all kinds of services, including pathology. So that's how we started and, in fact, continue to this day. The money came from the hospital. The money went to Baylor; Baylor paid the staff. But the main thing was that the pathologists here, with me being in charge, manage the entire laboratories.

Well, of course, then all the reimbursement changes occurred at the federal level, and managed care came in, and there were all kinds of challenges to income to the hospital. At the same time, it also became possible for pathologists to bill for their diagnostic services as professionals, instead of just taking a salary from the hospital or medical school. One could act as a practitioner. So we created a group practice at Texas Children's Hospital to bill for our services. The hospital would pay us to supervise, to make sure it was done properly, that the quality was good, and so on. That's still true, although not for individual tests.

When we started billing for professional services, of course we had additional income. So we distribute that income back to the hospital—not all of it, but we pay them back a certain significant part.

Some of it goes to the dean at Baylor, because all Baylor faculty who bring in money pay a tax, because the dean needs money from the clinical practitioners to pay for the non-clinical fields. In Pathology, of course, we have a mixture of the two, but in Biochemistry you don't bill patients; Anatomy, likewise. So that tax helps to support the academic programs of the school in general, and so we do that as well. And then whatever is left over, Dr. Lieberman gets a portion for Baylor, and I get a portion for the Department here.

None of this was part of anybody's education. It wasn't the education of the hospital directors, and it wasn't the education of the pathologists. It arose out of the changes in medical reimbursement. And it's different in different places.

—Milton Finegold, M.D.

Jumping and Running

There came a time when The Methodist Hospital, back in Mr. Bowen's days, felt that the health-care environment was changing, and that The Methodist needed to do some things to heighten or increase the likelihood that it would be here when it was all over. So what they chose to do was to offer consulting services, management services, around the countryside. Hell, they even went to Turkey. I don't know how far into Mexico they went, but it was an international consulting operation for a while, and it was certainly in Louisiana and several places in Texas.

The hospital started out offering consultative management services but expanded all the way up to and through actual owning of the hospital. San Jacinto is a prime example of a hospital that came into our possession. Basically, as

64. The core lab operates around the clock to provide routine chemistry, hematology, coagulation, urinalysis, blood analysis, endocrinology, tumor markers, cardiac markers, drug monitoring and toxicology tests for The Methodist Hospital, physician offices, and referring labs and hospitals.

Methodist entered into these management agreements, saw weaknesses in places, or absolute deficiencies, they took steps, as any prudent manager of a business would do, to ensure against that problem or a repetition of it.

In one particular case, Conroe, it became clear to the management that they needed a change in pathology, and so they came to Dr. Titus and said, "We want you to do the pathology." Dr. Titus resisted that fairly forcefully because he really didn't think it was an appropriate situation for an academic medical school. There were other people who thought the same thing. To make a long story short, even though Dr. Titus resisted it, it came down to Mr. Bowen. He said, "You know, do this, Jack—as a personal favor to me. I want you to do this."

So we were reluctantly coerced or led into what, if we'd been brighter, we would have jumped on and run with many years ago. It has turned out, as the world has turned, to be a smart thing, and a good thing, for us to do. We are a stronger department because of those kinds of things, and not just from a financial standpoint. So the impetus for our, call it outreach, or call it our expanding business opportunity, was Conroe.

Since Will Kyle has come, I think we have grown at a faster rate. Certainly it's a more open and integrated process. I can't remember exactly when we took over

Brazosport, but that's probably about the transition time. We've added Brazosport, Baytown, Sugar Land—that's new, relatively new—Huntsville, and Wharton, along with two or three surgery centers. I'm guessing we had Conroe, The Woodlands and San Jacinto, and that's it. So certainly the number of sites has grown.

We are a more cohesive team, better at dispersing responsibilities, so that we have more time to focus on what our opportunities are and to address them in a more rapid fashion. We have quarterly business meetings with the principals involved to try to decide what the best opportunities are. I know that it helps everybody to have those meetings. That started just since Will has come, and it makes it easier for everybody.

—Jamie Davis, Ph.D.

The Message

The thing that struck me about Baylor as a whole was how entrepreneurial the college was and remains, not only in the economic sense, but in the investigative and diagnostic sense. This is the place where you are expected to come and build and cooperate, but do it on your own. Everybody was hustling then, and they hustle now. At a faculty meeting today, Ralph Feigin announced that the rate of growth of Baylor's grant funding in the last couple of years has been faster than any other medical school in the United States.

I will never forget when I talked to Bill Butler just around the time I took the job. I was there with Bill Butler and Bobby Alford. They were negotiating with me, and I said, "Well, how many salary lines would I have to build these new programs we're talking about?"

Bill looked at me, and he said, "As many as you can raise money for."

So I got the message early, and of course it's worked very well for us as a Department.

The entrepreneurial nature of the Department had been developing since the early '80s when Jack Titus, who was the previous chair, was asked by The Methodist Hospital to develop a pathology program at Conroe Regional Medical Center and San Jacinto (Methodist Hospital) in Baytown.

65. Conroe was the beginning of the Department's outreach to expand Baylor's services to other regions.

Circumstances were this: The Methodist Hospital and The Methodist Corporation had been developing management contracts for different hospitals around the area. For the hospitals they were managing, they provided ancillary services—anesthesia, pathology, and radiology, or at least radiology and pathology. So we ended up going out there at the invitation of The Methodist Hospital.

After I got here, in '88 or '90 or '91, somewhere in there, it turned out that The Methodist realized that they were liable for the operations of the hospital if they had a management contract, and so they beat a hasty retreat, because for the cost of the management contract they were at incredible risk. Still it left us in place with a decade of quality experience out in Conroe, and so we stayed. There were three hospitals originally, which were Conroe, The Woodlands Hospital, and San Jacinto. San Jacinto is part of The Methodist Group, so that is a little different, but The Woodlands Hospital and Conroe were in that original cluster.

One of the things that we can do without interfering with the private docs practicing medicine is to provide a quality of pathology service that they cannot

66. With his *Hope* mural at Medical Center Hospital in Conroe, artist Robert Dafford of Lafayette, La., transforms a brick wall into a tranquil, uplifting Lake Conroe landscape.

get at a small community hospital, because we find seasoned, experienced pathologists. They live in the community, they work in the community, they are part of the community, and they are full-time Baylor employees, but in addition we provide backup service from our experts here in the Texas Medical Center. So if there is a blood-bank problem that no community pathologist could reasonably be expected to handle, they call David Yawn. If there is a microbiology problem, they call Jamie Davis or Charlie Stager. If they have difficult slides, they call the expert in the area, and they get same-day turn-around time without additional charge to the patient. (Usually if we send slides, let's say to M.D. Anderson, there is an additional charge to the patient for a secondary consultation.) We view the Community Pathology Associates consultation as an intra-group one, because we are all Baylor College of Medicine Pathology, and so there is no charge to the patient. That is how the process got started.

—*Michael Lieberman, M.D., Ph.D.*

Expansion

When I came here, Jack Titus—I'm not related to him—was the chairman, and the administrator was Wes Moreland. It was more of a sleepy academic department.

Primarily the mission of the Department was to train medical students, do medical research, and provide clinical services just at the Medical Center-based hospitals, such as The Methodist, Texas Children's, and Ben Taub. Now our role has expanded so dramatically out to Conroe, The Woodlands, Huntsville, Baytown, Lake Jackson, and Wharton, places like that, through the Community Pathology Associates outreach program. Now there is much more of an entrepreneurial spirit in looking for new sources of revenue to fund projects here within the Department, both for research and academic medicine.

67. Becky Patrick manages client relations and is of great help to Pathology Department customers.

We brought Becky Patrick on, not quite two years ago, to do some secretarial work for Dr. Wheeler. Then she became office manager in the front and is really focused a lot on client services. She handles our client relations. That was a turning point from the standpoint of having a formal department for handling client relations. It made a big difference to our internal and external customers.

—*David Titus*

He Gets On It

After Wes Moreland left, I was looking for somebody to be the new administrator, and I didn't like anybody in the catchment that I got. I realized I knew Will, so I invited him to come over. I laid out a vision, and he liked it. Will really complements my interests and skills, because he is very much a process person, very much a people person. He understands how to attend to people's needs and

68. Will Kyle is admired for his sound judgment and sense of ethics. Perhaps his greatest strength is his ability to understand what motivates people and how to provide for their needs.

to get the best out of them. I understand the importance of those things, but I don't do it very well, and so it's just fortunate.

He's also got a rock-hard ethical core. He's got very good judgment about what's appropriate and what's not, what's ethical, what will motivate people and still be fair. I don't think we could do better. Certainly given my interests and skills, I couldn't do better, and I think most departments here couldn't do better. He's got good financial skills, he's got good number skills, good accounting skills, but, you see, that's not his real strength. Or rather, there are lots of people who have those skills. His strength is to understand what motivates people and how to provide for that within the framework of what's appropriate for our class of institution.

I found him purely by luck because we used the same athletic facility. Sometimes we would find ourselves huffing and puffing on the treadmill next to each other. One of the great things about the treadmill is that people can run at different speeds and run together.

Will made the process of management much more inclusive. Now we have the quarterly meeting. Will and Jamie and Tom and I and Armand Martel and Jim Fletes and David Titus sit around and brainstorm about options and so on. The idea for that forum really comes out of Will's head, as does this sense of process. I'd be tempted to go off half-cocked, use half the story and make a snap decision. Of course, you do two things with process: One, you get better decision-making, but two, the sense of inclusiveness has been just a wonderful addition that he's brought. He instituted a weekly staff meeting with the support staff, which is a great morale booster, a great way to share information and get feedback from people. We didn't have that before; that's something else he did. And he's very responsive to all the physicians and scientists on our staff. It's not just that the big brass gets good treatment and the assistant professors get nothing. When people have needs, he gets on it and helps.

—Michael Lieberman, M.D., Ph.D.

Up to Speed

We are really pleased with Will. It is always kind of scary when you get a new boss. You wonder if you're going to have a job tomorrow, if he's going to get rid of some staff. But it actually never even felt that way after he started.

Coming from psychiatry, he was learning a whole new field. He mentioned to us several times that he was spending so much time reading, especially our contracts on our clinical side. He was also reading a lot on pathology so he would be up to speed.

—Ginger Jozwiak

Creating Resources

In a typical day, something meaningful usually gets done. Not because I did it, but because there are a lot of good folks that help our Department run. A typical day involves solving a problem with a patient, usually around a payment or billing issue. It involves resolving a staff conflict either based on resources or misunderstandings about what may need to be done. The "business of pathology" in an academic setting means that there is a business side, and there is a "support this primary mission" side. Generally they are one and the same, sometimes not. Almost always some part of the day is spent trying to be smart proactively about resolving something that either is a problem or eventually will be. A lot of effort goes into that. And how do we get paid for what we do, and how can we make sure we are getting paid a fair amount for what we do? What is the right thing to do with that money in terms of supporting Dr. Lieberman's vision for the Department? So I guess it is a day of decision-making within that framework.

Today I had a meeting where there were some pretty serious staff conflicts that needed to be resolved. Some are a bit emotionally charged and still not fixed. I'm not sure I can fix it, but I think I know as a group where we need to end up. I do try to look for that deeper meaning sometimes in the professional relationship, not the personal relationship, but the professional relationship. That is an important boundary to keep in mind. But it is probably wrong to say it was a fun thing to be involved in. That would be a bit perverse, maybe, but it would be an interesting thing to move people towards a different level of candor with their feedback with each other. That is a part of my day that I enjoy.

We have been able to manage our growth in a way that I think has been good for us. You can't run a successful academic department on tuition and grant money. It's not going to happen. You have to create resources that allow you to do the mission. Mike understands that, and he has let me help him with that. That has been the most rewarding thing to me, by far, in a somewhat difficult environment with several challenges; we have been very successful at growing the business of pathology within the context of our academic vision. It has been a lot of fun.

I've been lucky to have a number of good teachers here—Dilzi Mody, Armand Martel, Tom Wheeler, Mike Lieberman, and especially Jamie Davis. He's shared so many of his experiences, and his balanced wisdom has taught me so much. He's such an asset to the Department.

From a practical perspective, I think I've been able to assess opportunity, to make business decisions based on that assessment, and then act accordingly. From an administrative perspective, I've worked hard to build a sense of community.

I've worked to establish credibility, so that people are willing to work with us and willing to trust us, to think that what we tell them is true. We need to be responsible and accountable, to follow through with the things that need to get done. We have not always done a perfect job with that. We have let things slip through the cracks that should not have. Nothing major. But for the most part, we have done a good job of establishing administrative credibility. To me, nothing else happens if you don't have that.

There was a bit of a crisis which probably goes back to the issue of how I got here. My guess is that Mike is astute in his evaluation of people. I think he perceived me for what I am, and that is an honest person. That credibility was something he knew the Department needed. He was hoping that I would be credible and smart about it. Since we're five years into it, I guess we succeeded.

—*Will Kyle*

Quality

If I am doing something for the patient, then I think I am doing something for the Department. After all, quality is meeting or exceeding the expectations of your clients. Who are the clients or the customers of the Department of Pathology? Ultimately it is the patients out there, really, and the physicians also, the physicians who use our services, right? So I think that whenever I serve the patient, say, for example, if I am doing leukophoresis, removing all of these bad white cells in a patient's system, and I do it well and with compassion, I am reflecting the Department.

I may not be consciously doing it. I don't think: "I am going to do this well, just so the Department will be blessed." But I think if you look back, people would say ... I don't know that they would say, "*Yeah, that's the Department of Path-ology.*" (But) if there is a consistency about the quality of the service that we deliver as a Department, then I have contributed to that. The same way with our other customer, the physician out there who is taking care of the patient directly. I think they would feel the same way.

—*Gene Bañez, M.D.*

CHAPTER EIGHT

DERRING-DO

Danger! Intrigue! Revolution!

Conover

At Methodist we've served a lot of very important dignitaries from all over the world. Kings and queens and whatevers from various places. Movie stars, gangsters, and gangsters' girlfriends would come here. That is, a bunch of people who were incognito, incommunicado, guarded by their own secret service or our secret service. The president of Turkey, for example, was here at one time in the historical past, and he was, I'm told, one of the two or three most likely people to get assassinated. We were used to a lot of secret activities. It kind of becomes blasé after a while.

So one morning in April of 1976, Dr. Titus is saying to Phil Migliore and me that he needs to know something. "How can we assure," he says, "that a patient who's here, who will have to have laboratory specimens collected on him and presented down to the laboratory, won't be identified and the information that he's here released to the world at large?" I'm thinking, well jeez, who cares? But Jack's being very secretive about it, trying to get us to answer the question. "Can you give me assurance that one or two or three of our most trusted blood collectors either won't recognize this individual or will be able to keep this secret, even if

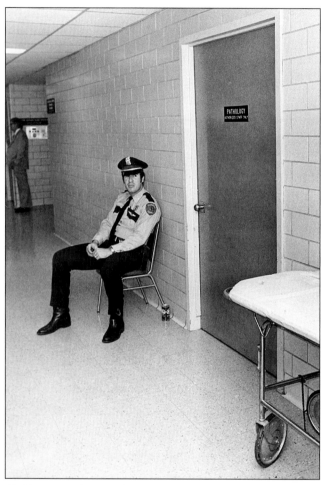

these people are going into the room and collecting information on this patient, whom we will call John Doe?" Actually the name that was being used was Conover. I've always wondered if maybe that wasn't some sort of telepathy right there. The con is over?

So we're sitting there trying to answer this hypothetical without enough information even to make a valid decision. And so finally I say, "Damn, Jack, I don't care who it is, but to be able to make a decision, we need to know more than you're telling us."

He said, "OK, there are only five or six people, chiefs of services around here, who may be involved in this patient's care and know who he is. I don't really want to have to

69. Houston policeman G.A. Olin guards the door to Methodist's pathology lab, where Howard Hughes' body was reportedly kept.

tell you, but so you guys can give me a valid judgment about how we handle this case, I'm going to tell you: Howard Hughes."

And I said, "Oh, shit." This was literally the only person in the world I could possibly ever have thought of that I really didn't want to know where he was—because it's going to leak. And then everybody who knows is a suspect.

I'm not all about celebrities. I'm aggravated by them more than anything else,

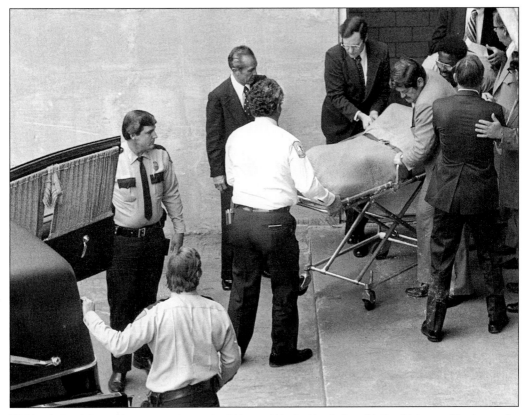

70. Hospital and funeral home attendants wheel Howard Hughes' body from Methodist to a waiting hearse for transfer to the funeral home on April 7, 1976. The autopsy revealed Hughes died of chronic renal disease.

but there you are, there's always one exception to the rule. Nobody in the world knew where Howard Hughes was, probably including Howard Hughes. It was a big secret. It was kind of like the Elvis thing now, except it wasn't tongue-in-cheek when it was Howard Hughes.

We don't really know whether he was dead before he ever got on the plane. He was in Acapulco. But anyway, we got a subsequent call that he had expired, and that he was still landing. He was brought here, and the autopsy was performed by Jack Titus and Malcolm McGavran.

Everybody from NBC to CBS to the *National Enquirer* was all over this hospital. You couldn't turn the corner without flash bulbs popping. Some fairly major bribes were being offered to everybody from housecleaning on up for any sort of information. There was no telling what a picture of the body would bring, because there were all sorts of horror tales about how long Hughes' toenails were and other weird speculation.

It was something that you can't really grasp until you see the human condition.

—*Jamie Davis, Ph.D.*

Desert Operation

The Shah of Iran was in Panama, and I was invited by his staff to come and maybe operate on him there. After I was down there and I saw him and saw the facilities and the resources there, I felt that it would be too risky. Finally I told them that I'd rather not do it there, because I didn't want to put him at that great risk. I left. A few days later, his sister called me and said that Sadat in Egypt had invited him to come there to be treated. Would I come to Egypt with my team to operate on him? And I agreed to do that. So I took my whole team over there.

—*Michael DeBakey, M.D.*

There We Were in Egypt

I went to Egypt with Dr. DeBakey in 1980. I went with Dr. Yawn and one of my technologists to help the Shah of Iran. It was quite a treat.

It was a very rapid decision. Anwar Sadat said he was going to protect the Shah, he was going to back him up. So that is where the Shah went—to a military hospital in Cairo. And then there was the problem of the medical team to help out. There were many people who did not want to expose themselves to that situation and also did not want to take the risk of having a possible complication with such a critical patient.

You know how Dr. DeBakey is. He will take on any challenge. Nothing is too big for him, so he did accept. I understand there were negotiations at a high level. Dr. Kissinger and others were involved in asking him to take on this responsibility.

Then he needed a team. Dr. Titus called, and he told me what he needed. I was the only one doing hemapheresis, so he asked if I would do it. I said, well, OK. They wanted David Yawn to come, too, and I said that I was also going to take my technologist. They might not have what I need in Egypt, and at least I could

71. The Shah of Iran, center, and Anwar Sadat arrive at Maadi Military Hospital on March 24, 1980. David Yawn, M.D., and Anita Werch, M.D., were among the support team for the Shah's operation.

have someone who works with me all the time. So there was an anesthesia team, the surgery team, and us.

They picked us up in the middle of the night in a black limousine, and off we went to Egypt in Oscar Wyatt's private plane. We were flown in directly. We were there with Wyatt and some lawyers. They were going to Africa, so they dropped us off. It was a fascinating time, a very fascinating time. It was when the Ayatollah had taken over. They were threatening the Americans, and there we were in Egypt, all of us.

The way we function here is so different. We are used to clean rooms and everything sterile and, you know, the way things should be. There we had to start scrubbing the rooms, big rooms. Also the electrical system was different, so we had to find a way of converting the current for the hemapheresis machine and the other machines. Dr. Yawn was very helpful in working with the engineers at adjusting the machine so we could work it.

72. Among the Shah of Iran's surgical and support team members from Houston were, *from left*, Sharon Storey, David Yawn, and Michael DeBakey, as well as, starting sixth from left, Ellen Morris, Betty Reiley, Gerald Lawrie, and Anita Werch.

They had lined up a number of recruits for platelets. There we went, making platelets for the Shah. The operation was successful, but we spent a whole week there.

We stayed in a hotel, and they would drive us back and forth. They were nice. After surgery and the patient got better, they took us to visit the pyramids, which were so fantastic. We went in a black limousine, so we felt like we were in a movie.

Dr. DeBakey may not remember, but when we were coming back on the same plane, everybody was nervous after a whole week being there. I was going to have Passover at my home, and most people (back home) had no idea where I was. Rumors were flying.

Dr. Titus was very nice. He was communicating with my husband to tell him that we were OK. During all this time, every day he talked to my husband. Jack was a riot.

—*Anita Werch, M.D.*

Out First

Late one night, I get a call from Dr. Titus. He says, "You're going to have to fly to Egypt." I had no idea what it was about. The limo came to my house. I packed and got my passport and a few dollars. It was because Dr. DeBakey was going to Egypt to do the Shah of Iran's splenectomy with the whole team. I went there with Dr. Werch to provide blood components for the Shah's surgery. We had to take a machine with us to collect platelets.

Oscar Wyatt had gutted his jet in the back. He had mattresses for us to sleep on. And we slept nonstop in his private jet from the airport to Cairo. They put me out of the plane first. I think it was because, if anybody was going to assassinate us, they would rather it be me than Dr. DeBakey.

The Shah's spleen was so big that it was using up all of his platelets, so that's why we brought the cell separator. When we got there, we knew that they had 220-voltage electricity, and we made the correct arrangements to switch the voltage, but they're supposed to have 50-cycle electricity versus 60-cycle, which is what's used in the United States. When we got there, the cycles varied all over the place, and the machine kept shutting down on us. We were sweating blood thinking, "What if we don't get these platelets?" Somehow, the Egyptian engineers came in, and we did all kinds of wiring things and made the machine work.

That was a hair-raiser which was very exciting and which I wouldn't want to repeat.

There were other trips like that with Dr. DeBakey. The last one was with him for backup for the Russian surgeons who did Boris Yeltsin's surgery. I think I was more scared on that trip, mainly because I thought, "Well, if something happens to Yeltsin, we might all—except for Dr. DeBakey—never be seen again." But actually, they treated us like kings there.

DeBakey had a long, long history of working in Russia with the Russian people. DeBakey's known for all the famous and rich kings and queens and persons he has operated on, but he also took a lot of indigent cases and still promotes that. He operated on some of the senior commandants with peripheral vascular disease, politicians during the communist era. So even before the communist era ended in

73. Michael DeBakey, M.D., *right*, consults with Russian President Boris Yeltsin in Moscow in September 1996. Yeltsin underwent heart bypass surgery early in November 1996.

Russia, DeBakey was highly thought of. He was like a patriarch for Russia. Even during the most severe part of the Cold War, they still respected and loved DeBakey.

The main surgeon who actually did the surgery on Yeltsin was a guy named Renat Akchurian who'd trained here at Methodist. He trained with DeBakey and Noon. He also had a cardiovascular anesthesiologist who trained here. That was the connection. A lot of their academic leaders in cardiac surgery actually came here and got training. But eventually during the communist era, they couldn't bring their wives, they couldn't bring any family, so the communists were assured they would go back. Now, of course, they can bring their families over.

We went to other countries that we consider Third World countries. I'm not going to say what they are, but we actually scrubbed floors with Clorox before the surgery. That wasn't Egypt; it wasn't Russia. The facilities in Russia for Yeltsin's surgery were—at least in that hospital, which is the major cardiovascular center there in Moscow—equal to anything we had in the United States. They just had only one room like that, while we've got 20 at Methodist. But limited resources on some of these trips were scary. We wanted to do the same quality of work there that we could do here. It was tough.

—David Yawn, M.D.

Plotting and Planning

When I was hired, I had applied for a job at the VA up in Albany. And they asked Dr. Gyorkey, who was chief of service at the VA here, to interview me as a pre-interview. Although they offered me the job then at Albany, it turned out, unbeknownst to anyone, really, that there was a job here. Since my husband was here at Baylor, I wanted to stay, and so I accepted it.

Why they had a position here and they did not know it—it seems like a weird thing—is because the person who had my job before me was called Ebrahim Yazdi. He's really quite famous now. He really had not been doing his job very often. Let me tell you, he was actually the American head of the Iranian Revolution.

When he left, he said he was going on vacation. He didn't quit or anything, but he was next seen on the cover of *Time* standing behind the Ayatollah Khomeini. Still, when I first came they just knew he wasn't coming back, but he had not gone to the revolution yet. I saw on my desk all these notes in Persian, because I took over his old desk, and he had all this writing. It was actually the plotting and the planning of that whole thing. I thought it was really sort of neat.

Then people started reconstructing what he had been doing. They could see that, "Oh yeah, he made a lot of calls, and he kept always talking, whatever." He used the free phone service that we get. There was the area network at the time for all the VA, I think. So in a way we indirectly and unknowingly supported the Iranian Revolution.

He came back, and I met him then. He was well-liked here. But then the next time he appeared was when the arms-for-hostages time came, and he was here again. Nobody knew about the arms-for-hostages deal, of course, so his cover was to come here and chat, chat, chat. But he really went up to Dallas and saw to those arms. That's where the arms were sent from, and he went up there.

—*Jill Clarridge, Ph.D.*

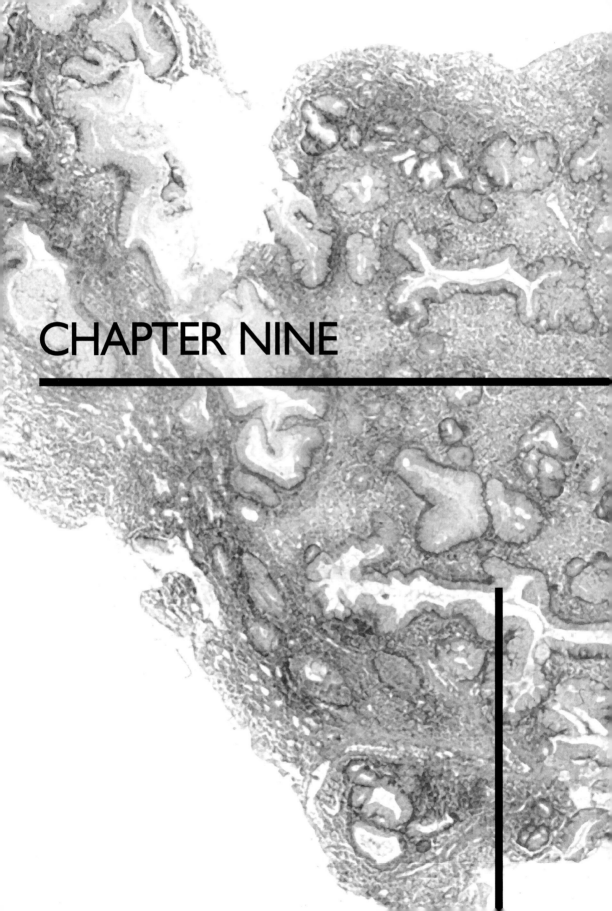

CHAPTER NINE

WATER

────

In late May and early June of 2001, Jamie Davis and Phil Migliore told me about the flood of June 15, 1976, when 10.47 inches of rain fell on the Medical Center in a 24-hour period. It was, they said, the 100-year flood.

On June 8, 2001, 25 years later almost to the day, the Medical Center (and Houston at large) suffered its second 100-year flood. This time the damage was even more extensive.

Baylor took in 16 feet of water. Approximately 30,000 rats and transgenic mice died, and 60,000 tumor samples were destroyed. Damage exceeded $100 million, and recovery took months.

While the Department suffered devastating losses, the faculty and staff nevertheless maintained most of the clinical services for the hospitals they served. How?

Picture a hotel ballroom decked out as a pathology lab and office, with a buffet running alongside one wall while tissue samples are delivered to another corner. It all takes place under the lights of crystal chandeliers. …

June 15, 1976
An Exciting Event

I guess things that I remember involve overcoming difficulties. The big flood, have you heard of the big flood? I think it was probably '76. I remember the flood—that was an important and somewhat exciting event. I think that is why some people join the Army at times of war. It wasn't necessarily exciting, but it was being alive, you know? And it was scary and exhilarating.

To bore you with some of the details: In the old days, rape or suspected rape victims who came to the Emergency Room here in effect got referred to us (the micro section) because we did the stains and looked for sperm. It was something that I really didn't like to do because of the risk of going to court to testify and all that sort of stuff. So in about '76, the City of Houston Police Department, working with the Health Department, had established a Rape Crisis Center. In the cases of suspected rape, you would call the Police Department, and they would send out somebody with a rape kit. You collected all the specimens in it, and the police took it with them to the crime lab. I was trying to convert the Emergency Room staff over to calling the Rape Crisis Center instead of us taking responsibility here. I was having a meeting with representatives from the Police Department, the Emergency Room, the City Health Department, etc., setting up this new protocol.

The meeting was down on the corner of the main building where Medical Records used to be. And the Emergency Room was down there, too. I came out of there at about 4 o'clock and started down the corridor, which is the other south corridor of the old main building as you go towards Fannin. I met a guy coming down the corridor. He was wet up his waist. I said, "Man, what happened to you?"

And he said, "I just crossed Fannin."

So I said that I had to see this. And I walked out to what now is the front of the hospital, and literally you could see the rooftops of cars under water out on Fannin. The water was 4 feet deep out there. And our fuse boxes were located in the sub-basement, along with our emergency generators. Water was 3 or 4 feet deep in the basement, so it was 8 feet deep in the sub-basement.

We had no power in The Methodist Hospital at all. So it was exciting. When

74. The Texas Medical Center experienced the "flood of the century" in 1976. Department members acted quickly, putting together a field strategy to take care of the needs of their clients.

the lights go out in surgery and the emergency lights don't come on, you are in deep doo-doo.

Power was out in this part of the city for probably three or four days. The hospital and other institutions here got jet turbines connected to generators. I think ours came from the military, because the military does field hospitals and that sort of stuff all the time. Huge jet motors were parked on bright red trailers by the side of the building, and you couldn't hear yourself think when you went outside. There were extension cords the size of your leg running into various places to get some electrical power.

It was in a warm part of the year. We had just the bare minimum of services available from the lab standpoint—as well as from the entire hospital standpoint. We had to go to KFC to get food for patients. Of course they discharged all the patients that they could. But we had very minimum electricity and therefore minimum capabilities for doing anything, as I remember, for three or four days.

That first evening, I went home about daylight the next morning. I think what we were trying to do is to make do with what we had, trying to run extension cords from whatever the available power was to some instruments and trying to isolate and determine what our capabilities were and what we could do about it. It involved calling other places around the city and outside of the area, because it basically was a Medical Center flood. So we were trying to establish networks for doing this, that, and the other. I don't remember those kinds of details. But we weren't sitting around drinking coffee during that period of time.

There was a lot of potentially serious flooding. There were a number of people who had to be saved, if you will, from the lower levels of the hospital. Women and children were down there in waist-deep water with the lights out. And you know it was dark. We had no air conditioning in a building that was not designed for ventilation. But we did have one cold room on emergency power, after we got it up, because of certain reagents and so forth. And you could take a break in the cold room.

My relationship with Mr. Bowen was fairly straightforward, *mano a mano*, with neither one of us giving much ground. During the flood, he was like a field commander, standing out by the Emergency Room with lights flashing on emergency vehicles and so forth. We were trying to put together a field strategy to take care of this, that, and the other. I was there to take care of the microbial-waste situation and the water.

It was like a field command when he said, "What are we going to do about the water, Davis?"

And I said, "You don't worry about the water—it's taken care of."

"All right," he said, "get to it."

So that was an exciting event.

—*Jamie Davis, Ph.D., May 31, 2001*

100-Year Rainfalls

It was like a battle zone. I have never been in a battle zone, but I figure if anything was like this, it was a battle zone. The disaster really became apparent to everyone at about 5 in the afternoon. It had been raining all day, very hard. And of course the water began to rise. Believe it or not, the water never overflowed from the bayou. We have had one overflow in this area, but it was not then. However, it became so full that the water in the street had no place to go. The streets began to flood, and when the bayou was doing its thing, the water began to back up in the Medical Center. It rose up so high against the building that it began to seep into the foundation of the basements, including the Baylor building, the library, Methodist Hospital, I don't know how many more.

At The Methodist Hospital, the emergency generators are in the sub-basement. The tunnel system that existed at that time was open—so there were no barriers—and the waters began to come into the basement. There was nothing to prevent them from going into the sub-basement, where the emergency generators were. The first thing that was lost was the city power, so the hospital switched to emergency power, but the generators became flooded, so by 5 all the lights were out.

At that time, we would start surgeries at 7 in the morning and finish at 9 at night. A lot of this was cardiovascular surgery, open-chest and all the rest of that, so when the power was lost, we had people on the surgery table. They finished under flashlights.

For the next week, there were no lights and no power available to The Methodist Hospital from the usual sources. During the night the rain had stopped. They brought in on semis at least two to three huge generators, which they parked out between the hospital and the garage. And all the doors were open because we had no temperature control. During the night they had to evacuate the patients, and there were no elevators, so they had to be brought down stairs. You had people in ICU, had people on the upper floors. They evacuated as many as they could, especially those who needed critical care, and tried to maintain the patients who were less healed. Some of those who weren't able to walk down stairs were able to stay.

We continued to operate our laboratory under emergency generators, but we were only allowed to select a few pieces of equipment. These generators had to be shared by the entire hospital. I guess at that time we were an 800- or 900-bed hospital. Not everything had been built by then. We wanted to provide electrolytes, things like sodium and potassium. We wanted to be able to provide blood gases—

that is, be able to check on those people who had trouble with oxygen content. We wanted to keep up one piece of equipment that was brand-new at the time and able to do individual tests on demand without having to batch them out. Previously we had to do everything manually or at best semi-manually.

All of this stuff for the first time was able to be performed by an instrument called the Automatic Clinical Analyzer—ACA—which was a Dupont instrument. All you had to do was take the specimen and pour it into a little cup and put it on the instrument. The instrument picked up the specimen and dispensed it into a prepackaged little cellophane pack that was able to do the test. It would turn all the tests around on a cycle, like a bicycle chain, and finally they went into the device that was able to take the reading. It had all the mathematics built into the system, so it calculated the result and printed it out on a piece of paper. We wanted to keep that operating. We weren't going to be able to do any routine types of things, so the ACA would enable us to do a lot of individual tests that we otherwise wouldn't be able to do.

We were living in the laboratories. There were maybe a few fans around that we could use, but the temperature in the labs was about 90 degrees, close to the limit that these instruments would operate and get accurate results.

The basement was where the autopsy room was. I was one of those individuals who went into the basement, because we did have some areas in the basement that were pathology-related. It turns out that because of flood waters, anyone who had gone into the basement had to get a tetanus shot. That was OK, because I hadn't had one in a long time. So I had to get a shot, along with a lot of other people who had ventured into the basement after the flood waters went down.

We were able to provide for the better part of the week some semblance of medical care for the patients still in the hospital at that time, but it was an experience that I or I don't think anyone else will ever forget.

All of the major buildings that were involved with flooding took steps to prevent a similar occurrence. It may not be obvious to all those who are walking by. I think the Baylor building is probably the best example of that, the Cullen Building that faces Fannin. They built embankments up along the sides of the building. This is one of the steps that were taken to put up a barrier to water creeping into the basement areas in the future. At Methodist, in the tunnel system, they also created barrier doors, sort of like submarine hatches. If it started to flood into the area, you could close off the doors to try to protect other areas against water damage, especially the emergency power.

We talk about 100-year rainfalls. That is a lot, especially within the time period. It wasn't a 24-hour period. We are talking about a three- to four-hour period when most of it came down.

Actually if we had that today, it might be a total disaster for a lot of the area. There has been so much building to the west of the city that, even now, the bayous fill up pretty quickly. There is some flooding over at Meyerland from time to time. Flooding is a danger pretty literally.

—Phil Migliore, M.D., June 4, 2001

June 8, 2001
Setback

Definitely the flood was one of my biggest challenges. This has been a hard two months so far. We lost so many cages. We lost almost 500 cages of mice, and just the week after that, I think we were all pretty exhausted from dealing with the flood.

Baylor is going to recover from the flood, but it is not going to be as great a place in five years as it could have been without the flood. It has probably set back a lot of people in different ways. People's careers have changed. People have decided to leave, not only from Baylor, but also from the Medical Center.

I have been lucky because although our animal room was affected, we did not lose as much as some people lost, partly because I waded down into the water on flood day and rescued 150 cages of mice.

I don't think I was supposed to be down there. Dr. Tinkey, the associate director of Comparative Medicine, and I went down to the vivarium and rescued 150 cages. I said, "Peggy, I need to get into my room to see what is going on," and we went down there. There were a number of cages that were flooded up to the next rack. So we went in there and rescued actually some of our most critical mice.

It was one of my saddest moments to be there and see everything below that

75. Remnants of Tropical Storm Allison inundate the Texas Medical Center in 2001. Looking north, the Fannin underpass at Holcombe is filled; clearance under the overpass exceeds 14 feet.

point and know it was dead, even some of the mice on the fourth row from the top. But I think that our room was the only one that was spared the fourth row because Peggy and I went down there.

We were only down there for a couple of minutes, but it was a really sad moment in my life. You know, you work 10 years building up something, and to see all this destruction. I am not sure if some of the stuff that we are doing will be able to recover from the flood. It changes some of the directions that we are going with our research.

—*Martin (Marty) Matzuk, M.D., Ph.D.*

Lost

We lost 30 to 40 percent of our mice. We also had freezers that lost power for several days, and we lost things in there. We are sharing space with someone who was in the basement of one of the older buildings and lost absolutely everything—

computers, data, notebooks, reagents, precious cell lines, everything. I'm not sure I just wouldn't stay at home in bed and not want to get up.

—*Gretchen Darlington, M.D.*

Pretty Bad

I had a little room over at Baylor. That's where I started my lab, but then we grew a little bit more, and so I asked Dr. Lechago if I could move into his lab in the Neurosensory Building basement. And he said yeah, so we started taking over. We took over half to three-quarters of it. He didn't have a fellow at that time, so it was OK with him. So we did a lot of work there. We had a freezer; we had a lot of material, a lot of work that we had done.

And then the infamous Tropical Storm Allison came around. What can I tell you? It was pretty horrendous. One of the things that I had asked before that day, because I had heard stories of the previous flood, was, "What happens when the next one comes around?" So we had transferred some equipment upstairs, but we still had quite a bit of it down there. That night it was pretty obvious that it was going to flood, you know, and it happened.

The next morning we were all crying. I came to the hospital around 10 in the morning because I didn't sleep at all that night. The first thing I did was to go upstairs to see if I could help anyone. I found Seth Lerner. We thought about the tissue bank. The tissue bank is on the fourth floor of the Fondren Brown Building. In the prostate area it holds 30,000 specimens from about 4,000 radical prostatectomies—12 years' worth of work. And it's frozen tissue. There was no electricity. If we didn't do anything, it was gone. So Seth and I started scrambling and seeing what we could do. We talked with a lot of people. We started looking for a generator so we could feed at least those freezers to keep them up. When we went there, they were still cold. We didn't open anything, because we were afraid of letting the heat into the freezers. We just touched them, and they were still cold, and it was still pretty good, can't complain.

They wouldn't let us bring generators in because there was really no place to put them that night. So after a lot of talking, a lot of moving around, we really stuck around the hospital. We got the chief of engineering at Methodist to agree

76. A workman pumps flood waters from the basement of the Cullen Building following Tropical Storm Allison in June 2001. Baylor College of Medicine took in 16 feet of water.

to feed those generators with lines from the only other building that had electricity that day. It took a while, but after a few hours they had electricity, but they only had electricity for about an hour or so because it was too much power, so it would keep popping. So we started a rotation to stand in front of the freezers to save the tissue. Mohammad Sayeeduddin came in, and he helped with that, and the rotation actually lasted for two weeks. Marcus Wheeler helped, because even though we had electricity, there was very little electricity to go around the whole hospital, and this was a very high-maintenance project. It required a lot of electricity, and essentially we kept losing electricity all the time, but it was OK.

The other problem was that the freezers work usually in an air-conditioned environment. It was over 90 degrees inside. Sometimes it got to 100 degrees. The freezers were supposed to go to -80 degrees, and they just couldn't handle going to -80 from 100, so we blew one freezer, and we had to get another one.

We tried to move the freezers to another building, but we couldn't because the elevators were not working, so there was no way of getting them out of there. There were no elevators working at all.

It was a total disaster. I mean, we came to the hospital, and you're talking no lights, and forget about air conditioning. It was really hot and humid and horrible, and we had to go into all these areas with flashlights. There was nothing left, no lights, nothing.

The tissue, after about two weeks of that, we did save that tissue. That's one thing we did.

I can't remember which day we actually were able to go down to my lab and see what had happened. Once we were able to get there, everything was destroyed, and we had nothing left. Literally, we had water to

77. After Tropical Storm Allison, Baylor College of Medicine closed while staffers scrambled to restore services. Damage exceeded $100 million.

the roof. It was pretty bad. There was nothing left there, nothing left. It was a total disaster. You couldn't do anything. We didn't try to salvage anything. It was just impossible.

The service part of our story is another story on its own. We couldn't work here, because we had no electricity. So we couldn't look into the microscopes. No air conditioning. There was no water, because the whole water system at Methodist was contaminated. The second day after the flood, they started pumping water. We knew that we weren't going to get a lot of tissue samples, because there weren't any. I mean, the hospital was closed. But we still had the Baylor lab, and we knew that we were going to keep getting samples there. I think this is the second day after the flood, or the third day after the flood, that we came in and tried to organize. I remember there was a meeting in Tom's office, and Mike was there, and Will was there. We were trying to see what in the world we could do. What were we going to do with the specimens that came in? We had no idea. We didn't have a

78. Cleanup efforts after Tropical Storm Allison took weeks as teams worked to restore labs and offices to working condition. Notice the water-level marks on the walls of this hallway.

lab. We couldn't work at Baylor, either, because the whole Baylor building was down. No water, no electricity, no heat, no nothing. So we were looking for an alternate lab to send material to. We talked with several big labs, and we got actually several of them to agree, but then after a while we decided that we could do it in-house, and we found some space at Baylor in the new Taub building that had some power. The college gave us some space, so we decided to set up the lab there.

We needed someplace where the pathologist would be able to sit down and look, and we couldn't do it at Baylor. We needed transcription. I don't remember who suggested renting one of the rooms in the Marriott, but that's what we did. We set up a whole little organization. It was pretty impressive.

There were several issues. One was actual space. The first day, they gave us two adjacent little conference rooms, and then they kicked us out the next day. So they took us to the long conference room, the ballroom, and that's where we stayed for about two or three weeks.

79. Staff members worked diligently, setting up a makeshift department in a ballroom of the Marriott. The Department was operational within three days.

What we were going to do with transcription was a big deal. We could dictate cases, but how do you keep track of cases? There were a lot of legal issues. So I remember I asked Subhendu Chakraborty if he could set up all the Macs that we have—if he could set up an intranet to connect the Macintosh computers with each other and connect that to the server, which is actually a Mac. Then the cases would be put into the server, and it would be legal and on record. So it was doable. Tom Wheeler's son, Dayton, and Carlos Talavera and Subhendu worked really, really hard, and they set it up, and it was pretty good. We took microscopes, we took computers, we took all the Macs that we could find. I had two in my office. Even Dr. Lieberman's portable computer was used.

That first day, not a lot of people were here. Actually, during the first few days, not a lot of people were here. Dr. Lieberman and Will were carrying things, Becky was here, Tom. A few others. We were just carrying things back and forth to the hotel and setting things up. By the end of that second day, we were all pooped, but it was set up. On the third day, we were up and running.

From there on, it was just a matter of doing the work. Work kept coming, and people started coming back slowly, and then it was too noisy and people couldn't concentrate, but it worked out OK.

Slowly we started coming back here to Methodist. We were the last part of the hospital to get electricity back, because there was a problem, something in the basement. We didn't get air, though, so when we came back here, we could look into our scopes, but we didn't have air for a long time. It was pretty bad.

—*Gustavo Ayala, M.D.*

The Second Thing

I've been here for nearly 12 years. I had been given an assignment, and I feel that I've carried it out as far as I can, and right now, there is very little challenge in terms of new things. I find myself losing—I don't know the word—relevance, if you will. I know it's a funny thing to say, because people like me, and I'm very well-considered and all that, but when I talk about relevance, I mean in terms of being able to effect change and lead into new territories. So that's one thing. I get very restless if I don't feel that I'm changing and moving.

The second thing is the flood.

Because of the amount of work I had here at Methodist, one of my goals, which was to eventually get an NIH grant for my research, was never truly fully realized. I was starting to come out of the hole, so to speak, in '97, '98. At that point I had lots of material, several good projects, I had a fellow, and my wife was my research assistant. I was trying to get some molecular stuff together. I had some preliminary results that were very, very good on gastric cancer and gastritis.

Then a sea of calamities happened, one after the other. First, in 1998 my wife died suddenly, two weeks after a coronary bypass. She was diabetic. So that liquidated my laboratory in terms of who was running it. My excellent fellow, Dr. Nirag Jhala, was supposed to spend a second year after he had gathered all the materials and the protocols and all that, but he could not keep his J-1 visa renewed. He had to go after an O-1 visa that he was offered in Alabama, and he's now an assistant professor there. In the meantime I had found an excellent physician, a research assistant, but her husband got a great job in Austin. She left. That essentially closed my laboratory, although I was sharing the space and the equipment with Dr. Ayala and other people.

80. Juan Lechago, M.D., left, and Gustavo Ayala, M.D., whose labs in the basement were destroyed by the 2001 flood, concentrate on their work over the hubbub at the Marriott.

Then came the floods in June, and the laboratory and all its materials, all its equipment, all its reagents, all its records, all its computers, everything was under water and destroyed and gone. So that was the second thing that kind of left me. There went any hope for autonomous research. Mind you, I'm still working very closely with Dr. Younes, my former fellow. We are working very hard on several of his projects, and some of them I will take to Cedars Sinai. But it's not the same thing.

Right after the flood, we were working out of the Marriott Hotel. And I had my cellular phone there. A few weeks before, Cedars Sinai had called me saying, "Juan, we just lost our GI pathologist. The GI Department in this hospital is enormous and very influential, and they are really, really very upset about this. Do you know some nationally recognized GI pathologist who would be mobile and come here?" I said I'd think. I'd check around. I'd ask. And when the flood happened, something snapped in my head, so I grabbed my phone there at the Marriott and called and said, "Arthur, are you still looking?"

He said, "Oh, yes! Yes! Yes! Do you have a name?"

I said, "Oh, yes. I have a name."

Well, he was kind of surprised. He said, "Oh, wow! When, when can you come?"

—Juan Lechago, M.D.

Carrying On

I certainly think that Will Kyle did a wonderful job of getting things up and running almost immediately after the flood, but certainly, for some time during that period and afterwards, we were waiting for things to settle down from the cleanup and all. I'm not sure what word to use. "Depressing" may be not exactly the right word, but sort of discouraging, even though of course we didn't let it show. I personally felt a great loss, even though I tried not to let that show. We had to carry on, and we did. Everything is going to work out and has worked out, I think.

—Phil Cagle, M.D.

What We Remember

I remember sitting around with Tom and Gustavo and thinking about how to do this, about using the Marriott. It grew out of the three or four of us talking. If we rented the ballroom, we were close enough that we could run over to Baylor and also use the histology facilities at Texas Children's. We made the decision that we had to keep a presence, not only for any Methodist things that might have to be done, but also because of all of our outside hospitals. Many of those were almost unaffected by the flood, so they would still be sending us consults and special stains, and all the surgery centers for which we did the processing and the cutting and the slide-making, as well as the interpretation, they would all be sending

81. Chairman Michael Lieberman, M.D., Ph.D., studies a slide and oversees operations at the Marriott. At night, staffers slept on roll-away beds to protect the Department's patient records.

us stuff. So we hit upon a relatively simple solution, which was to keep the pathologists and the operations close.

We were fortunate that Texas Children's never went down. They operated on emergency power, so we could get things cut, mounted, and stained there, and eventually we were able to use some of the space here at Baylor. But principally, as I recall, Gustavo Ayala and Subhendu Chakraborty were able to get a local area network going. We could not use all of our computer capacity, but at least we could fax reports out. We just lugged microscopes across the bridge from Methodist to the ballroom and plugged them in. Then we just cannibalized some stuff from Baylor and some stuff from Methodist and put it all together. One of the things that really made it work was Gustavo's ability to write some simple programs that allowed us to print out facsimiles of our path reports so that we could get things on them.

One thing worth noting is that we also brought our Easy Path server. Easy Path is the program that keeps track of all the Baylor specimens. So there we were with those microscopes, which are worth a minimum of $10,000 each, and all these computers. All of that could be replaced, but we also had the server, which had patient information on it, and all our programs. So we got two roll-away beds, and we had a couple of people, Marcus Wheeler and I forget who else, stay on alternate nights, because we were terribly afraid that we would lose the patient records.

With respect to Pathology, honestly, there have been relatively few permanent effects. Our revenues were down for a few months because, of course, when the hospital did not operate, literally operate in the sense of surgical operations, we had fewer specimens to look at, and when there are fewer specimens and fewer patients, we bill less. On the other hand, most of the peripheral hospitals that we serve were almost unaffected. So we had a slight dip in revenues but nothing that wasn't easy to cover in terms of our cost.

For Baylor and Methodist as a whole, there have been some profound changes. Methodist lost several hundred thousand square feet of space that is below grade that they are only going to restore for light use, with a few exceptions. Baylor lost 100,000 square feet of space. The school is still struggling with FEMA and the idea of getting reimbursed and what to do. The school is building walls at certain heights to raise the flood level to something like 51 or 52 feet. I have forgotten the exact calculation, but I think it is the 500-year flood plain that they are raising it to.

Some good things have come out of it. The hospital was in the midst of doing a total reassessment of its space needs and planning for the future, but this, of course, really accelerated the process and got them to focus. The other good thing is that there has been a real effort to clean up and spruce up a lot of the aging parts of the physical plant, using things like new wiring or new paint and carpet.

The biggest single catastrophic loss for the college and the hospital is cash. All of this takes money, and of course the hospital had no revenues, just the way the physicians had no revenues. The Medical School lost revenues because all of us pay a dean's tax to the Medical School. If we don't have receipts, we are not paying taxes.

Speaking for Pathology, the effects of the flood a year later are invisible in aggregate. There are still some people, like Gustavo and Juan Lechago, who has

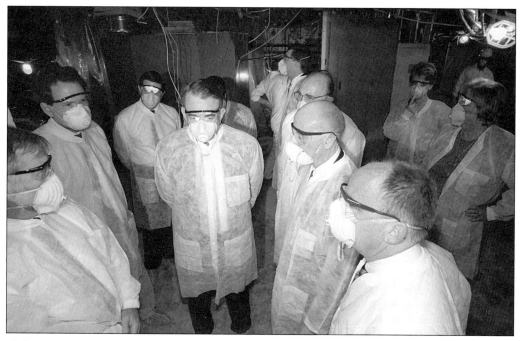

82. From left to right: An unidentified man, U.S. Reps. Ken Bentsen and Tom DeLay, Health and Human Services Secretary Tommy Thompson, Dr. Michael DeBakey, Dr. Ralph Feigin, and U.S. Rep. Kevin Brady tour the flood-damaged lower levels of Baylor College of Medicine. Those on the tour wore environmental suits as a precaution against mold exposure. The tour also made stops at The Methodist Hospital and Memorial Hermann Hospital.

now gone, who felt it severely, but most people can hardly remember there was a flood. It's interesting. The flood, of course, was a local event that all of us experienced, both at home and at work. September 11 is something that we experienced indirectly by television and the newspapers. And yet in everybody's mind, September 11 looms so much larger. It is an interesting study in remembrance and values. The flood was an act of nature, an act of God, but September 11 was a direct assault on America and American values. What we remember does say something about who we are as a people and how we view things.

—*Michael Lieberman, M.D., Ph.D.*

In the Old Days

One advantage to my job—some people might call it a disadvantage—is that we're kind of isolated up in Microbiology at Methodist. There was no elevator, one telephone, and not much of anything else, and the stairwell was pitch-black from 4 up. So you'd come up here in the morning, and you didn't leave until that afternoon. Occasionally I would go across the street just to see how things were going, but there was more activity probably over in the Marriott around the surg path activities and probably more innovative kinds of things. I mean, I think that, as a Department, it was one of the remarkable things that we did.

What we did up here in Micro was basically persevere. Probably the only interesting facet of my experience during that period of time, beyond just the aggravation of not having the wherewithal to do much of anything, is that I was, at least on one occasion, the only individual who remembered doing blood cultures in a non-automated fashion.

In the really old days, you took an Erlenmeyer flask with a cotton stopper in it and put some blood in it and put it in an incubator, and you shook it up a couple of times a day and looked at it to see if it had become turbid, i.e., indicating some bacterial growth.

We evolved from that up to the point now where our blood cultures are performed in a constantly monitored situation, where about every 10 minutes, each blood culture in the machine is looked at electrophotometrically. In the old days, they were looked at once or twice a day when you picked them up. That was a relatively insensitive way to detect growth. However, if you have been trained in the last 10 or 12 years, you may never have seen manual blood cultures, and therefore you have no experience or recollection of what one does without automated equipment.

So here we are: The automated equipment doesn't work, and the question is, "What do we do?" Having been doing this for 35 or 40 years, I knew how to change the whole process to do blood cultures.

We also had to haul five-gallon bottles of water up the stairs, and, of course, the toilets didn't flush, so once or twice a day we had to go downstairs. There was not much really remarkable beyond the fact that people came to work and did what they could under less-than-what-one-would-expect-in-this-century working conditions.

Certainly not everybody would have been able to accomplish what happened at the Marriott. Not every group of people would have had the willingness and the *esprit de corps* to make that work. Everybody stayed in good spirits. That's my view of this flood.

In many respects, even though the physical damage to the Medical Center was much greater than it was in '76, I guess it was less exciting to me this time than the time before. Maybe I'm just tougher than I was, or less excitable.

—Jamie Davis, Ph.D.

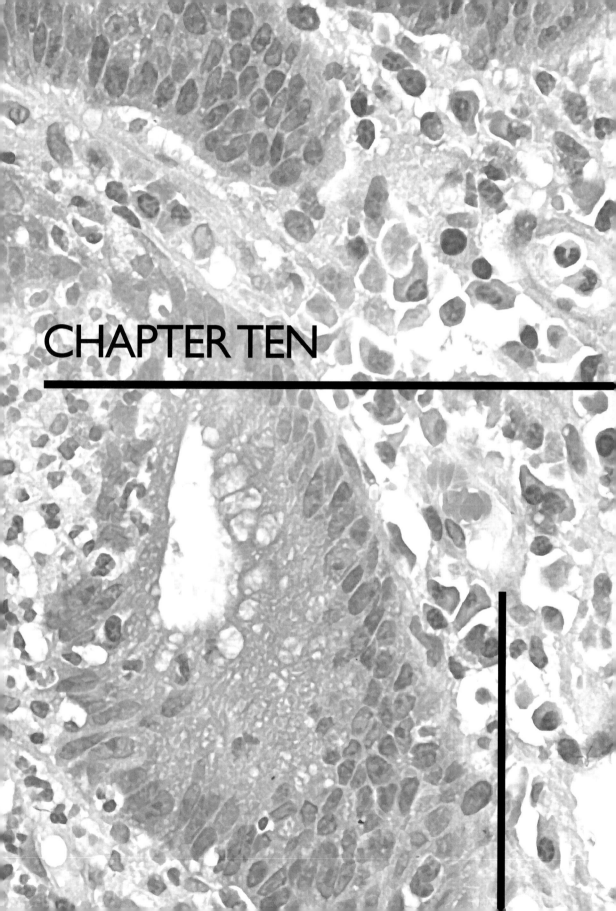

CHAPTER TEN

THE FUTURE

This chapter will be fun to read in 50 or 100 years. What did we guess correctly? What could we not possibly have imagined?

It's Inevitable

I think the future of pathology at Baylor will be like the future of pathology in the U.S.A. and the world. Dr. Lieberman and other persons like him will keep it going roughly the way it is, with more and more instrumentation and electronics, so it's going to be very automated. I would guess that sometime the microscope, as we see it now, will sort of disappear and be a museum piece. Probably everything will be somehow on video or digital. In other words, instead of looking at the slide on a microscope and have the light come from below, some camera is going to digitize it and flash it on a screen. There will be remarkable change. It's inevitable that it will happen. I suppose if I could come back 10 years from now, 15 years from now, I wouldn't even recognize pathology.

Some things will probably stay. I would think that as time goes on, if a person has an operation and needs a sample of tissue taken, there will probably have to be somebody like a pathologist trained to take that sample of tissue and process it. Now the processing may be absolutely different from what it is now, but it would have to be processed somehow. You would have to have a person like that who is going to interpret whatever the digital thing shows.

So there will always be a person like a pathologist. They may not call him that anymore, but somebody is going to have to interpret whatever the machinery puts out. The computers are going to take over, in a sense. All we have to do is learn how to use them to our advantage, and I think "to our advantage" would probably be to the patient's advantage, too.

If I came back here even five years from now, I probably wouldn't recognize what was going on.

—*Harlan Spjut, M.D.*

Small Percentage

I think the Department is going to continue to grow. Twenty years ago, when I went to the Christmas party, I knew everybody. Now I know just a small percentage. Under Lieberman's leadership we have grown, especially in the areas of molecular biology and in basic research. I think we're going to continue growing in those areas. The faculty will grow and become more and more diversified and more and more sub-specialized. So I will soon be a dinosaur.

—*David Yawn, M.D.*

A Great Need

One speaker in particular whom I have heard several times over the years at national conferences, who is probably 10 years older than me, talked very pessimistically about an individual pathologist sitting down at a scope in the future and diagnosing things. He thinks it is going to be very much based on lab technique and leaving the pathologist potentially out of the picture. I'm not that pessimistic.

I would recommend pathology as a specialty for somebody in medical school without any hesitation. The job market was very tight 10 years ago or so, and people were telling me when I was in medical school that it would be a mistake to go into pathology. But I don't think that is the case at all anymore. Now granted, there is no direct patient contact, although in selected areas there can be, and I hear medical students say over and over again they really liked pathology in the classroom and found it very interesting, etc., etc., but they (and these are young kids) want the direct patient contact, which is fine. There is a great need for that, and that is what most physicians do. But there is still a need for people to go into pathology, and if you like pathology that much, there are still little niches where you can have direct patient care, like fine-needle aspiration or doing apheresis procedures.

I wouldn't be surprised if there is a predominance of women, which I think is great. I am probably very sexist, but I think that women in general, again in general, are much more in tune with detail than men, in general, are. There are certainly excellent male pathologists, and I don't want that to be misinterpreted, but a lot of what I do is following up on little stupid, nitpicky things that takes no intelligence to do, like being sure that stain gets done, this one gets done, and then incorporated into the report. I have to think women oftentimes are better at that than men.

—*Chris Finch, M.D.*

Like Football

I genuinely believe that Baylor Pathology is on a huge upswing. Most of the basic science researchers are in our late 30s or early 40s, a pretty young group. If you look at the life cycle of science, you know that age group is really just in the beginning or middle part of their careers, and generally once things get going, it is easier to build. Mike Lieberman has put together a really good young group of scientists who work on very interesting stuff and who are going to move forward. I came from a department that has more total NIH funding, but it was a very old department. A lot of the big people were in their 60s, and at some point, things just kind of peter out.

It's like football teams or basketball teams. A department goes through a cycle where they have a bunch of good young people and they are on an upswing, and as they get older, they have reached their maximum funding. There is a tremendous clinical base here in terms of pathology practice, the amount of surgical pathology practiced, the provisions and clinical services. Both sides of the Department are in very solid positions to go forward.

—*Michael Ittmann, M.D., Ph.D.*

A Wide Choice

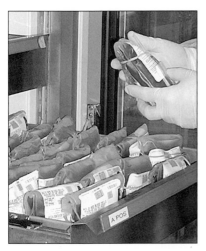

83. Although red cells will continue to be used, genetically produced components will become increasingly important.

My area is transfusion medicine, and I can foresee that we are going to have a large number of different genetically produced blood components, like preparations that are going to replace regular platelets. But we are still going to use red cells for a while, for a long while. We have some synthetics and some protein carriers of oxygen and the hemoglobin solution. But we are going to have a much wider choice. We may change the way we do compatibility. Everything is going to evolve. There is never a dull minute, never.

—*Anita Werch, M.D.*

Investigation

The future of pathology lies in investigation. It has such great opportunities and resources. It will also provide basic support, particularly to other disciplines in correlative research or cognitive research where there'll be multiple disciplines involved. The Department of Pathology has a great opportunity to do that—and is doing it, as a matter of fact. It has a great potential for future development.

—*Michael DeBakey, M.D.*

What Is Going to Happen

The future is genetics. Now I look at slides under the microscope. I make diagnoses, whether it be a human disease or a mouse what-have-you. I determine from

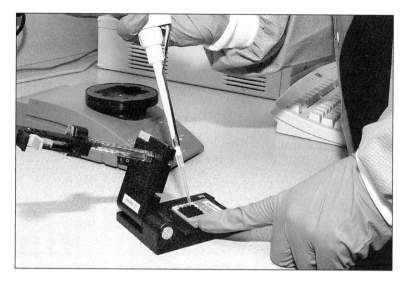

84. A DNA specimen is prepared for polymerase chain reaction testing. Genetics will take on an increasingly important role in the pathology of the future.

what I see what else we might do besides looking at a routine slide or a routine stain. Maybe there are other stains I can use to characterize the chemistry of the tissue; maybe I can use an antibody to determine what proteins are being expressed there and not elsewhere. I can cut out pieces of tissue from the slide with a laser dissection microscope and then extract it and give it to another lab to do molecular analysis. I can send the tissue away for genetic studies on frozen material when I know what kind of tissue it is.

The genetic revolution is going to take over. In chip technology, people will take a well with 96 plates on it or a medium of some kind, and they will have 8,000 gene sequences on that in little holes. They would pour the tumor-tissue DNA in there and see where it binds and which genes are expressed excessively or not as much. Or they look at the messenger RNA, which reflects gene expression, and they will convert that to DNA in the test tube from the tumor or from the patient or from different parts of the tumor. (I am assuming that it is tumor for the moment; it doesn't have to be tumor.) Then they will compare a genetic expression from the tumor and the rest of the tissue.

The most common cancer in pediatrics is acute leukemia. When we look at leukemic cells, they look very similar. We can do cytochemistry, and we can do this and that, but what we really need is to find out what the translocations are between one gene and another in different chromosomes. That creates a new product that is responsible for the development of the leukemia. How those translocations occur is not at all clear, but if they occur and the cells grow at the rate that they shouldn't, then they could be between, say, chromosome 15 and chromosome 17. And if you get that particular translocation, that leukemia would do very well, and you don't need to use very harsh poisons. But if you have a different one, it is going to do very badly, and our standard treatment isn't going to work. So we have to use something else. That is what we need to make the decision right away, at the start. That is going to happen everywhere.

Polymerase chain reaction amplification of small amounts of DNA will also guide us. Right now it would take us three, five, seven days to grow up a fungus. You can't afford to wait; you have to know what is going on. If you can use molecular tools to make the diagnosis, and you take out three days of waiting, that can make a difference. That is what is going to happen. Everything in pathology is going to be genetic-based. In no time.

Except for giving blood for transfusions. That is expensive stuff and highly technical. Lots of machinery. Pathologists are still going to have a role in looking at initial blood smears. No one chip is going to contain all the genes, so which chip should we use for each situation? We will still have a tissue-based or attributional role, and we are still going to look at stools under the electron microscope, because it is very fast and cheap.

—*Milton Finegold, M.D.*

Bridge People

Right now we've got two very fine groups, a very strong basic science group and a very strong hospital pathology group. I should say "groups," since there are many hospitals and many different kinds of research.

A goal is to develop more people in that middle ground who can work comfortably with basic science and with diagnostic pathology. More bridge people. More people who can do translational research, who can do clinical research. My other goal is to see some of the people who are now junior grow into national leaders in the sense that Dina Mody and Mary Schwartz and Tom Wheeler have in one generation, and in the generation before them people like Abe Ramzy, Juan Lechago, and Milton Finegold.

So that's another goal—that the people in the 30- to 40-year-old bracket develop and mature the way the people in the 40- to 50-year-old bracket are maturing. One thing I need is some help from the school, because I need more research space. Money I can always figure out how to raise, but space, I'm absolutely dependent on the school to make a dream of a stronger and even better-known department come true.

—Michael Lieberman, M.D., Ph.D.

Standing By

The other day, Dr. Ramzy, who has a very fine sense of humor, started giving me a hard time. I said, "Abe, after listening to you, I am leaving here with a mixture of joy and happiness." But actually, it's very difficult to leave this place because of the way I've been treated. First of all, Mike Lieberman not only delivered all he promised, but went well beyond that. Most of my colleagues are not only colleagues, but personal friends. I've had wonderful times in this place, and I had very sad ones when I lost my wife. Curiously, it was the sad times that put even more in evidence the human quality of the people. It made me appreciate them even more than I did before because of the way they stood by me.

I'm going to leave because I need new challenges, because I have a little bit of a new life and all those things, but I'm leaving a place with lots of people I truly respect and admire. I feel that from the bottom of my heart.

And this Medical Center is unique. Texans speak big, but they put their money where their mouth is. You must hand this to them.

—Juan Lechago, M.D., Ph.D.

AFTERWORD

By Michael W. Lieberman, M.D., Ph.D.

In reading what people have said about each other and the Department, I am overwhelmed by gratitude for having the opportunity to work with so many colleagues whose generosity and graciousness are represented by their comments in these pages. I am also proud to be the custodian of so much accumulated wisdom and accomplishment. If I ever doubted that our Department is committed to excellence, this narrative puts those doubts aside.

My personal thanks to Amy Storrow for accomplishing what at many times seemed to me an impossible task—organizing the voices and perceptions that capture the growth and change of the Department over 60 years. Every page of this book represents her intelligence and skill. What inevitably gets lost in an oral history project like this are some events and lives that by happenstance or plain bad luck are not represented in the stories of their colleagues. With apologies for unintended omissions and an emphasis that may not feel accurate to others, I note the Department's debt to some additional people.

John J. Moran and Rose Moran, the parents of John A. Moran and Jean

Cunningham, began the work of the Moran Foundation that John A. Moran has so ably and passionately embraced. As John mentions in his narrative, the foundation has helped many young faculty start research careers—often by giving them their first grant. The vision of the Moran family in setting up and expanding the Moran Foundation has been a boon for our young faculty.

Dr. Dennis Woznicki had just joined the faculty when I came. His untimely death robbed all of us of so much laughter and warmth. It was a pleasure to establish an annual lectureship in his honor in 1991. Dr. Corpus Ortegosa, who preceded Dr. Raymond McBride in leading the pathology program at Ben Taub General Hospital, was ill with colon cancer when I arrived. I remember vividly his unfailing support and wisdom; the Department has perpetuated his memory by establishing an annual lectureship in his honor. Ray, who had been recruited by Dr. Jack Titus for his talents in immunology, was running the teaching program when I came. With Corpus' death I appointed Ray to run the program at Ben Taub, which he continued doing until he was offered an irresistible position in Italy. Dr. Alden (Bud) Dudley was chief of Pathology at the VA Medical Center under Dr. Jack Titus and continued in this position for a number of years under my stewardship until taking a position in New Jersey. He and his wife, Mary, added zest and enthusiasm as well as leadership to the Department.

The first person to take me to lunch when I arrived in Houston in the summer of 1988 was Dr. Richard Hausner, a former faculty member, then as now in private practice in greater Houston. His knowledge of the landscape of pathology both locally and nationally has continued to inform my leadership of the Department. Richard also introduced me to Dr. Jerry Wilkenfeld, a fine pathologist and colleague in practice in the community. Dr. Bill Hill, also in private practice, was a supporter of the Department and provided funds for an annual lectureship in anatomic pathology.

The modesty of Dr. Jamie Davis in chronicling our history greatly underrepresents his crucial role in working closely with Jack Titus and me in shaping the Department. He sets a standard for judgment and integrity to which most of us can only aspire. Dr. Marty Matzuk helped the Department recruit Dr. Jim Musser out of his residency at the University of Pennsylvania. Jim quickly established a nationally recognized research program in infectious disease and strengthened our microbiology program at The Methodist Hospital. His recruitment by NIH to reorganize a large program in bacterial pathophysiology was a significant loss for the Department. We are fortunate that he has recently rejoined the Department. The leadership and organizational skills of Dr. Armand Martel and Dr. Jim Fletes should not go unrecognized; they have helped ensure a standard of care in our Department of which we are all proud. Absent from the narrative is the outstanding science of Dr. Tom Cooper; fortunately for us, his many contributions to molecular biology are well represented in the scientific literature. The recruitment of Dr. David Bernard in 1999 in clinical pathology and laboratory medicine at The Methodist Hospital has been of enormous benefit to patients, colleagues, and trainees. His efforts there have been among the most important recent initiatives in the Department. No summary of my debts would be complete without mentioning Judy Henry, the administrative director of the laboratory at The Methodist Hospital; she is a trusted colleague who has given me unfailingly good advice and saved me from disastrous mistakes on more than one occasion.

A word about Will Kyle and his staff. I mention in my own narrative what a pleasure it has been to work with Will. His contributions and those of his senior staff—Dilzi Mody, Ginger Jozwiak, and Becky Patrick—should not be taken for granted. There is a tendency for us physicians and scientists to think mostly about what we do and to undervalue the contributions of others. Busy pathologists and scientists frequently forget that administrative leadership is essential. Will and his team have provided the infrastructure that has been essential for our medical and scientific excellence.

I would leave the wrong impression about our Department if I did not note specifically how absolutely dependent we pathologists and scientists are on the careful and patient work of the people who work with us. In no small measure, our success is the result of their hard work. We could not function for a day without the support staff, the secretaries, the dieners, the technicians and animal-care people, and the drivers, who perform a thousand tasks each day and are unfailingly cheerful and kind even when we professionals occasionally cross the line. There is no way to express their contribution to our efforts.

It is impossible to list the contribution of every individual in the Department in detail; even to do so in an afterword would distort the purpose of the book, which is to capture the Department's history in the words of those who made it and witnessed it. I hope that by listing a roster of the faculty and staff of the Department for 2003, this book will give a sense of how many individual contributions it takes to make a great department.

Whatever the future may bring, it will certainly involve people. We've said little in these pages about young people—residents, post-doctoral fellows, and pathology fellows. The book has been about our past and our present. Yet they are clearly the future. To the extent that the past is prologue, I am confident that the future will be bright. What role telepathology will play or what place genomics or proteomics will have in the future is certain in only one respect—they will all eventually be supplanted. The role of the electron microscope, which during Dr. Bob O'Neal's tenure was the latest and most modern technique in pathology, has been reduced to just another tool by immunohistochemistry and molecular biology. What will remain a constant is the need for human talent, for engaged minds to develop new ways to attack old problems and to reformulate our vision of disease. What is underrepresented in the body of this book are the thousands of hours we spend each year educating and mentoring our trainees—it is a task in which every member of the Department is engaged every day. Our most important task for the future, one to which we must respond if we are to continue to lead in pathology, is to identify, attract, and educate able young people. They are the only coin of the realm. Who would buy a used pathology department?

I am proud of what the men and women who work with me have accomplished. I am confident that if we meet the future with as much drive and imagination as we have demonstrated in the past, the future of Baylor Pathology will be bright.

CHRONOLOGY

1845: The Republic of Texas charters Baylor University.

1900: The University of Dallas Medical Department is founded, although no University of Dallas exists. Student fees are $75 in tuition per session, $5 to register, and $25 to graduate. The school designs a curriculum that lasts the two years required for licensure. Classes are first held at Temple Emanu-El in Dallas.

1901: Pathology classes are taught by "Ulrich" for two hours a week to first- and second-year students. Ulrich's status on the faculty is unknown.

1902: E.A. Blount, M.D., is professor of pathology, histology, and bacteriology, and lecturer on dermatology. Dr. Blount is one of the original stockholders in the corporation.

1903: The Medical School affiliates with Baylor University in Waco, Texas, and the name is eventually changed to Baylor University College of Medicine.

1904: Pierre Wilson, M.D., succeeds Dr. Blount. He is professor of histology, pathology, bacteriology, gynecology, and abdominal surgery and is also listed in some records as professor of clinical surgery.

"... Pathology being one of the most important, we have planned a course in every way similar to that of Johns Hopkins. The students will be taught by lectures and demonstrations. The classes will be subdivided into sections and given thorough laboratory instruction; graded Pathological research and teaching suitable to the needs of each class will be our desire."

–Catalogue, 1904 [1]

1907: Alfred E. Thayer, M.D., succeeds Dr. Wilson as professor of pathology and bacteriology.

1909: Baylor University assumes financial responsibility for the Medical School and integrates it into the university.

1911: Walter H. Moursund, M.D., joins the faculty as an assistant professor of pathology.

1912: The pathology professorship is vacant. Marvin D. Bell, M.D., is assistant in pathology.

1913: The Medical School organizes itself by departments. Dr. Moursund becomes professor of pathology and bacteriology.

1915: The Department of Bacteriology and Preventive Medicine splits from Pathology to become its own department.

1917: The departments are recombined. J.H. Black, M.D., becomes professor of pathology and bacteriology. Dr. Bell becomes associate professor of bacteriology and clinical pathology.

1919: George T. Caldwell, M.D., is appointed professor of pathology and chairman of the Department. His wife, Janet Caldwell, M.D., is also a pathologist. At first she assists him in the laboratory; later she is director of the lab at Baylor University Hospital.

"[Dr. George T. Caldwell] was a forceful, demanding teacher, sometimes rather pointed in his remarks yet highly respected by his students. [He] had a nervous mannerism which the students enjoyed and abetted. As he entered the student laboratory, he would kick to the side anything which happened to be in the doorway. The students would plant some article, a match, wad of paper, or perhaps a candy-bar wrapping, in the doorway and then wager among themselves as to whether or not Dr. Caldwell would kick the article aside. It is said he very rarely failed to do so."

—Walter Moursund[2]

1921: The State Pathological Society of Texas is formed. It later changes its name to the Texas Society of Pathologists.

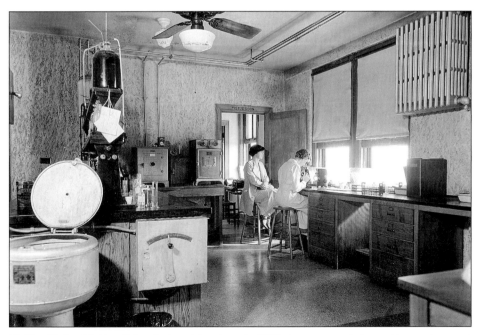

85. The Methodist Hospital pathology laboratory in 1922 shows an orderly working environment devoid of the technological advances that are now a standard part of every pathology lab.

1923: Pathology is again separated from the Department of Bacteriology, Hygiene, and Preventive Medicine.

1927: Dr. Caldwell resigns as chair to move to Mineral Wells, Texas. Rodger J.B. Hibbard, M.D., is acting professor of pathology and chairman. Stuart A. Wallace, M.D., joins the Department as an assistant professor.

1928: Maurice L. Richardson, M.D., is professor and department chairman.

1929: Dr. Wallace leaves Baylor.

86. Dr. George T. Caldwell, M. D., was chairman of the Department in Dallas for 21 years.

1930: Dr. George T. Caldwell returns to Dallas and is reappointed to the faculty as professor of pathology and chairman of the Department. He holds these positions until 1943.

1936: The American Board of Pathology is created. It begins its certification program.

Dr. Wallace rejoins the Pathology Department as an assistant professor.

1939: Edward H. Cary, M.D., charters the Southwest Medical Foundation, a nonsectarian organization dedicated to supporting the Medical School.

1942: Dr. Wallace is promoted to associate professor.

1943: The Baylor University Board of Trustees voids its contract with the Southwest Medical Foundation over the issue of the foundation's assumption of a nonsectarian medical school.

The Baylor Medical School administration realizes that the Southwest Medical Foundation is in an excellent position to start its own medical school and knows that the Baylor University College of Medicine cannot do well in such a situation. D.K. Martin, a Baylor trustee, takes a midnight train to Houston to meet with John Freeman, a board member of the M.D. Anderson Foundation. Interested in bringing a strong medical school to Houston, the Anderson board offers Baylor $1 million in cash to pay for a building and $100,000 a year for 10 years to assist with operating costs. The Houston Chamber of Commerce contributes $500,000 over a 10-year period.

Faculty and students feel their loyalties torn. Most stay in Dallas. Dr. Moursund, now the dean after a tour of duty as professor of hygiene and preventive medicine, has just two months to pack up the Medical School and move it to Houston before classes resume in July. The students help to pack. Sixty-five truckloads of equipment are moved to Houston during a time when gasoline is rationed because of World War II.

New construction is not allowed during the war, so the school rents an old Sears, Roebuck building on what is now the corner of Montrose Boulevard and Allen Parkway. The dissecting tables for anatomy classes are in the former "notions" area of the store.

Dr. Wallace becomes chair of the Pathology Department. He ships his entire collection of pathology specimens from Dallas, including 100,000 microscopic slides, and unpacks them in Houston. Dr. Wallace holds the first endowed professorship at the Medical School, the Fulbright Professorship of Pathology. Irene Fulbright endows the chair. She also gives Dr. Wallace a Cadillac, as befits his new station in life. It is too large to fit in his garage.

87. Stuart Wallace, M.D., served as the first chairman in Houston.

"That this was all done in memory of and in appreciation of your husband and our good friend, Mr. Fulbright, makes mellow with memories the entire donation.

Your gift will now join the gifts of Judge Baylor, Sam Houston, and other patri-
archs as all of them together served, down through the years, ambitious youth from
around the world."

—*Letter to Irene Fulbright from Pat Neff,*
President, Baylor University, 1944[3]

The Department of Pathology has two full-time employees: Dr. Wallace and Anna Haley, a tissue technician who worked with Dr. George Caldwell in Dallas and is married to Melvin Haley, M.D. Later that year, Paul Wheeler, M.D., from Washington University, and S.E. Kerr, M.D., join the faculty.

The school begins its classes on July 12, 1943. There are 60 freshmen, 38 sophomores, 15 juniors, and 16 seniors. The school is sustained, in part, by the Army's and Navy's medical training programs, which order their students to Houston, although some would prefer to stay in Dallas.

The school's operating budget in 1943-44 is $250,347.

1944: Joyce Davis begins her medical studies in the former Sears warehouse.

1945: Ground is broken for the Medical School building at the heart of what will become the Texas Medical Center, the dream of M.D. Anderson.

1946: The College of American Pathologists is founded.

Baylor begins to offer residencies in pathology.

1947: H. Roy and Lillie Cullen announce they will give $800,000 to the school. Over the next seven years, they give a total of about $2.5 million, enough to complete and equip the building, which is named after them.

The Texas Society of Pathologists creates the George T. Caldwell Award for scientific distinction.

88. The Cullen Building, named after H. Roy and Lillie Cullen, who gave about $2.5 million to Baylor University College of Medicine over the course of seven years, was dedicated in 1948.

1948: The Cullen Building is dedicated April 22-24.

> *"This building, modern in every detail, provided the space and facilities for more effective conduct of a complete program of medical education and research, the fulfillment of a long hope of those who had carried on, sustained by faith and loyalty."*
> —*Walter Moursund*[4]

Michael E. DeBakey, M.D., accepts the position of chairman of the Surgery Department at Baylor. He makes the first formal arrangements to affiliate the school with a hospital, the Veterans Administration Hospital.

Dr. Wallace contracts to provide pathology services for The Methodist Hospital. Baylor will be paid $10,000 per year. The opportunity exists because when Methodist's pathologist, Martha Wood, M.D., fell ill, Paul Wheeler, M.D., from Baylor worked as her temporary replacement. Methodist was pleased with Wheeler's work.

The Baylor Pathology Department agrees to supervise the laboratory at San Jacinto Memorial Hospital.

1949: Dr. Wheeler, beloved pathology professor, dies.

"Long range project on Gerontology (aging) in dogs:
A pure bred dog colony has been started. These animals are to be maintained under
approximately the same conditions as humans, viz—they are to be inoculated
against contagious diseases, they are to be fed well, but with variation in diet, and
a number comparable to the number of humans will be subjected to minor or
major surgery. With a pure strain one hopes to determine differences in chemical
changes, vitamin needs, and tissue changes as life progresses. It is especially hoped
that something definite can be learned about heart disease, kidney disorders, and
arteriosclerosis, plus also cancer."
—From the Pathology Department's Report on Research, April 1949[5]

The Houston Society of Clinical Pathologists is founded on July 22.

1951: The school's operating budget has risen to more than $700,000. Enrollment is 355, and there are 678 voluntary faculty members. The school's 114 investigators work on 189 research projects.

Dr. Wallace is president of the Texas Society of Pathologists.

1952: Dr. Moursund resigns as dean.

"[The Eye Pathology] laboratory and the one in New Orleans are the only two in
this section of the country, and it has been requested by the Armed Forces Institute
of Pathology that we undertake to process all eyes from Texas. This indicates that
the Armed Forces Institute of Pathology, where the major share of eye pathology is
done in the country, considers this laboratory adequate and sufficient to process these
eyes."
—Stuart Wallace, Annual Report, Department of Pathology, 1952[6]

1955: S. Donald Greenberg, M.D., arrives as a resident. There are now 12 residents in Pathology.

89. An aerial view from 1957 shows Baylor College of Medicine's Cullen Building, top center, at the heart of the growing Texas Medical Center.

"... I want to congratulate you on having an energetic and ambitious son, who is taking full advantage of his opportunities, and seems to be making considerable progress on one or more of the projects which he has undertaken. ..."
— *From a letter to Philip B. Greenberg, M.D., from Stuart A. Wallace, M.D.*[7]

1957: Jack Abbott, M.D., serves the first of two terms as president of the Houston Society of Clinical Pathologists.

1959: Dr. Wallace wins the George T. Caldwell Award from the Texas Society of Pathologists.

1960s: Tension between the Baptists of Texas and the school intensifies. The use of federal funds to finance the school's new wings disturbs some on the grounds of separation of church and state. The Baptist General Convention of Texas gives the Medical School approximately $100,000 each year, but the school's annual budget is now $10 million to $20 million. Membership of the school's executive committee is limited to Baptists, a policy that makes it difficult to secure local funding from non-Baptists.

1960: *"One of the greatest accomplishments by the Personnel Committee of the*

College, assisted by the Dean, was the obtaining of a new Chairman of perspicacity, research ability, and new ideas to the Department.

"I wish to thank these people for taking their time and effort in obtaining a new Chairman. Also I wish to express my everlasting gratitude to the Dean, the Trustees, and all concerned for allowing me to stay on as a Full Professor with tenure. I wish also to commend the full-time, part-time, and clinical members for their immense loyalty to the Department and to me, especially since 1957, when I had a great deal of illness. May God bless them all."

—Stuart Wallace, Pathology Department
Annual Report, 1960-61 [8]

Franz Leidler, M.D., is president of the Houston Society of Clinical Pathologists.

1961: Robert M. O'Neal, M.D., succeeds Dr. Wallace as chair of the Pathology Department.

Approximately 900 square feet in the Department are converted for research by moving Dr. Wallace's pathology museum into the student laboratories and building a chemistry laboratory and electron-microscopy suite. The labs are known as the Sam Taub Memorial Laboratories; funds for them are donated by Ben Taub.

"In a much more practical but very important way, an electron microscope will help our College of Medicine by making this department attractive to young men of high quality seeking a place to begin or continue careers in academic pathology. By this means we should be able more easily to obtain research grants from outside agencies and soon establish a sound foundation of research in morphology."

—Robert M. O'Neal [9]

Harold Wood, M.D., is president of the Houston Society of Clinical Pathologists.

The Department has 15 full-time faculty members. Nine are conducting research, four with the help of funding from the federal government.

Six residents leave the program, four residents remain, and four more are expected the following year.

The department performs 486 autopsies and 6,419 tissue specimens, smears, and cell blocks. The clinical laboratories perform 531,941 tests.

A graduate program in experimental pathology starts. It has one student, Joyce Rowland Marshall, who seeks an M.S.

1962: Harlan Spjut, M.D., arrives at Baylor on July 1. Matthew Noall, M.D., Erwin Rabin, M.D., and Minoru Suzuki, M.D., also join the Department.

1963: Carl J. Lind, M.D., is president of the Texas Society of Pathologists.

"In order to provide an increasingly sought service and to aid in efficient perform-ance of research projects, the services of the histology laboratories of the Department of Pathology are available to all departments to perform routine tissue stains and standard histochemical technics [sic] on a basis of $.75 (seventy-five cents) per slide."

—Memorandum from Robert M. O'Neal, M.D.,
to all departments at Baylor.[10]

Dr. Spjut receives notice that the School of Cytotechnology at Baylor has been approved for the "training of two students concurrently."

1964: The Jewish Institute for Medical Research, Jesse H. Jones Hall, and M.D. Anderson Hall open. The Department gains 1,200 square feet of research space.

Berne Newton, M.D., serves as president of the Houston Society of Clinical Pathologists.

90. Robert M. O'Neal, M.D., third from left, was chairman of the Department in 1965. Former chairman Stuart A. Wallace, M.D., fourth, died in a Department conference room later that year.

1965: Dr. Wallace dies in the Pathology Department conference room on October 13.

"Stuart Allen Wallace, Distinguished Professor Emeritus of Pathology, died on October 13, 1965, while attending a seminar in his department. That he was so engaged, even though severely disabled, was characteristic of this devoted scholar. He had been serving Baylor University College of Medicine for 38 years and, as one of the group with the spirit and vision of explorers, had successfully brought our Medical College through great difficulties into its present strength. The academic ideas that were his are those of which we are proud, and those standards which he despised, we despised.

"This man was a friend to all of us, and we marvel at the forces that created such an unselfish being, a model of honesty, insight, wisdom, and modesty. We do not expect to find another man so created. But because of Stuart Wallace we will find many men a little closer to his mold."

—Robert M. O'Neal, M.D., in Aesculpulian, 1965 [11]

Sid Anderson, M.D., and Robert Fechner, M.D., join the Department. Han-Seob Kim, M.D., joins the Department as a resident.

William T. Hill, M.D., is president of the Houston Society of Clinical Pathologists.

1966: Medicare and Medicaid go into effect.

The School of Medical Technology is rebuilt at Ben Taub Hospital. Bruce W. Jarvis, M.D., runs it.

1967: Dr. Fechner heads up the residency program.

Melvin D. Haley, M.D., serves as president of the Houston Society of Clinical Pathologists.

1968: The Baptist General Convention of Texas votes to sever ties with the Medical School. The school has a deficit of $800,000.

Dr. DeBakey becomes dean of Baylor University College of Medicine. In a 1977 interview, he would recall, "In 1968, Baylor University College of Medicine was about to collapse. An increasing deficit, insufficient financing, and a demoralized faculty placed Baylor in a critical position in the late 1960s. Two deans and seven departmental chairmen had resigned."[12]

Enrollment in the School of Medical Technology expands from nine to 12 students; it is filled to capacity.

The Department now has five electron microscopes, eight automatic ultramicrotomes, five darkrooms, three spectrophotometers, two ultracentrifuges, and two gas chromotagraphs.

Dr. Hill is president of the Texas Society of Pathologists.

Harvey S. Rosenberg, M.D., is president of the Houston Society of Clinical Pathologists.

1969: Dr. O'Neal resigns as chair of the Pathology Department. Other faculty who leave include Bruce W. Jarvis, M.D.; John J. Ghidoni, M.D.; Chao N. Sun, Ph.D.; Marion M. Campbell, M.S.; and Harold W. Jordan, M.D.

Dr. Spjut is appointed acting chair on August 1. Jochewed Werch, M.D., takes over the School of Medical Technology from Dr. Jarvis.

Joyce S. Davis, M.D., serves as president of the Houston Society of Clinical Pathologists.

91. Michael DeBakey, M.D., inventor and world-renowned surgeon, brought many changes to Baylor during his tenure as dean.

There are 15 residents continuing in or joining the Department.

Dr. DeBakey proposes to the state Legislature that Baylor double its enrollment. He will ensure that Texas residents make up 70 percent of each class, a step designed to ease the doctor shortage in Texas. Gov. Preston Smith signs a bill authorizing a contract with Baylor College of Medicine for the training of new physicians at the same rates as University of Texas medical schools in Dallas and Galveston. However, no money is appropriated for the program.

1970: Carl J. Lind, M.D., wins the George T. Caldwell Award from the Texas Society of Pathologists.

Donald Weilbaecher, M.D., joins the Department as a resident.

1971: Dr. Lind is president of the Houston Society of Clinical Pathologists.

For fiscal year 1971-72, Baylor receives $2.5 million in tuition aid from the State of Texas.

On August 31, Dr. Spjut resigns as acting chair.

On September 1, William C. Roberts, M.D., is appointed chair of the Department. However, he never arrives at Baylor.

Dr. Spjut resumes serving as chair on March 1.

Edith Hawkins, M.D., is a first-year resident.

Among other monies for research, one grant is from the Hycel Corp. for $1,500 to evaluate the accuracy of an automated screening process in the detection of cervical atypia.

92. Jack Titus, M.D., Ph.D., left the Mayo Clinic to become chair of the Pathology Department.

1972: Jack Titus, M.D., Ph.D., succeeds a relieved Dr. Spjut as chair on September 1. He is named W. L. Moody Professor.

Residents who join the Department include David Yawn, M.D., and Carlos Bedrossian, M.D.

There are now 48 full-time faculty members. The Department performs 1,700 autopsies and prepares and evaluates 42,000 surgical specimens (among them 3,200 frozen sections), 71,000 cytology specimens, and approximately 8 million clinical tests.

1973: S. Donald Greenberg, M.D., serves as president of the Houston Society of Clinical Pathologists.

1975: John D. Milam, M.D., is president of the Houston Society of Clinical Pathologists.

Malcolm McGavran, M.D., arrives at Baylor.

1976: In April, Howard Hughes' autopsy is performed at The Methodist Hospital by Dr. Titus and Dr. McGavran.

On June 15, 10.47 inches of rain falls on the Medical Center in a 24-hour period. It is thought to be the worst flood ever to hit the area. In consultation with the Federal Emergency Management Agency, the Medical Center installs flood-protection systems to protect against water that rises one foot above the level of this flood.

93. The flood of 1976 prompted the installation of better flood-protection systems.

1977: Dr. Titus serves as president of the Houston Society of Clinical Pathologists.

1978: Dr. Milam is president of the Texas Society of Pathologists.

1979: Milton Finegold, M.D., arrives at Texas Children's Hospital.

1980: Dr. Yawn and Dr. Werch travel to Egypt with Dr. DeBakey as part of a team that performs surgery on the ailing Shah of Iran.

1981: Dr. Milam wins the George T. Caldwell Award from the Texas Society of Pathologists.

1987: On September 1, Dr. Spjut once again becomes acting chair when Dr. Titus returns to Minnesota.

1988: Dr. Spjut resigns as acting chair when Michael W. Lieberman, M.D., Ph.D., takes over as chair.

1989: Dr. Hill wins the George T. Caldwell Award from the Texas Society of Pathologists.

Dr. Greenberg wins the Harlan Spjut Award from the Houston Society of Clinical Pathologists.

94. Michael Lieberman, M.D., brought a commitment to basic research to the Department when he became chair in 1988.

1991: Thomas Wheeler, M.D., is president of the Houston Society of Clinical Pathologists.

Dr. Rosenberg wins the Harlan Spjut Award from the Houston Society of Clinical Pathologists.

1992: Dr. Spjut wins the George T. Caldwell Award from the Texas Society of Pathologists.

1993: Dr. Lieberman is president of the American Society of Investigative Pathology.

Dr. Titus wins the Harlan Spjut Award from the Houston Society of Clinical Pathologists.

1994: Ibrahim Ramzy, M.D., is president of the Texas Society of Pathologists.

1995: Dr. Milam is president of the American Board of Pathology.

1997: Dr. Joyce Davis wins the George T. Caldwell Award from the Texas Society of Pathologists.

Linda K. Green, M.D., is president of the Houston Society of Clinical Pathologists.

95. The Cullen Building today appears deceptively calm; research projects and teaching affecting the future in all areas of health care are conducted within its walls.

1999: Dr. Ramzy, wins the Papanicolaou Award from the American Society of Cytopathology.

2000: Martin M. Matzuk, M.D., is named Stuart A. Wallace professor of Pathology.

96. Water from Tropical Storm Allison fills the area outside the Cullen Building.

2001: On June 8, Tropical Storm Allison hits Houston. At Baylor, approximately 60,000 tumor samples are destroyed, and 30,000 transgenic rats and mice die. Damage exceeds $100 million, and lost research time is immeasurable. The Pathology Department sets up temporary headquarters in the ballroom of the Medical Center's Marriott Hotel. It continues to serve its clients from outlying hospitals.

Mary Schwartz, M.D., is named to the Robert M. O'Neal Chair of Pathology, Thomas Wheeler, M.D., is named to the Harlan J. Spjut Chair of Pathology, and Dina Mody, M.D., is named to the Ibrahim Ramzy Chair of Pathology.

Research space in the Department totals approximately 21,000 square feet.

2002: Dr, Edith Hawkins retires. Vicky Gresik, M.D., has her lab coat bronzed.

2003: Thomas Cooper, M.D., is named S. Donald Greenberg Professor of Pathology. Clay Goodman, M.D., is named to the Walter Moursund Chair and Michael Ittmann, M.D., Ph.D., to the William Tiggert Chair.

James Musser, M.D., Ph.D., returns to Baylor as professor of pathology and is named to the James R. Davis Chair of Pathology.

[1] Courtesy Baylor College of Medicine Archives

[2] Walter Moursund, *History of Baylor University College of Medicine* (Houston: Gulf Printing Co., 1956) p. 68

[3] Courtesy Baylor College of Medicine Archives

[4] Moursund, p. 150.

[5] Courtesy Baylor College of Medicine Archives

[6] Courtesy Baylor College of Medicine Archives

[7] Courtesy Baylor College of Medicine Archives

[8] Courtesy Baylor College of Medicine Archives

[9] Courtesy Baylor College of Medicine Archives

[10] Courtesy Baylor College of Medicine Archives

[11] Courtesy Baylor College of Medicine Archives

[12] Ruth SoRelle, *The Quest for Excellence: Baylor College of Medicine, 1900-2000* (Houston: Baylor College of Medicine, 2000), p. 110

2003 FACULTY AND STAFF

Faculty

Adekunle Adesina, M.D., Ph.D., Associate Professor, Pediatric and Molecular Neuropathology, TCH

Craig Allred, M.D., Professor, Breast Cancer, Pathology, BCM

Mojghan Amrikachi, M.D., Assistant Professor, Anatomic Pathology, TMH

Rose Anton, M.D., Assistant Professor, Anatomic and Surgical Pathology, TMH

Dawna L. Armstrong, M.D., Professor, Neuropathology, TCH

Hazel L. Awalt, M.D., Assistant Professor, Surgical Pathology, Woodlands

Gustavo Ayala, M.D., Associate Professor, Anatomic Pathology, TMH

Ashok Balsaver, M.D., Associate Professor, Anatomic Pathology, Diagnostic Clinic

Eugenio I. Bañez, M.D., Associate Professor, Hematology, Clinical Pathology, BTGH

Marcia Barnes, M.D., Assistant Professor, Surgical Pathology, San Jacinto

Roberto Barrios, M.D., Associate Professor, Pulmonary and Renal Pathology, BCM

Amy L. Bauer, M.S, Instructor, Physician's, Assistant, TMH

David Bernard, M.D., Ph.D., Assistant Professor, Clinical Chemistry, TMH

Meena Bhattacharjee, M.D., Assistant Professor, Pediatric Neuropathology, TCH

Cory Flagg Brayton, D.V.M., Associate Professor, Comparative Medicine, BCM

Gregory J. Buffone, Ph.D., Professor, Chemistry, Lab Management, TCH

Philip T. Cagle, M.D., Professor, Pulmonary Pathology, TMH

Joiner Cartwright Jr., Ph.D., Assistant Professor, Electron Microscopy, BCM

Mario Cervantes-Vazquez, M.D., Assistant Professor, Clinical Pathology, Woodlands

Subhendu Chakraborty, M.S., Instructor, Surgical Pathology and Cytopathology, TMH

Jeff Chang, M.D., Ph.D., Associate Professor,

Hematopathology, TMH

Haiyun Cheng, M.D., Ph.D., Assistant Professor,
Research in Environmental Carcinogens, BCM

Patricia Chevez-Barrios, M.D. Assistant
Professor, Ophthalmic and Surgical Pathology,
TMH

Deborah Citron, M.D., Assistant Professor,
Anatomic and Clinical Pathology, BTGH

Donna Coffey, M.D., Assistant Professor,
Anatomic Pathology, TMH

Lisa Cohen, M.D., Assistant Professor,
Anatomic and Clinical Pathology,
CPA - BCM

Thomas A. Cooper, M.D., Professor,
Molecular Biology, BCM

Gretchen J. Darlington, Ph.D.,
Professor, Molecular Pathology, BCM

James R. Davis, Ph.D., Associate Professor,
Microbiology and Virology, TMH

Richard Davis, Ph.D., Assistant Professor,
Developmental Biology, BCM

Susan Davy, M.D., Assistant Professor, Clinical &
Surgical Pathology, Conroe

Megan Dishop, M.D., Assistant Professor, Surgical
and Autopsy Pathology, TCH

Hanna El-Sahly, M.D., Assistant Professor,
Tuberculosis Research, BCM-Graviss

April A. Ewton, M.D., Assistant Professor,
Anatomic Pathology, TMH

Daniel Farkas, Ph.D., HCLD, Associate Professor,
Molecular Diagnostics, TMH

Chris Finch, M.D., Assistant Professor, Anatomic
Pathology, BTGH

Milton J. Finegold, M.D., Professor, Pediatric
Pathology, TCH

Diego Fiorito, M.D. Assistant Professor,
Cytopathology and Surgical Pathology,
San Jacinto

James Fletes, M.D., Assistant Professor, Surgical
Pathology, Brazosport

Ramon Font, M.D., Professor, Opthalmology,
NEUR

Scott A. Goode, Ph.D., Assistant Professor,
Developmental Genetics, BCM

J. Clay Goodman, M.D., Professor,
Neuropathology, TMH

Edward A. Graviss, Ph.D., Associate Professor,
Epidemiology/TB Study, BCM

Linda K. Green, M.D., Professor, Anatomic
Pathology and Cytopathology, VAMC

Mary V. Gresik, M.D., Associate Professor,
Hematopathology, TCH

M. Carolina Gutierrez, M.D., Assistant Professor,
Anatomic Pathology, BTGH

Geetha Habib, Ph.D., Associate Professor,
Molecular Pathology, BCM

Lileah F. Harris, M.D., Assistant Professor,
Surgical Pathology, San Jacinto

Lawrence J. Hartley, M.D., Assistant Professor,
Anatomic and Clinical Pathology, Matagorda

Michelle M. Hebert, M.D., Assistant Professor,
Surgical Pathology and Hematology,
Huntsville

M. John Hicks, M.D., Ph.D., D.D.S., Professor,
Electron Microscopy, Pediatric Pathology,
TCH

Michael Ittmann, M.D., Ph.D., Professor, Prostate
Pathology, VAMC

Laura P. Jimenez-Quintero, M.D., Assistant
Professor, Surgical Pathology, Woodlands

Subbarao V. Kala, Ph.D., Assistant Professor,
Toxicology, BCM

Debra L. Kearney, M.D., Assistant Professor,
Cardiovascular Pathology, TCH

Han-Seob Kim, M.D., Ph.D., Professor,
Anatomic Pathology, BTGH

Beatriz M. Kinner, M.D., Assistant Professor,
Anatomic Pathology, VAMC

Michael Koehl, M.D., Assistant Professor,
Anatomic and Clinical Pathology, Huntsville

Bhuvaneswari Krishnan, M.B.B.S., Associate
Professor, Surgical Pathology and
Cytopathology, VAMC

T. Rajendra Kumar, Ph.D., Assistant Professor, Molecular Pathology, Biology, BCM

Geoffrey A. Land, Ph.D., M.S., Professor, HLA, TMH

Claire Langston, M.D., Professor, Pulmonary Pathology, TCH

Rodolfo Laucirica, M.D., Associate Professor, Surgical Pathology, Cytopathology, Flow Cytometry, BTGH

Christopher Leveque, M.D., Assistant Professor, Blood Banking, TMH

Michael W. Lieberman, M.D., Ph.D. Professor and Chairman, Neoplasia, BCM

Barbara Lines, M.D., Assistant Professor, Surgical Pathology, Conroe

Dolores Lopez-Terrada, M.D., Assistant Professor, Anatomic and Clinical Pathology, TCH

Joyce Maldonado, M.D., Assistant Professor, Surgical Pathology, Cytopathology, San Jacinto

Graeme Mardon, Ph.D., Associate Professor, Developmental Biology, BCM

Armand H. Martel, M.D., Assistant Professor, Anatomic Pathology, Conroe

Martin M. Matzuk, M.D., Ph.D., Professor, Molecular Pathobiology, BCM

Dina R. Mody, M.B.B.S., Professor, Cytology, Surgical Pathology, TMH

Syed Mohsin, M.D., Assistant Professor, Breast Cancer Pathology, BCM

Jacqueline Monheit, M.D., Assistant Professor, Anatomic and Clinical Pathology, CPA

Seema Mullick, M.D., Assistant Professor, Anatomic Pathology, Sugar Land

James M. Musser, M.D., Ph.D., Professor, Human Bacterial Pathogenesis, BCM

Thu Ngo, M.D., Assistant Professor, Anatomic Pathology, VAMC

Mary L. Ostrowski, M.D., Associate Professor, Cytopathology, Surgical Pathology, Flow Cytometry, TMH

Ching-Nan Ou, Ph.D., Professor, Chemistry, TCH

Mustafa Ozen, M.D., Ph.D., Instructor, Prostate Pathology Research, VAMC

Edwina J. Popek, D.O., Associate Professor, Placenta and Perinatal Pathology, TCH

Peter Powaser, M.D., Assistant Professor, Anatomic and Clinical Pathology, Wharton

Suzanne Powell, M.D., Assistant Professor, Surgical Pathology, TMH

Joseph F. Pulliam, M.D., B.S., Instructor, Medical Student Teaching, TMH

Syed Fiaz Quadri, M.D., Assistant Professor, Clinical Pathology, Matagorda

Jon Reed, M.D., Associate Professor, Dermatopathology

Emilie Rouah, M.D., Assistant Professor, Surgical Pathology, BCM

Abdus Saleem, M.B.B.S., Professor, Hematology and Coagulation, TMH

Mary R. Schwartz, M.D., Professor, Surgical Pathology, Cytopathology, Dermatopathology, TMH

Steven Shen, M.D., Ph.D., Assistant Professor, Surgical and Autopsy Pathology, TMH

Anna E. Sienko, M.D., Associate Professor, Anatomic Pathology, TMH

Richard N. Sifers, Ph.D., Associate Professor, Molecular and Cell Biology, BCM

George J. Snipes, M.D., Associate Professor, Anatomic and Neuropathology, BCM

Harlan J. Spjut, M.D., Professor, Surgical, Orthopedic, Gastrointestinal Pathology, BCM

Charles E. Stager, Ph.D., Associate Professor, Microbiology, BTGH

Nina Tatevian, M.D., Assistant Professor, Pediatric Pathology, TCH

Jun Teruya, M.D., Assistant Professor, Clinical Pathology, TCH

Perumal Thiagarajan, M.D., Professor, Hematology, VAMC

LuAnn Thompson-Snipes, Ph.D., Assistant Professor, Research on Cellular Immunity, TCH

Nikolaj Timchenko, Ph.D., Associate Professor, Molecular Pathology, BCMN

Luan D. Truong, M.D., Professor, Nephropathology, TMH

James Versalovic, M.D., Ph.D., Assistant Professor, Microbiology, TCH

Gordana Verstovsek, M.D., Assistant Professor, Anatomic Pathology, VAMC

Donald G. Weilbaecher, M.D., Assistant Professor, Cardiovascular Pathology, TMH

Jochewed B. Werch, M.D., Associate Professor, Transfusion Medicine, BTGH

Thomas M. Wheeler, M.D., Professor, Urologic and Surgical Pathology, Cytopathology, TMH

Anne Shumate Witson, M.D., Assistant Professor, Surgical Pathology, Brazosport

Ying Wu, Ph.D., Instructor, Molecular and Cell Biology Research, BCM

Wei Yan, Instructor, Molecular Pathology Research, BCM

David H. Yawn, M.D., Professor, Transfusion Medicine, TMH

Mamoun Younes, M.D., Professor, Tumor Markers and Gastrointestinal Pathology, TMH

Pamela S. Younes, MHS, Instructor, Physician's Assistant, TMH

Qihui A. Zhai, M.D., Assistant Professor, Anatomic Pathology, TMH

Staff

Iman Abdi, Research Assistant I, Dr. Graviss

Julio Agno, Lab Animal Technician III, Dr. Matzuk

Tammy Akif, Administrative Coordinator II, BCM

Wanda Alexander, Senior Office Support, Specialist, BCM

Francine Allen, Research Assistant I, Dr. Cagle

Barbara (Bobbie) Antalffy, Senior Research Assistant, TCH, Dr. Armstrong

Margo Anton, Research Technician III, TMH, Dr. Wheeler

Joseph Apostol, Cytotechnologist, BCM

Donna Atwood, Coordinator, Veterinary Services, BCM, Dr. Lieberman

Gabriel Ayala, Research Technician III, Dr. Cagle

Shirley Baker, Senior Administrative Coordinator, BCM

Shantel Bearman, Clerical Assistant, BCM, Histology

Allison Belcher, Research Technician II, TCH, Dr. Langston

Yvetter Boney, Academic Coordinator, BCM

Nivla Boyd, Medical Transcriptionist II, BCM

Francis Bui, Computer Systems Administrator I, BCMA

Thanh-Tung Bui, Research Technician II, BCM, Dr. Graviss

Donnie Bundman, Research Associate, BCM, Dr. Cooper

Heather Burgess, Research Technician II, BCM , Dr. Mardon

Rebecca Burks, Laboratory Technician II, Conroe

Asma Burney, Histology Technician I, BCM, Histology

Peter Calkins, Research Associate, BCM, Dr. Lieberman

Concepcion Cantu, Clinical Technician II, BCM, Dr. Graviss

Lei Chen, Research Technician I, TCH, Dr. Thompson-Snipes

Xuebo Chen, Research Associate I, BCM, Dr. Snipes

Xiujie Cheng, Laboratory Technician I, BCM, Dr. Mardon

Min Cho, Research Technician II, BCM, Dr. Goode

Sandra Christiansen, Histology Lab Manager, BCM

Trishina Clark, Senior Clerk I, BCM, Histology

Hong Dai, Research Associate, BCM, Dr. Ayala

Shana Davis, Research Technician II, TCH, Dr. Armstrong

Krista Diekman, Research Technician II, BCM,
Dr. Sifers

Michelle Doby, Laboratory Assistant, BCM,
Histology

Xiu-Rong Dong, Research Associate, BCM,
Dr. Majesky

Mary Edwards, Histology Technician III, TMH

Diana Forrister, Medical Transcriptionist,
Diagnostic Clinic

Henry Francis, Assistant Clerical Administrator,
BCM

Joleen Francis, Professional Fee Coder, TMH

Jacqueline Furr, Histology Technician III, BCM,
Histology

Regina Garcia, Administrative Support,
Coordinator II, BCM

Andrea Gardley, Histology Technician I, BCM

Leticia Garza, Histology Technician II, BCM

Lori Gomez, Research Technician II, VAMC,
Dr. Ittmann

Lucy Gonzalez, Administrative Support,
Coordinator II, TMH, Dr. Bernard

Sylvia Gonzalez, Senior Administrative
Coordinator, BCM

Tiffany Goudeau, Clinical Technician II, BCM,
Dr. Graviss

Pauline Grennan, Histology Technician III,TCH,
Dr. Finegold

Miriam Guajardo, Administrative Support,
Coordinator I, TMH, Dr. Bernard

Grace Hamilton, Histology Lab Supervisor, BCM

Jin Han, Post-doctoral Associate, TMH,
Dr. Wheeler

Mark Harding, Research Technician II, BCM,
Dr. Mardon

Kelly Hart, Medical Transcriptionist II,
Dermatopathology

Yi Hsiao, Electron Microscopy Technician, BCM

Horng-Wen (Erica) Hsieh, Special Projects, BCM

Yanhong Huang, Post-doctoral Associate, TCH,
Dr. Versalovic

Jun-ichiro Ishii, Research Associate, TMH,
Dr. Wheeler

Lorretta Jackson, Research Coordinator II, BCM,
Dr. Graviss

Paige Jackson, Director, Clinical Business Services,
BCM

Nicholas Jennings, Research Technician II, BCM,
Dr. Lieberman

Kirsten Johnson, Research Librarian, BCM,
Dr. Cagle

Willie Johnson, Senior Clerk I, BCM, Histology

CarolinaJorgez, Research Associate, BMC,
Dr. Matzuk

Ginger Jozwiak, Senior Administrative
Assistant II, BCM

Geeta Kala, Research Associate, BCM,
Dr. Lieberman

Carol Kempen, Administrative Secretary II, TMH,
Dr. Ramzy

Syed Khalil, Project Coordinator, BCM,
Dr. Graviss

Ava Kibbe, Histotechnologist III, BCM, Histology

Deanna Killen, Histology Lab Supervisor,
BCMS, Histology

Michal Klysik, Research Technician I, BCM,
Dr. Matzuk

Bernard Kwabi-Addo, Research Associate, VACM,
Dr. Ittmann

William Kyle, Administrator, BCM

Andrea Ladd, Post-doctoral Associate, BCM,
Dr. Cooper

Alvaro Laga, Research Post-doctoral, BCM,
Dr. Cagle

Anhouyen Le, Research Associate II, VAMC,
Dr. Thiagarajan

Linda Lester, Administrative Coordinator, VAMC,
Dr. Genta

Rile Li, Research Associate, TMH, Dr. Wheeler

Sandra Li, Research Technician II, TCH,
Dr. Versalovic

Xiaohui Li, Research Technician I, BCM,
Dr. Matzuk

Yi-Nan Lin, Graduate Student, BCM,
Dr. Matzuk

Weili Liu, Postdoctoral Associate, BCM,

Dr. Lieberman

Yan Liu, Research Technician II, BCM, Dr. Sifers

Remigio Lopez, Histology Technician II, BCM

Yoshiro Lozano, Research Technician I, BCM,
Dr. Younes

Ruth Luna, Research Technician, TCH,
Dr. Versalovic

Hongbin Luo, Post-doctoral Associate, VAMC,
Dr. Ittmann

Lang Ma, Research Associate I, BCM,
Dr. Matzuk

Xiaoping Ma, Laboratory Assistant, BCM,
Dr. Kumar

Xin Ma, Post-doctoral Associate, BCM,
Dr. Graviss

Sabina Magedson, Laboratory Technician I,
BCM, Histology

Jason Martin, Research Assistant I, TMH,
Dr. Wheeler

Toshiki Matsuura, Post-doctoral Associate, BCM,
Dr. Matzuk

Weldon Mauney, Research Coordinator, BCM,
Dr. Graviss

Pamela McShane, Research Coordinator III,
TMH, Dr. Bernard

Brooke Middlebrooks, Research Technician II,
BCM, Dr. Mardon

Dilzi Mody, Administrative Associate II, BCM

Felton Nails, Histology Supervisor, TCH,
Dr. Finegold

Ralph Nichols, Senior Electron Microscopy
Technician, TCH, Dr. Hicks

Anna Nunez, Senior Office Support Specialist,
BCM, Dr. Younes

Henry Nwaugbala, Histology Technician III,
BCM

Sandra Oaks, Senior Administrative Assistant,
BCM, Dr. Lieberman

Samuel Ogbonna, Project Intern, BCM,
Dr. Matzuk

Amiko Ohashi, Post-doctoral Associate,
Dermatopathology, Dr. Reed

Paul Olsen, Research Technician II, BCM,

Dr. Graviss

Wayel Orfali, Post-doctoral Associate, BCM,
Dr. Snipes

Yuly Orozco, Research Coordinator, BCM, Dr.
Graviss

Shirita Ozan, Laboratory Assistant,
Dermatopathology

Xi Pan, Research Associate, BCM, Dr. Graviss

Stephanie Pangas, Post-doctoral Fellow, BCM,
Dr. Matzuk

Kartik Pappu, Research Technician II, BCM,
Dr. Mardon

Kenya Parks, Research Technician II, BCM,
Dr. Graviss

Shakun Parti, Histology Technician I, BCM

Becky Patrick, Senior Administrative Coordinator,
BCM

Brian Patrick, Project Intern, TMH, Dr. Wheeler

Rebecca Penland, Research Assistant II, VAM,
Dr. Genta

Kathryn Pepple, Graduate Student, BCM,
Dr. Mardon

Tuan Pham, Research Technician II, BCM,
Dr. Mardon

Michael Powell, Project Intern, TMH, Dr. Ayala

Tony Prejean, Research Coordinator, BCM,
Dr. Graviss

Mahdis Rahmani, Research Assistant I, BMC,
Dr. Younes

Allison Rainer, Senior Research Assistant, BCM,
Histology

Paula Ramirez, Administrative Secretary I, TMH,
Dr. Wheeler

Robert Reich, Research Technician III, BCM,
Dr. Graviss

Susan Robbins, Pathology Laboratory Supervisor,
BCM, EM

Nicole Robertson, Medical Transcriptionist II,
BCM

Angshumoy, Roy, Graduate Student, BCM,
Dr. Matzuk

Dorene Rudman, Histology Technician II, TCH

Sajida Salar, Histology Technician II, BCM

Melinda Sanchez, Medical Transcriptionist II, BCM

Passion Sanders, Student Helper, TMH, Pamela Younes

Mohammad Sayeeduddin, Histology Lab Supervisor, TMH, Dr. Wheeler

Zahida Sayeeduddin, Research Technician I, TMH, Dr. Wheeler

Shea Scott, Histology Technician III, BCM

Ricky Simon, Laboratory Technician I, BCM, Dr. Lieberman

Gopal Singh, Senior Research Assistant, BCM, Dr. Cooper

Shari Stark, Special Project, BCM, Dr. Lieberman

Dai Su, Senior Research Assistant, TCH, Dr. Finegold

William Swanniutt, Computer Operator, Ld, BCM

Matthew Swulius, Research Technician II, BCM, Dr. Sifers

Przemyslaw Szafranski, Post-doctoral Fellow, BCM, Dr. Goode

Linda Tang, Research Technician II, BCM, Dr. Matzuk

Beril Tavsanli, Research Technician (Graduate Student), BCM, Dr. Mardon

Larry Teeter, Research Associate, BCM, Dr. Graviss

David Titus, Business Developmental Director, BCM

Frederick Ubberrud, Computer Operator, Ld, BCM

Tinika Ussery, Laboratory Assistant, BCM

Frank Valdez, Clinical Technician II, BCM, Dr. Graviss

Mirna Vasquez, Laboratory Technician II, Conroe, Dr. Martel

Angela Vogel, Histology Technician III, BCM

Annetta Walker, Histology Laboratory Supervisor, Dermatopathology

Jianghua Wang, Post-doctoral Associate, VAM, Dr. Ittmann

Yu Wang, Research Technician I, TMH, Dr. Wheeler

Jun Wei, Post-doctoral Associate, BCM, Dr. Goode

Pandora Williams, Research Coordinator, PCMA, Dr. Graviss

Natalie Williams-Bouyer, Research Associate, BCM, Dr. Graviss

Linda Williamson, Laboratory Technician I, BCM, Histology

Jamar Willis, Messenger, BCM, Histology

Constance Wright, Laboratory Technician I, TCH, Dr. Langston

San-Pin Wu, Graduate Student, BCM, Dr. Majesky

Xuemei Wu, Post-doctoral Associate, BCM, Dr. Matzuk

Chen Xia, Post-doctoral Associate, VAMC, Dr. Ittmann

Donna Zawada, Administrative Coordinator III, BCM, Dr. Graviss

Hong, Zhang, Pathologist's Assistant, BCM

Min Zhao, Research Associate, BCM, Dr. Goode

RESIDENTS AND FELLOWS

July 1, 2002 - June 30, 2003

Allen, Timothy M.D.

Arbab, Farinaz M.D.

Bayer-Garner, Ilene M.D.

Buckleair, Linda M.D.

Chen, Albert M.D.

Chen, Alice M.D., Ph.D.

Chen, Henry M.D., Ph.D.

Coffey, Donna M.D.

Cope-Yokoyama, Sandy M.D.

Dishop, Megan M.D.

Ehrlich, Michelle (Post-sophmore fellow)

Eldin, Karen M.D.

Granville, Laura M.D.

Han, Bing M.D., Ph.D.

Helekar, Bharati M.D.

Huttenbach, Yve M.D.

Jaffee, Ian M.D.

Kozovska, Milena M.D., Ph.D.

Kunda, Anand M.D.

Lin, Jefferson M.D.

Liu, Liang M.D., Ph.D.

Montalvo, Cristina M.D.

Newman, Apple M.D.

Parrott, Michael Brandon (Post-sophmore fellow)

Perna, Ashley M.D.

Rust, Megan M.D.

Schmiege, Lorenz M.D., Ph.D.

Sheehan, Andrea M.D.

Shen, Yang Angela (Post-sophmore fellow)

Smith, Megan M.D.

Snyder, Tamela M.D.

Stewart, Paul (Post-sophmore fellow)

Sule, Norbert M.D.

Tops, Terrill M.D.

Vejabhuti, Choladda M.D.

Wells, Linda M.D.

Ye, Ying M.D., Ph.D.

Yorke, Rebecca M.D.

Young, David M.D., Ph.D.

ILLUSTRATION SOURCES

1. Courtesy of Ibrahim Ramzy, M.D.
2. Baylor College of Medicine
3. Courtesy of Tom Wheeler, M.D.
4. Courtesy of Milton Finegold, M.D.
5. Courtesy of Tom Wheeler, M.D.
6. Baylor College of Medicine
7. Baylor College of Medicine
8. Baylor College of Medicine
9. Baylor College of Medicine
10. Baylor College of Medicine
11. Baylor College of Medicine
12. Baylor College of Medicine
13. Baylor College of Medicine Archives
14. Baylor College of Medicine Archives
15. From *Round-Up,* 1946, Baylor College of Medicine Archives
16. Baylor College of Medicine Archives
17. Courtesy of Robert O'Neal, M.D.
18. Baylor College of Medicine Archives
19. Baylor College of Medicine
20. Baylor College of Medicine
21. Baylor College of Medicine Archives
22. Courtesy of Amy Storrow
23. Baylor College of Medicine
24. Baylor College of Medicine Archives
25. Baylor College of Medicine Archives
26. Baylor College of Medicine Archives
27. Courtesy of Michael Lieberman, M.D., Ph.D.
28. Baylor College of Medicine
29. Richard Carson Photography
30. Baylor College of Medicine
31. Courtesy of Michael Lieberman, M.D., Ph.D.
32. Baylor College of Medicine Archives
33. Baylor College of Medicine Archives
34. From *Round-Up,* 1950, Baylor College of Medicine Archives
36. Baylor College of Medicine Archives
37. John P. McGovern Historical Collections and Research Center, Houston Academy of Medicine, Texas Medical Center Library
38. Baylor College of Medicine
39. Baylor College of Medicine
40. Courtesy of Tom Wheeler, M.D.
41. Baylor College of Medicine
42. Courtesy of Tom Wheeler, M.D.
43. Baylor College of Medicine
44. Baylor College of Medicine Archives
45. Richard Carson Photography

46. Baylor College of Medicine Archives
47. Baylor College of Medicine Archives
48. Courtesy of Phil Cagle, M.D.
49. Baylor College of Medicine Archives
50. Baylor College of Medicine Archives
51. Courtesy of Tom Wheeler, M.D.
52. Courtesy of Tom Wheeler, M.D.
53. Baylor College of Medicine
54. Courtesy of Jamie Davis, Ph.D.
55. Baylor College of Medicine
56. Baylor College of Medicine
57. John P. McGovern Historical Collections and
    Research Center, Houston Academy of
    Medicine, Texas Medical Center Library
58. Baylor College of Medicine
59. Courtesy of John A. Moran
60. Baylor College of Medicine
61. Baylor College of Medicine
62. Baylor College of Medicine
63. Courtesy of Jan Finegold, M.D.
64. Baylor College of Medicine
65. Baylor College of Medicine
66. Baylor College of Medicine
67. Baylor College of Medicine
68. Baylor College of Medicine
69. Associated Press/Wide World Photos
70. Associated Press/Wide World Photos
71. Associated Press/Wide World Photos
72. Courtesy of David Yawn, M.D.
73. Baylor College of Medicine

74. Baylor College of Medicine Archives
75. The Houston Chronicle
76. Baylor College of Medicine
77. Department of Publications and
    Communications, Baylor College of Medicine
78. Baylor College of Medicine
79. Baylor College of Medicine
80. Baylor College of Medicine
81. Baylor College of Medicine
82. The Houston Chronicle
83. Baylor College of Medicine
84. Baylor College of Medicine
85. John P. McGovern Historical Collections and
    Research Center, Houston Academy of
    Medicine, Texas Medical Center Library
86. Baylor College of Medicine Archives
87. Baylor College of Medicine Archives
88. Baylor College of Medicine Archives
89. Baylor College of Medicine
90. Baylor College of Medicine
91. Baylor College of Medicine
92. Baylor College of Medicine Archives
93. Baylor College of Medicine Archives
94. Baylor College of Medicine
95. Baylor College of Medicine
96. Baylor College of Medicine

Chapter 1 and Chapter 6 micrographic
images courtesy of Ibrahim Ramzy, M.D.
All others courtesy of Baylor College of Medicine.

INDEX

Abbott, Jack, 42, 44, 118, 119, 247

Ackerman, Lauren, 5, 115, 116, 117, 118, 124

Adams, Gordon, 38

Adels, Morton, 35

Alford, Bobby, x, 35, 45, 54, 63, 79, 134, 180

Alvord, Buster, 31

Anatomic pathology, 20, 51, 89, 108, 238

Anderson, Sid, 44, 119, 123, 251

Antalffy, Bobbie, 158

Armstrong, Dawna, x, 22, 23,139

Ayala, Gustavo, x, 22, 62, 216, 219

Bañez, Gene, x, 25, 88, 120, 129, 135, 136, 187

Barrios, Roberto, x, 75, 165

Bauer, Walter, 118, 123, 124, 125

Baylor College of Medicine, ix, x, 17, 36, 52, 62, 182, 257

Baylor College of Medicine Archives, ix, x

Baylor University, 11, 30, 45, 48

Bedrossian, Carlos, 133, 134, 253

Bell, Marvin, 240

Ben Taub Hospital, 42, 48, 57, 58, 60, 62, 74, 99, 100, 101, 126, 145, 183, 214, 236, 248, 251

Bernard, David, 237

Berry Program, 8

biochemistry, 20, 24, 80, 89, 178

Birnbaumer, Lutz, 154

Black, J.H., 240

Blailock, Zack, 35

blood banking, 3, 57, 89, 111, 136, 143, 144, 232

blood processing, 144

Blount, E.A., 239

Bowen, Ted, 49, 50, 51, 53, 55, 58, 137, 178, 179

Brown, Arch, 89

Bucci, Robert, 84

Butler, William, xi, 61, 63, 71, 180

Cagle, Philip, xi, 3, 4, 15, 108, 133, 134, 218

Caldwell, George T., 240, 241, 242, 244, 247, 252, 254, 255

Caskey, Tom, 151

Cell Biology, Department of, 17, 153

Chakraborty, Subhendu, 215, 219, 259

Chapman, Frank, 89

Clarridge, Jill, xi, 132, 199

clinical pathology, 48, 52, 139

Clinicopathological Conference, 83

Clostridia, 147

Community Pathology Associates, 29, 175, 180-183

Conroe, Texas, city of, 179-183

Cooper, Tom, 237, 257

Cullen family, 244, 245

Darlington, Gretchen, xi, 63, 91-93, 152, 153, 155-157, 210, 211

Davis, Jamie, x, xi, 178, 180, 182, 186, 191-194, 203-206, 221-223, 236

Davis, Joyce, xi, 11-13, 20-22, 25, 36, 40, 41, 80-85, 88, 89, 244, 255

Davis, Phil, 82, 83

DeBakey, Michael, xi, 11, 35, 38, 41, 44, 45, 48-52, 54-56, 70, 71, 122, 137, 194-198, 221, 230, 245, 251, 252, 254

diabetes, 16, 124, 126, 130

dieners, 99, 237

Dresden Award, 94

Drosophila, 169-171

Edwards, Robert, xi, 97-99

electron microscopy, 29, 40, 43, 131, 232, 238, 248

Eileen Murphree McMillin Blood Center, 138

Emory University, 2

entrepreneurship, 162, 175-183

Evans, Ricky, 99

Fechner, Robert, xi, 44, 46, 117-119, 123, 124, 128, 134-137, 251

Feigin, Ralph, xi, 63, 71, 122, 125, 138, 139, 180, 221

Finch, Chris, xi, 23-25, 86, 99-101, 228, 229

Finegold, Milton, x, xi, 9-11, 15, 17, 56, 60-63, 116, 117, 124, 125, 138, 139, 143, 149, 150-155, 176-178, 230-233, 254

Fletes, Jim, 185, 237

Flood of 1976, 203-209

Flood of 2001, *see* Tropical Storm Allison

Friday afternoon slide conference, 88

Fulbright, Irene, 23, 243, 244

Gaines, Rick, 72

Galen, 18, 20

Garcia, Regina, 35

Genta, Robert, xi, 15-17, 166, 167

Ghidoni, John, 39, 252

Goodman, Clay, 257

Graham, David, 17, 166

Green, Linda, xi, 129-131, 255

Greenberg, S. Donald, 40, 50, 128, 132-135, 246, 247, 253, 255, 257

Gresik, Vicky, 257

Gyorkey, Ferenc, 131, 132, 199

Haley, Melvin, 244, 251

Halpert, Bela, 43

Hamilton, Grace, xi, 147-149

Hausner, Richard, 236

Hawkins, Edith, xi, 12, 13, 61, 90, 91, 139, 253, 257

Helicobacter pylori, 17, 166, 167

Hematology, *See* blood banking

Henry, Judy, xi, 59, 60, 27

Hill, Bill, 236, 251, 255

Hughes, Howard, 191-194

Human Genome Project, 151

Hycel, 160-162, 253

India, country of, 3, 4, 125

Italy, country of, 16, 167, 236

Ittmann, Michael, xi, 229, 230, 257

Jarvis, Bruce, 144, 251, 252

Jaworski, Leon, 161

Jefferson Davis Hospital, 31, 38, 41, 42, 82, 89

Jesse E. Edwards Registry of Cardiovascular Disease at the St. Paul Heart and Lung Center, vii

Jones, Faye, xi, 150, 151

Jozwiak, Ginger, xi, 185, 237

Kaufman, Raymond, 147

Kerr, S.E., 244

Khomeini, Ayatollah, 199

Kim, Han-Seob, xi, 74, 251

Krishnan, Bhuvaneswari, xi, 118

Kyle, Will, x, xi, 66, 72-74, 179, 183-187, 218, 237

Langston, Claire, 134, 139, 154

Laucirica, Rodolfo, xi, 185-187

Leadership, 29, 50, 56, 70-73, 228, 236, 237

Lechago, Juan, xi, 22, 108, 211, 216-218, 220, 233

Leidler, Franz, 248

Levi, Primo, 126

Lieberman, Michael, x, xi, 18-20, 29, 61-75, 86, 107, 108, 111, 121-123, 143, 151, 162, 164, 165, 168, 171, 175, 178, 180-186, 215, 218-221, 227-229, 232, 233, 235-238, 255

Lind, Carl, 249, 252, 253

M.D. Anderson Cancer Center, 8, 9, 53, 131, 182

Majesky, Mark, xi, 20, 21, 66, 67, 94, 95, 163, 164

Managed care, ix, 72, 177

Mardon, Graeme, xi, 94, 168-171

Martel, Armand, 185, 186, 237

Matzuk, Martin, xi, 69, 73, 167, 168, 209, 210, 236, 256

Mayo Clinic, the, 47, 52, 59

McGavran, Malcolm, 4, 12, 15, 56, 115, 117, 119, 123-131, 134, 136, 193, 254

McIntosh, Henry, 48-50, 52, 53

Medicaid, 177, 251

Medical Technology program, 145, 151, 153

Medicare, ix, 175, 177, 251

Methodist Hospital, the, 4, 5, 41, 42, 44, 45, 48, 49, 55-58, 62, 66, 82, 83, 89, 107-109, 118, 120, 123, 136-138, 145, 147, 153, 165, 178-181, 183, 191-193, 198, 204, 207, 208, 211, 213, 216, 218-221, 237, 245, 254

Migliore, Philip, xi, 6-9, 144-146, 191, 206-209

Milam, John, 254, 255

Minnesota, state of, 61

Mississippi, state of, 37

Mody, Dilzi, xi, 67, 68, 237

Mody, Dina, xi, 3-6, 63, 96, 128, 129, 232, 257

Moran Foundation, 160-162, 236

Moran, John A., 160-162

Moran, John J., *see* Hycel

Moreland, Wes, 183

Moursund, Walter, 240, 241, 243, 245, 246, 257

Musser, Jim, 236, 257

National Institutes of Health, 17, 152, 159, 161, 216, 229, 237

Nature, 167

Neff, Pat, 244

Newton, Berne, 249

Nursing, 23, 37

O'Neal, Robert, xi, 29, 32, 36-46, 84, 115, 116, 118, 122, 123, 132, 133, 238, 248-250, 252, 256

Oaks, Sandy, xi, 64, 65, 74, 171

Olson, Stanley, 33, 41, 42, 45

Ortegosa, Corpus, 236

Overstreet, John, 118

Panama, country of, 36, 37, 94

Paraguay, country of, 21, 22

Patrick, Becky, x, 25, 183, 215, 237

Picasso, Pablo, 129

Quincy, M.E, viii

Rabin, Erwin, 39, 249

Ramzy, Ibrahim (Abe), xi, 5, 63, 87, 91, 111, 233, 255-257

Recruitment of staff, 59, 63, 108, 125, 138, 139, 151, 152, 154, 156, 236, 237

Residency program, 15, 36, 39, 40, 45, 63, 79, 95, 129, 251

Rett Syndrome, 159

Richardson, Maurice, 242

Roberts, William, xi, 46-51, 253

Rochester, New York, city of, 9

Rosenberg, Harvey, 35, 57, 90, 135, 136, 252, 255

Sadat, Anwar, 194, 195

Saleh, George, 110

Salt Lake City, Utah, city of, 6

Sayeeduddin, Mohammad, 212

Schwartz, Mary, xi, 5, 56, 57, 63, 69, 73, 95-98, 111, 125-128, 232, 256

Science, 153

Sears building, 79-81, 243

Shah of Iran, 194-197

Shurberg, Barbara, 136, 137

Sifers, Rick, xi, 18, 68-70, 154, 157, 158

Slide conference, 89

Spjut, Harlan, xi, 5, 6, 29, 35, 37-40, 47, 50, 56, 62, 63, 69, 85, 86, 115-125, 128, 227, 228, 249, 252-256

St. Louis, Missouri, city of, 12, 31, 37, 38, 40, 44, 82, 83, 116, 127, 134

St. Luke's Hospital, 47, 62, 154

Stager, Charlie, 182

Stewart, Leroy, 99

Stout, Arthur P., 116

Strongyloides, 17, 166

Surgery, 5, 10, 11, 42-44, 50, 106, 110, 118, 132, 180, 195-198, 205, 207, 218, 240, 245, 246, 254

Surgical Pathology, 89, 97

Suzuki, Minoru, 40, 249

Teaching, 11, 12, 22, 23, 31, 38, 40-42, 61, 74, 85, 98, 118, 127, 128, 153, 236, 240, 256

Technology, ix, 10, 79, 86, 145, 155, 156, 231, 251, 252

Temple Emanu-El of Dallas, 239

Texas Children's Hospital, 13, 57, 58, 62, 90, 136, 177, 178, 183, 218, 219, 254

Texas Medical Center, 46, 53, 56, 61, 64, 182, 183, 203, 205-207, 209, 210, 223, 233, 236, 244, 247, 254, 256

Thayer, Alfred E., 240

The New England Journal of Medicine, 14

Titus, David, xi, 183-184

Titus, Jack, vii, viii, xi, 12, 25, 29, 47, 51-61, 63, 64, 71, 90, 122-124, 136-138, 151, 179, 180, 183, 191, 193, 194, 196, 197, 236, 253-255

Transgenic mice, 157, 165, 168, 203

Tropical Storm Allison, 203, 209-223, 256

Tuberculosis, 30, 36, 37

United States Air Force, 8

United States Army, 6, 80, 83, 138, 139, 204, 244

University of Dallas Medical Department, 239

University of Pennsylvania, 124, 236

University of Pittsburgh, 7, 19, 20

University of St. Thomas, 23

University of Tennessee, 14

University of Washington, 17, 20

Utah, state of, 38

Venezuela, country of, 36

Veterans Administration Hospital, Cincinnati, 17

Veterans Administration Hospital, Houston, 48, 50, 199

Vogel, Hannes, 139

Wallace, Stuart, 29, 30-35, 69, 83, 88, 89, 122, 175, 242-248, 250, 256

Washington University, 37, 115-118, 123-126, 135, 244

Weilbaecher, Don, 89, 252

Welch, William, 9

Werch, Jochewed (Anita), xi, 43, 68, 86, 143, 144, 194, 197, 238, 252, 254

Wheeler, Dayton, xi, 109, 110, 215

Wheeler, Marcus, 220

Wheeler, Paul, 11, 82, 244-246

Wheeler, Thomas, x, xi, 13-15, 49, 58, 62, 63, 73, 106-109, 120, 186, 215, 232

Whipple, George, 9

White, Yolanda, xi, 151

Wilkenfeld, Jerry, 236

Wilson, Pierre, 239

Women, 12, 56, 82, 83, 118, 136, 206, 229, 238

Woo, Savio, 17, 153

Wood, Harold, 248

Wood, Martha, 245

World War II, 36, 80, 162

Worthington, Marion, 56, 57

Woznicki, Dennis, 236

Yawn, David, xi, 51, 52, 57, 89, 90, 115, 119, 126, 130, 131, 136-138, 182, 194-198, 228, 253, 254

Yazdi, Ebrahim, 199

Yemen, country of, 16

Yow, Ellard, 31